From the author.

THE CHRISTIAN APPROACH TO ISLAM

MOHAMMEDANS AT PRAYER IN A MOSQUE

THE CHRISTIAN APPROACH TO ISLAM

BY

JAMES L. BARTON

FOREIGN SECRETARY OF AMERICAN BOARD OF
COMMISSIONERS FOR FOREIGN MISSIONS.
AUTHOR OF "DAYBREAK IN TURKEY," ETC.

College of Missions Lectureship
Fifth Series

THE PILGRIM PRESS
BOSTON   CHICAGO

THE PILGRIM PRESS
BOSTON

TO

THE VALIANT BODY OF

MISSIONARIES WHO HAVE LABORED AND SACRIFICED

IN MOHAMMEDAN COUNTRIES

AND TO THE

MULTITUDES WHO WILL YET DEDICATE THEMSELVES

TO THE

REDEMPTION OF THE WORLD OF ISLAM

THIS BOOK IS DEDICATED

PREFACE

The substance of this book was delivered in a course of lectures at the College of Missions in Indianapolis, Indiana. The original lectures have been thoroughly revised and re-written. The extended discussion in the daily press and the many articles appearing in various magazines and reviews reveal the interest the public is taking at this time in the Mohammedan question. There is a real revival in the study of Islam on the part of the general public, and a new inquiry within the Church as to the Church's relations and obligation to Mohammedanism in the face of the revolutionary events that have taken place in the Mohammedan world during the last four years.

The world war is having a more startling effect upon Mohammedanism than upon any other of the great religions. The three outstanding Moslem centers, Cairo, Mecca and Constantinople, have been in the heart of the conflict. The Caliphate has been overthrown and the call for a holy war rejected, while Moslems have been actively engaged on both sides of the great conflict. The old Mohammedan world with its boasted solidarity is no more. No longer do the nations of the earth, as for twelve centuries, stand in terror before the united forces of Islam. While Islam is still a mighty religion, it no longer is an international menace. Millions of Mohammedans will continue to believe in their religion and worship Allah, but few will persist in their dream of Moslem world domination. Through the only call ever issued for a universal holy war Mohammedanism made its supreme and final effort for national supremacy and failed.

The author is under great obligations to Prof. George A. Barton, Ph.D., LL.D., of Bryn Mawr College, who has carefully revised the manuscript from the point of view of the best

Oriental scholarship. Professor Barton was at the head of the School of Oriental Research in Palestine and is the author of many notable works upon Assyriology, Biblical archæology and interpretation, and the history of religions. He wrote the whole of the chapter upon " The Mohammedan Conception of God," contributed important parts to two other chapters and read the final page proof of the entire book.

J. L. B.

Boston, October, 1918.

CONTENTS

PART I.—EXTERNAL HISTORY

PART II.— MOHAMMEDANISM AS A RELIGION

of Allah to Jehovah. Denial of Mohammed's conceptions by Qaderites and Mutazillites. Transformation of Jewish conception of God by Jesus. Johannine conception of God. Emergence of trinitarian doctrine. Ways of holding trinitarian doctrine. Its significance.

PART III.— RELATIONS TO CHRISTIANITY

Some Christian truth should take precedence. The following should not be pressed at the outset: namely, Immaculate Conception; sonship, divinity, death and resurrection of Jesus Christ; fatherhood of God; redemption only through Christ; Christianity as the only true religion; the use of wine at the sacraments. Prejudice to be overcome. High morality demanded. Failure of Christianity to win the western world. A belief that Christianity has reached the height of its power. Composite authorship of the Scriptures. The relation of Christian nations to Mohammedan countries. The following truths of Christianity which appeal: Unity of God; divine omnipotence coupled with divine goodness; the miracles of Christ; Christian eschatology; the nobility of the teachings of Jesus; the fact that Jesus practised what he taught; Christianity expressed in benevolent deeds and unselfish character; secret prayer and worship; Christian benevolent institutions; worship free from casuistic demands; the Christians' Book; social regeneration; Christ fulfilling highest human aspirations; Christ, mediator and intercessor.

Practical method of approach to Moslems essential. The Mohammedan head and heart must be won. Special missionary preparation more essential here than for any other people. The general lines of approach; the Bible in the vernacular, specially prepared Christian literature, Christian education in all grades and departments. Emphasis on medical missions. Personal contacts and relations. Oral presentation. Its method and theme. Organizations of Moslem clubs. Use of pictures. Employment of Christian music.

A concerted plan essential. Only half-hearted effort hitherto. Plans must meet the new conditions. Complete survey of Moslem world needs to be prepared. A Mohammedan prayer cycle. Discussion of the failure of Islam as a religion. Agreement among missionary societies on standards of preparation for missionary work. Schools in Moslem countries for preparing new appointees. Willingness of the church to meet the cost. Removal of methods of restrictions against work for Moslems. International and interdenominational cooperation. Program of Christian occupation.

Proclamation of the Shereef of Mecca.

LIST OF ILLUSTRATIONS

PART I
EXTERNAL HISTORY

PART I

EXTERNAL HISTORY

THE CHRISTIAN APPROACH TO ISLAM

PART I — EXTERNAL HISTORY

Introduction

Mohammedanism has furnished a fruitful field for writers and lecturers on religion, especially since the beginning of the present century. It is one of the three great religions which gather around a person. These are Christianity, centering in Jesus Christ; Buddhism, originating with Gautama, called the Buddha; and Mohammedanism, which sprang from and is identified with the life and teachings of Mohammed.[1] The striking features of Islam, which call for investigation and discussion, are different from those of Buddhism and Christianity, but are, perhaps, equally numerous. This is due in part to the fact of the uniqueness of the teachings of Mohammed, and in part to the great and varied body of tradition that has grown up alongside of the Koran. A knowledge of this tradition is necessary to a proper understanding of the teachings and especially of the practices of Mohammedanism.

There is another reason why, during the last fifteen years, the attention of the world has been strongly turned toward Islam. It is preeminently the religion of the people of the Near East. Its adherents occupy the southern shore of the Mediterranean, the length and breadth of the Turkish Empire and Persia, and are numerous in the Balkan peninsula and in Russia. Thus, in the development of Western civilization and the advance of Christianity and modern education, an unusual contact has been inevitable between Moham-

---

[1] Zoroastrianism and Taoism also are religions which involve faith in a person, but the numbers of their adherents do not place them with the three mentioned.

medanism and the Western world. Islam has consequently compelled attention, not only as a religion but as a force dominating society and as a motive in the organization and conduct of the national life of a people. Conditions growing out of the European war, which has brought so emphatically to the front the Mohammedan Turkish Empire and the relation of that empire to its non-Mohammedan subjects, again demand a reinvestigation and restudy of Mohammedanism as a national and social force.

Previous discussions of Mohammedanism have approached it with a different purpose from that which we here entertain. Many books have been written covering a much wider range of study and investigation. They have usually been devoted to some phase of one of the following topics:

(1) The life of Mohammed and the rise of Islam.
(2) The doctrines and history of Mohammedanism.
(3) The contrasts and affinities which exist between Mohammedanism and Christianity.
(4) Sources of power and the weaknesses of Mohammedanism.
(5) The extension of Mohammedanism in the world.
(6) Reports of recent Conferences upon the subject of Islam.

One might naturally ask, therefore, whether there is need for another book on Islam when it has been so thoroughly covered.

There seems, however, to be no general treatment of the *Christian Approach to Islam*. The discussions hitherto have been primarily historical, theological and philosophical, and only remotely practical.

All that has preceded will be and must be of supreme importance to the Church which looks upon the great Mohammedan world as a field for preaching the Gospel of Jesus Christ, and it must necessarily form the ground-work and basis of our discussion in this volume.

The reports of the Christian Conferences held in Cairo and Lucknow, where the practical approach to Mohammedanism was extensively discussed, throw light upon this problem. Then, too, magazines like *The Moslem World*, a quarterly devoted to this subject, published in New York under the editorship of Dr. Zwemer; the *International Review of Missions*, published in Edinburgh under the Continuation Committee of the Edinburgh Conference; the *Missionary Review of the World*, published in New York; the *East and West* and the *Church Missionary Review*, published in London; the *Islamic Review*, published in Woking; the *Revue du Monde Mussulman*, published in Paris; *Der Islam*, published in Strassburg; *Blessed be Egypt*, published in Cairo, have provided, during the last few years, a large number of articles and a vast amount of information bearing upon the Christian approach to Islam.

The practical Christian studies Islam, not simply to learn its history and doctrines and philosophy but in order to obtain a knowledge of the best method of successfully reaching Mohammedans with the gospel. We do not approach our subject at this time, therefore, because we are interested in the history or even the social or the national strength and weakness of the Mohammedan religion and its philosophy, but we take up the discussion in order that we may learn, if possible, how to bring to the Mohammedan mind and heart as it exists today, in every Moslem country of the world, the saving knowledge of Christ.

The field is too large for a thorough discussion in a single volume. The Mohammedan world is too extensive and diversified, in race, environment, temperament and practice, to allow of an exhaustive treatment here. We have great diversity among Mohammedans in North Africa, Egypt, Turkey, the Balkans, Persia, Russia, Afghanistan, Turkestan, India, China, the Philippines, Java, Sumatra, etc., each worthy of separate and independent investigation.

The old theory, that the Gospel of Jesus Christ, being the same for all men and for all time and for all lands, should therefore be presented in precisely the same way to all people, everywhere and always, has been exploded. We are learning that Christ himself approached different classes of people in a different way but always with the same eternal message. He did not talk to the fishermen in the same way that He talked to the Pharisee. Paul had one address for the Greek philosophers at Athens and another for the Jews. A careful study of the New Testament will reveal the fact that Christ and His disciples shaped their message to the character of the audience addressed. The purpose of the message was to win the audience, and all who have given attention to the psychology of teaching realize the importance of having the message adapted to the thinking, the environment, the traditions, and even the social life of those to be won. A missionary who would go to the Hindus and devote time to convince them that there is a devil, or to the Moslems to persuade them of the existence of one great supreme God, or to the Confucianists to argue at length on the importance of children obeying their parents, or to the Chinese to endeavor to prove to them the majesty and power of the God of heaven, — would be looked upon as strangely deficient in the knowledge of the people whom he was attempting to instruct and persuade.

The effective presentation of Christianity, especially to those of another race and religion, is universally recognized as a task of great delicacy, requiring knowledge and sympathetic understanding, upon the part of the preacher, of the mind and belief and desire of the man approached. We are now seeking from the world of Islamic history, belief, and experience, that which will aid us in making a successful approach to the great heart of Islam.

Dr. D. S. Margoliouth makes the following statement[2]

[2] See *Mohammedanism* in the "Home University Library," p. 7.

regarding the names constantly employed in the discussion of our subject:

" *Islam* is the infinitive, and *Muslim* or ' Moslem ' the participle, of a verb which signifies ' to deliver ' or ' to commit entirely ' some thing or person to some one else; authoritatively interpreted in this context as ' to deliver the face to God,' i.e., to turn to God only in prayer and worship, to the exclusion of all other objects of devotion. Hence the words are equivalent to 'monotheism' and ' monotheist.' Their invention is ascribed in the Koran to Abraham, and the Christian apostles are said to have claimed this designation. There is, however, no historical evidence of their existence before the time of Mohammed, after whom the system is also called *Mohammedanism,* and who coupled with the proposition that God is One, ' there is no God but Allah,' another no less important: ' Mohammed is the messenger of Allah.' A Moslem or Mohammedan is, then, one who accepts the proposition that an Arab named Mohammed or Ahmad, son of Abdallah, of the city Meccah, in Central Arabia, who died A.D. 632, is the main and indeed ultimate channel whereby the will of the Creator of the world has been revealed to mankind."

CHAPTER I

NUMBERS AND DISTRIBUTION

Mohammedanism is one of the great religions of the world, although the latest to appear. There have been different classifications of the religious world, yet there is substantial agreement upon what may be called the principal religions. Omitting Fetichism as the name applied to the uncorrelated and unorganized religious beliefs and practices of the cruder tribes of Africa and the races upon some of the Pacific Islands and of other parts of the uncivilized world, there are nine well-defined forms of religious belief and practice.

Professor Hume of the Union Theological Seminary in New York has recently arranged and tabulated the followers of these nine leading religions of the world, accompanied by a statement as to their geographical location. Dr. Hume's summary is as follows:

Hinduism	217,000,000	British India only.
Shinto	24,000,000	Japan only.
Judaism	11,000,000	Over the world.
Zoroastrianism or Parsee religion	100,000	Western India, mostly Bombay.
Taoism	43,000,000	China only.
Buddhism	137,000,000	Ceylon, Thibet, Burma, Siam, Malay Peninsula, China, Japan, and Mongolia.
Confucianism	250,000,000	China and Japan.
Christianity	588,000,000	Europe, North and South America, Australasia, parts of Asia.
Mohammedanism	230,000,000	Arabia, Persia, Turkey, India, Africa, China.

It will be noted that Professor Hume classes Confucianism as a religion, which many question.

8

This makes the total of the followers of the nine above-named religions 1,500,000,000. It is impossible, however, to draw a clear line between the Taoists, Buddhists, Shintoists and Confucianists, since throughout Japan and many parts of China large masses of the population belong to two and frequently to three of these orders. A man in Japan may at the same time be a good Shintoist, Buddhist and Confucianist. Large populations in Japan are born Shintoists, receive their ethical instruction from Confucius, and when they die are buried by a Buddhist priest in a Buddhist cemetery. Making due allowance for double enumeration, these tables leave as followers of the less organized religions or Fetish worshipers perhaps 200,000,000.

According to this table, only Confucius and Christ have more followers than Mohammed. If we eliminate Confucianism from the great religions and class it as a cult or a philosophy, only Christianity claims more followers than Islam, and Hinduism is the only other religion that even approximates these in number; and Buddhism, while numbering more than all the followers of the remaining religions named, still stands considerably below.

The three great religions, therefore, in the order of the number of their followers, are *Christianity*, *Islam* and *Hinduism*, and these three embrace nearly two-thirds of the world's population.

The total population of the Moslem world is a matter of conjecture rather than of actual statistics. The discrepancies in the different statistical surveys attempted by various authorities are as disconcerting as they are surprising. Most of the estimates have been made by Western writers, although we have one or two instances of an attempted census by the Moslems themselves. In *El Moayyad* (Cairo) for November 9, 1909, the total population of the Moslem world is given at 270,000,000; but it is evident that the figures are largely guesswork, as the numbers in China are put at 40,000,000, in Africa at 70,000,000, and in Russia as high as 24,000,000.   In another case, to which Dr. H. H. Jessup called attention in the Lucknow Conference in 1911, the Sublime Porte, under the Hamidian régime, carefully copied a survey of the Moslem world published in the *Missionary Review of the World* in 1898, and gave it as an accurate census taken under the supervision of the Sultan and at his expense!

The following table gives the totals of the Moslem world population as estimated by various authorities.

Brockhaus, " Konvers.-Lexikon," 1894	175,000,000
Hubert Jansen, " Verbreitung des Islams," 1897	259,680,672
S. M. Zwemer (Miss. Review of the World) 1898	196,491,842
Allgemeine Missions Zeitschrift, 1902	175,290,000
H. Wichmann in Justus Perthes' Atlas, 1903	240,000,000
Encyclopedia of Missions, 1904	193,550,000
" The Mohammedan World of Today " (Cairo Conf. 1906)	232,996,170
Martin Hartmann, 1910	223,985,780
C. H. Becker, in Baedecker's Egypt (last German edition)	260,000,000
Lucknow Conference Report, 1911	200,000,000

We shall undoubtedly be upon safe ground if we assume that there are now from 200,000,000 to 230,000,000 Mohammedans in the world representing about one seventh of the world's population and occupying many different countries. In an introductory survey read at the Lucknow Conference referred to, Dr. Zwemer carefully discussed the numbers and distribution of Moslems, without attempting to include all of the countries in which followers of Mohammed are found. We here present a table compiled from many sources showing where the most of them dwell with the approximate number in each country.

Country	Numbers	Government
India, Burma and Ceylon	67,000,000	British
Russia	20,000,000	Russian
China	10,000,000	Chinese
Java	28,000,000	Dutch

Country	Numbers	Government
Sumatra	3,000,000	Dutch
Egypt and North Africa	22,000,000	British, Italian, French
Central and South Africa	40,000,000	British, French, Portuguese, Spanish and Independent
Turkey, Balkans and Arabia	18,000,000	Turkish, British and Independent
Persia	9,000,000	
Turkestan, Bokhara,	7,000,000	Independent
Madagascar, Mindanao, So. America, United States, Europe, etc.	5,000,000	Various governments
Total	229,000,000	

Assuming that these figures are approximately correct, we find that some 91,000,000 Mohammedans are under British rule. This makes Great Britain the greatest Mohammedan power. Of this total number, 68,000,000 are in Asia and 23,000,000 in Africa. France governs some 16,000,000; Italy, 2,000,000; and Germany, at the outbreak of the war, about the same number. The Dutch have in their colonial possessions some 36,000,000 and Russia, 20,000,000. This gives a total of 167,000,000 Moslems under the leading European and so-called Christian nations. Less than 14,000,000 of the remaining are under the Caliphate of the Ottoman Empire and none of the remaining constitute anywhere a Moslem nation that can justly claim national independence.[1] This fact is worthy of consideration at the outset of our discussion as it is of prime significance. Mohammedanism in its origin and, for centuries in its practice, has been a theocracy which claimed the right of religious and political domination. As a national or political force its chief demonstration in modern times has been the Ottoman Empire, of which Islam was the state religion and the basis for the laws and the administration of the state. For 500 years we have had in the history of the Ottoman Empire an exhibit of what Islam

[1] Since this was written Mecca has become an independent state.

is able to do for the state or nation, with its consequent results.

Gradually and without special attempt, national Christianity as such has supplanted Mohammedanism, the governing force of Moslem peoples and races has passed from the Moslems to Christians, and Islam as a ruling and political force has almost disappeared from the earth. It should be here made plain that few if any of the Moslem peoples that live under Christian flags are made to feel governmental restraints and restrictions in the practice of their religion. They are given as full religious liberty as they ever enjoyed under Moslem rule.

In considering the Moslem world we must remember that about 14 per cent (or one-seventh) of the entire population of the world are Moslems. A glance at the preceding tabulation will show how widely they are distributed along both sides of the equator in Asia and Africa, reaching north of this belt of greatest heat in Turkey, Russia, Persia, Afghanistan and China. The large majority of the Mohammedans are tropical by birth and nature, and mostly Asiatics or Africans. At the same time they reveal a capacity and tendency to emigrate and occupy permanently areas outside of the heat belt, while considerable numbers have always lived in temperate zones.

The relations of the Moslem populations of the various countries in which they dwell to the local government differ in different countries. Under British rule in India the Mohammedans have the fullest liberty, not only for the practice of their religion, but in national affairs. A Mohammedan may attain to the highest position in the government open to natives of the country and it has sometimes been charged by the Hindus that Moslems were given preferential consideration. In military affairs there are undoubtedly grounds for the complaint. It is worthy of note that the British do not attempt to colonize upon Moslem territory and thus dominate local affairs through resident citizens of Great Britain. They organize a local government which is temporarily under the leadership of Englishmen, but which, in theory at least, is in the control of the citizens of the country governed and ultimately to become free from British domination. On the other hand, the French have attempted to establish French colonies in Algeria in which Europeans become controlling citizens of that country. Algeria sends deputies to the French Chambers, making that country an extension of France into Africa. All Moslem countries occupied by Russia were made an integral part of the Empire possessing the privilege of sending representatives to the Duma. The Dutch follow in the main the practice of Great Britain in the control of its Moslem possessions. Large liberty is given them to use their religious laws in the administration of justice among Moslems with the least possible interference with their religious prejudices and practices. Those practices only are interfered with which infringe upon the liberties and rights of others and run counter to the practices of civilized laws.

Even the integrity of the Moslem's religion has sometimes been safeguarded as in the British Sudan, where Christian missionaries are not permitted to work for and among the Moslem populations, but only among the pagan tribes. The Dutch Government has put no such restrictions upon the missionaries; neither have the British in other countries. Where a European country has exercised only a protectorate over a Mohammedan country, as Russia over Persia, France over Morocco and Tunis and England over Egypt previous to the great war, all religious matters and a large liberty in the control of internal affairs have been left to the local Mohammedan authorities, although the protecting country has endeavored to secure justice for all classes and liberty of conscience in religious belief and practice.

Mohammedans have little cause for complaint at the way

they have been governed by the Christian powers of Europe, except that they have not been able to employ coercive measures upon the non-Moslem inhabitants of the country nor use government processes to prevent Mohammedans from purchasing Christian books and attending Christian places of worship. They have also found it difficult to use force upon Moslems who were slack in the practices of their faith or who even became Christian. To such as refuse to recognize the right of the individual to the exercise of private judgment in matters of religion, this has seemed a hardship, even an unwarranted interference upon the part of the government, but the larger number of Moslems have not been slow to recognize the fairness and justice of the position. No Moslem people who have for any length of time experienced the freedom and prosperity that invariably follows Christian rule would be willing to return to a Mohammedan government. The readiness and unanimity with which the Moslems of Egypt rallied to the support of Great Britain at the outbreak of the European war, even when this arrayed them as enemies of a Moslem power, is a demonstration of their appreciation of the Christian government of Egypt and their unwillingness to return to Ottoman rule.

Islam, unlike the other great non-Christian religions except Buddhism, is not and cannot be confined to any one country or race. It is distinctly an expansive religion, as its history clearly reveals and as its present practices show. It is a missionary religion. By a missionary religion we mean, in the first place, one that is capable of being propagated among other peoples. Hinduism cannot be thus propagated, since, in order to become a Hindu, one must be born into the faith. There is no process by which an alien can so change himself as to be accepted into the circle of Hinduism. Judaism is not a missionary religion, certainly not as it has been practiced for nineteen centuries.[2] The name has come to signify

---

[2] Judaism was a missionary religion during the two or three centuries just previous to the beginning of the Christian era.

a race, and for one to attempt to become a Jew would be looked upon as absurd as for a leopard to try to change his spots. These religions may be called ethnic in that they belong to a race in a peculiar sense, and have come to be regarded as a race characteristic.

In the second place, a missionary religion is one in which its followers not only assume that their religion can be propagated, but who feel under certain obligations to make disciples of those outside. Buddhism is of this class, since, through its devotees, the religion has spread from southern India into Ceylon, Burma, China, Korea, and Japan, although during recent generations there has been little effort upon the part of Buddhists to propagate their faith.

Christianity is a missionary religion on every count. This fact does not here need elucidation. Mohammedanism is also of this class for reasons as patent and cogent as those that support the claim for Christianity. Whatever may have been, or may be, the motives that have prompted the disciples of Islam to extend their faith, and the methods by which it has been accomplished, the fact remains that Mohammedanism is capable of being propagated among alien peoples and races, and the followers of Mohammed believe it to be their duty and privilege so to extend a knowledge of their faith as to enlist new devotees. All this is true in spite of the fact that the word " missionary " as we use it does not occur in the Koran. The one passage that can be quoted as inculcating a missionary propaganda is in Sura III, verse 100, " Let there be people among you who invite to the best religion."

CHAPTER II

SPREAD OF ISLAM

The phenomenal success of Mohammed as the founder of a new religion was due not wholly to his own ability, enthusiasm and courage, but was, in a large measure, owing to the surroundings into which he was born and the opportunities that those surroundings afforded. It is an example, by no means unique in history, of the power of environment in making a man and in the development and success of his mission.

At the birth of Mohammed, in the year 570 A.D., the civilized part of Western Asia was divided between two empires, both of them of enormous strength, namely, the Persian empire and the so-called Roman empire of Constantinople. They were rivals of each other and were in constant conflict. Arabia was in part between them and was sometimes subject to one and sometimes to the other, so far as the independent spirit of the Arab could be subject to any nation. The Roman Empire was by name and profession Christian, but as distance increased from the center, the character of the Christianity professed by its subjects was corrupted by conflicting heresies so that the essential character of the teachings of Jesus Christ was distorted almost beyond recognition. There was constant revolt against the established religion and control from Constantinople, and to this was added the unrest which the inhabitants of Arabia manifested under Roman political power. It is manifest that neither the religious nor the political power of Constantinople held firm hand on the thought and life of the inhabitants of the Arabian peninsula. Their natural political attitude was that of rebellion, and their religious attitude that of heresy.

16

On the other hand, the religion of Persia had developed into a kind of dualism, represented by the spirit of light, Ormuzd, and the spirit of evil, Ahriman. The Sun was venerated as the symbol of the power of light, accompanied by a superstitious worship of fire and of the heavenly bodies; while the spirit of evil or darkness became almost personified as the force to be resisted.

The Arab, being subject first to one and then to the other of these powerful neighbors, caught some fragments of the religion represented by each. Zoroastrianism and Christianity had their followers in Arabia, while there were many colonies of Jews who had settled there before the time of Christ and who, in a general way, represented the Jewish faith; but the dominant creed of the inhabitants of Arabia was a crude polytheism in which the Arabs were gradually losing faith.[1] They were coming to believe in one Supreme Deity, but subordinate to Him was a host of inferior divine personages who were looked upon as intercessors.

This barren development of early Semitic religion had its center in the temple in the sacred city of Mecca. The holy black stone, an aerolite from heaven, said by tradition to be a relic of an earlier temple built by Abraham and Ishmael, had sacred connections with Paradise. It was supposed to have been given to Adam and to have been an object of veneration to the day of Mohammed. In the city of Mecca was also the holy spring, Zem Zem, which, according to tradition, broke forth to save Hagar and Ishmael from perishing of thirst, and to this the devout Arab came to worship the God of Abraham.

Just before the rise of Mohammed there had developed a dissatisfaction with the national religion among the more reflective and discerning of the inhabitants of Mecca and the surrounding areas. One of the most ancient biographies of

[1] Cf. J. Wellhausen, *Reste arabische Heidentums*, 2te, Aus., Berlin, 1907, or G. A. Barton, *A Sketch of Semitic Origins, Social and Religious*, New York, 1902, pp. 123–135.

Mohammed gives an account of four men who, without revelation, perceived the error of idolatry. It is reported that these four men refused to bow the knee before the image of the Kaaba, and went out in search of the purer faith of Abraham. Tradition reports that two of these four became Christians; the third embraced Islam, but later went to Abyssinia and there became converted to Christianity; the fourth renounced and condemned all the gross superstitions of his countrymen, but remained in a sceptical condition of mind to the time of his death.

In his *Christianity and Islam*[2] W. R. W. Stephens sums up the situation in the following words:

" Arabia was on the edge of two great rival empires, both weakened by protracted and exhausting contests. The crisis of the struggle, indeed, was contemporaneous with the preaching of Mahomet. Heraclius the Roman Emperor overthrew the Persian power in 629. The Roman Empire was itself weakened in the border provinces by this exertion; the Persian Empire never recovered. The Arabs had been partially subject to one or other power, but never absorbed politically or religiously by either.

Gross superstition and licentiousness prevailed, but a spirit of discontent and scepticism was at work. There was no national unity. Each tribe was a separate, independent atom.

The opportunity then was favorable for the action of some master mind which should first of all weld the jarring elements of life in Arabia itself into a compact body; then proceed to annex to it the great neighboring Empire of Persia, already prostrate by its rival; and finally to subdue the weakened fringes of that very rival, the Roman Empire.

This was the work of Mahomet."

Until after the flight to Mecca, Mohammed endeavored to propagate his new religion by persuasion rather than by force. His was a quiet, persistent search for favorable soil in which to sow the seed. After only eight years at Medina, when success had crowned his armed campaigns, the prophet is reported to have addressed a manifesto to the world inviting all mankind to submit to Islam. Ambassadors were sent to

[2] New York, 1877, pp. 13 and 14.

present these messages in person. Tradition declares that this message was as follows, quoting from the one said to have been sent to Emperor Heraclius:

" In the name of God, the Merciful, the Compassionate, Mohammed, who is the servant of God and his apostle to Heraclius the Emperor of Rome. Peace be on whoever has gone on the straight road. After this I say, verily I call you to Islam. Embrace Islam and God will reward you two-fold. If you turn away from the offer of Islam, then on you be the sins of your people. O people of the Book, come towards a creed that is fit both for us and for you. It is this — to worship none but God and not to associate anything with God, and not to call others God. Therefore, O ye people of the Book, if ye refuse, beware. We are Muslims and our religion is Islam."

This would indicate that Mohammed saw a vision of world conquest for his new religion, and so began by asking certain sovereigns to accept him as a prophet of God, and inviting all the world to the same privilege. From this time onward, the sword played a large part in the dissemination of Islam.

While Mohammed set out to found a new religion, he also established a new political order, different from anything that then was or that had previously existed. Starting with the idea that he wished only to convert his brethren to belief in one God, he overthrew the government of both Medina and Mecca, and, for the tribal rule by which the leading families shared in the conduct of public affairs, he substituted a theocratic monarchy centering in himself as the representative of God on earth.

Missionaries with the sword multiplied their activities, as success crowned their endeavors, to win neighboring tribes. Biographers of saints report that vast numbers were converted by the power of preaching the Gospel of Mohammed, although it is difficult not to believe that, in many instances at least, if reports are true, an army was waiting to strike in case the preacher's eloquence and persuasiveness failed to bring about the desired results. It is impossible to distinguish, in the narrative of the many conquests of Islam during the first century after the death of Mohammed, how much was due to religious zeal and how much to greed and political ambition.

Other methods have been employed by Mohammedans for propagating their faith, such as the purchase or forcible seizure of non-Moslem children in times of plague, famine, war and massacre, or even in times of no special disturbance, and rearing them in the Mohammedan faith. The Janissaries at Constantinople are a case in point. The children of Christians were taken regularly to replenish the ranks of this special body-guard of successive Sultans of Turkey. Another method employed to increase the number of Moslems was the plurality of wives and the use of captive women of non-Moslem races as concubines. These two methods of propagation were conspicuously employed, and even to the present time are in use by the Turks.

It must be borne in mind that there is no distinctive Moslem race or people. While Mohammed was an Arab, as were the early converts, no attempt was instituted to make Islam an ethnic religion. Jews were among the early converts, and as conquests increased, other races were added and intermarriage followed, since Islam claimed to recognize no race or class. To the present time, willing or enforced conversions from among Christian and other people have produced a mixture that bears the marks of a great variety of contributing races. Probably today the Arabs present the purest Moslem race, while Mohammedans in China are mostly Chinese.

Before the death of Mohammed the greater part of Arabia had submitted and produced a political unity that had never before been experienced in the Peninsula, creating from a great number of disconnected and often hostile tribes the semblance of a nation under one leader. With astonishing speed a political organism emerged, subordinating the clan system to the larger idea of religious unity. It is no wonder, in the face of such success, that Mohammed began to see visions of world conquest, or that his followers caught the idea and began to act upon it.

One naturally asks the question whether the zeal of Mohammed and his immediate successors was due more to religious enthusiasm, or to love of conquest? This question will probably never be satisfactorily answered, since undoubtedly motives were hopelessly mixed. Large numbers of those who comprised the victorious armies of the faithful had yielded only under external pressure, succumbing in the hope of worldly gain. Pride in new-found strength, with assurance of booty, accompanied by a hitherto unexperienced conception of a common religion, spurred on the armies and their leaders to renewed activities and deeds of daring which led to rapid conquest.

It is an interesting fact that Mohammedanism extended itself in the first century East and West along the belt of greatest heat. There seems to have been little effort to propagate the new religion in regions north or south of 30 degrees of latitude. Unlike all other religions, it may be called the religion of the tropics, although there is nothing in its teachings or practice that would seem to exclude it from temperate and even from frigid zones. It has in European Turkey, in much of Asiatic Turkey, and in Russia and Turkestan, held its own considerably north of the limit named, as it has also done in China, but still the fact remains that the great mass of Mohammedans are found today, and have always been found, in tropical countries. It should be noted in passing that the people within the region named for the last five centuries have contributed practically nothing to the development and social, intellectual or commercial advancement of the human race. Mr. Alleyne Ireland says of them:

"The people of this belt have added nothing whatever to what we understand by human advancement. Those natives of the tropics and subtropics who have not been under direct European influence have not during that time (five centuries) made a single contribution of the first importance to art, literature, science, manufacture or invention; they have not produced an engineer or a chemist or a biologist or a historian or a painter or a musician of the first rank." [3]

These facts must be taken into consideration in all plans and efforts made for the elevation and Christianization of this people; this is a large part of the Moslem problem and may suggest at least one of the reasons why previous endeavors in this direction have been so meagre of tangible results. Islam was born under a tropical sky and seems to shrink from the rigor of a colder zone.

It was manifestly the thought of Abu Bekr, the successor of Mohammed, that a campaign of conquest was intended by his chief and that the responsibility of carrying out that intention rested upon him. An army was dispatched to Syria, the first of a series of remarkable campaigns in which, under his successors, Syria, Persia, and North Africa were conquered. The ancient kingdom of Persia was overrun and some of the fairest provinces of the Roman Empire were seized.

Dr. Zwemer notes three periods in the spread of Islam, the first, from the death of Mohammed (632 A.D.) to 800 A.D.; the second, covering the Ottoman and Mongol period, from 1280 to 1480 A.D., and the third from 1780 to the present time. These may be called the Apostolic period of rapid expansion, the Medieval period of centralization, and the Modern period of mystical revival and of national decline.

During the first, or Apostolic period, the disciples with irresistible zeal carried their faith and sway throughout Arabia, across Syria, Egypt, Tunis, Tripoli, Algeria, Morocco, and into Spain. At the same time Persia was brought under the sway of the prophet, while preachers of Islam were making converts in Canton and Western China and in parts of India. It is impossible here to explain at length or to attempt a

[3] Ireland, *The Far-Eastern Tropics*, Boston, 1905, p. 4.

description in detail of the tremendous energy and enthusiasm of the armies of Islam, as they swept with fanatical energy and zeal, North, East and West, conquering everything that blocked their way and creating within a century after the death of the prophet an empire greater in extent than that of Rome at the height of its power.

It would be an interesting study to search for the secret of the power of this new religion by which it was able to accomplish such marvelous results. Many explanations are given, such as, the corrupt, divided state of Christianity, depriving it of power of resistance; the disorganized condition of non-Christian peoples and their dissatisfaction with their religions; the fanatical zeal of the recent converts to Islam; the ambition of the Caliphs to create and govern a great Moslem theocracy; the use of the sword to win converts to the new faith, and the license given to the conquerors to gratify lust and to acquire booty. There is no doubt that every one of these reasons, besides many others, contributed to the rapid rise and extension of Islam throughout the regions named, during the first period of conquest. At times one or more of these conditions contributed in a conspicuous manner, while in other places and under other conditions different motives prevailed.

It is probably true that, in most if not in every instance of conquest, the offer of Islam was made to the unbelievers. If they accepted, they were expected to join the ranks of the invaders. If they refused to embrace the religion of their threatening foe, they might be put to the sword or compelled to pay heavy tribute for the privilege of continuing to live. Even to the present day, this custom of an annual tax to a Mohammedan Government is in practice and is required of all non-Moslem subjects that they may have the right to live. It is called the life tax.

The entrance of Islam into China was less violent. There is a tradition that Mohammed mentioned China as a place

from which knowledge could be obtained. It is known,
however, that in the 6th century there was considerable
trade between China and Arabia, which was further extended
in the 7th century, then also reaching into Persia. In the
Chinese Annals of the province of Kwangtung, of which Canton is the capital, bearing date 618–907, the following passage
occurs:[4]

"At the beginning of the T'ang dynasty there came to Canton a large
number of strangers, from the kingdoms of Armam, Cambodia, Medina and
several other countries. These strangers worshiped heaven and had
neither statue, idol or image in their temples. The Kingdom of Medina
is close to that of India and it is in this kingdom that the religion of these
strangers, which is different from that of Buddha, originated. They do
not eat pork or drink wine and they regard as unclean the flesh of any
animal not killed by themselves. . . . Having asked and obtained from
the emperor permission to reside in Canton, they built magnificent houses,
of a style different to that of our country. They were very rich and obeyed
a chief chosen by themselves."

China was reached not only by the merchants who followed
the sea routes of trade but also by Moslem diplomats who
came by way of Persia.

In 638 A.D. Africa was entered by Moslem preachers,
and the propagation of Mohammedanism in that country is
still going on. In fact there is today no country in which
such conquests are being made as here. During the first
period the northern part of Africa was conquered, and in 710
the Arabs crossed into Spain. In the modern period, Mohammedan propagandists went west from Egypt and from
the Northeast as far as Chad, while slave dealers penetrated
from Zanzibar as far as the Great Lakes. The modern movements into Africa are led by the slave dealer and the Arab
trader, and by the Senousi brotherhood, which began in 1843
and is called the Jesuit order of Islam. They are found in the
Libyan Oases, Fezzan, Tripoli, Algeria, Senegambia, the

4 Quoted by Arnold in *The Preaching of Islam*, pp. 294, 295.

Sudan and Somalia. They represent one of the strongest modern advance movements among Moslems.

Within a hundred years after the death of Mohammed, an adventurous Arab chief advanced into India as far as Sind, and settled in the valley of the Indus. His successors were dislodged but again an Afghan chief named Mahmud at the very beginning of the 11th century began a series of raids on India. He was a savage leader and one of his chief objects was apparently the winning of the fabulous wealth of the country. He was the first Moslem chief to obtain a permanent footing in that country, and toward the close of the 12th century one of the generals of Muhammed, the successor of Mahmud, took the city of Delhi, which was then the seat of one of the strongest Hindu powers. The northern provinces of India were overrun as far as Benares. After Mahmud's death the Moslem empire thus begun fell in pieces while the Indian provinces still remained Mohammedan. Various dynasties succeeded and during the reign of the Tujhlak Dynasty, Tamerlane crossed the Afghan borders and captured and sacked Delhi. This was in 1399. In 1526 the Moguls (another spelling for the Mongols) invaded India. For more than two centuries they ruled over the greater part of India.

The Medieval period embraces the rise of the Ottoman and the Mogul Empires. This phase of Islam is of special interest at this time. The early records of the Mongols have not been preserved. The Mongol historian declares that they sprang from a blue wolf. The first name widely known in history is Jenghiz Khan, the eighth in descent from their first king. This man was born on the banks of the Onon river in 1162, and was placed upon the throne when thirteen years of age. In 1206 at an assembly of the notables of his kingdom he set himself at their head and shattered his only remaining enemies upon the steppes of Mongolia. Spurred on by this victory, he planned an invasion of the empire of

the Kin Tartars, who had wrested Northern China from the
Chinese Sung Dynasty. He met with success in all his battles
in Mongolia and, breaking through the Great Wall of China,
he entered the province of Kansu.   In 1213 he dispatched
three armies to overrun the empire. He was eminently
successful.   The army of Jenghiz knew no defeat. Its progress in every direction was unchecked.   When satiated with
blood and booty, it stayed its conquest and turned backwards.
Jenghiz Khan was one of the greatest conquerors the world
has ever seen.   Starting as the chief of a petty Mongol tribe,
he saw his armies victorious from the China Sea to the banks
of the Dnieper.   His empire rested upon no stable foundation, and so it dwindled away under the hand of his immediate
degenerate successors, leaving nothing behind to indicate the
triumph of his personal victories.

As a result of the Mongol invasion of Persia and Southern
Russia, we have the Turks in Europe and Western Asia, since
it was the armies of Jenghiz that drove the Osmanli ancestors
from their home in Northern Asia and caused them to invade
Bithynia.

Timur, or Tamerlane, a direct descendant from Jenghiz
Khan, nearly two centuries later accomplished a notable
conquest until he had resubjugated the whole of Central and
Western Asia, from the Chinese Wall to the Mediterranean,
and from the Siberian Steppes to the mouth of the Ganges.
The series of Mogul Mohammedan Emperors who established
and maintained in India for several generations the Great
Mogul Empire sprang from the line of Jenghiz Khan and
Tamerlane.

Space will not permit our tracing in detail the story of
the Mogul Emperors in India, which plays so conspicuous a
part in the development of Mohammedanism in that country.   We may add, however, that, until about 1200 A.D.,
Hindu princes ruled in petty principalities, when the first
Mohammedan invasion into the northern provinces took

place. This was the beginning of Moslem rule, culminating in the Great Mogul Empire, which was brought to the zenith of its power by the Emperors Akbar, Jehangir, Shah Jehan and Aurangzeb, and which declined and disappeared under Muhammed Shah and Alamgir.

The story of the splendor and power of the Mogul Emperors is of interest, both because of their Moslem faith, and because of the large number of Mohammedans over whom they held sway. These ancient empires have since been merged into a more orderly government under the rule of England, but the Moslem populations remain.

The Malay Archipelago was not entered until the 14th century, when the northern coast of Sumatra was occupied. Then Java became a Moslem mission field and soon was sending missionaries to the Spice Islands. Even today, Moslems and Christians are competing for the conquest of the remaining pagan tribes in these Islands, which is also the case in many parts of Africa.

Islam entered Burma from India through merchant missionaries; this was also the case in Russia and in all places where Mohammedanism is now advancing. Outside of Turkey, the sword at the present time plays but little part in the propagation of Islam. In Burma, the Malay Archipelago and many parts of Africa, the increase in the number of Mohammedans from conversion is alarmingly large.

The Ottoman Turks are descendants of many and extensive tribes emanating from the tablelands and plains of Central and Western Asia. These were pastoral, predacious, nomadic and warlike. They had various names, such as Turkomans, Kirghises, Usbecgs and Nogays, as well as many others derived from the district occupied or from a conspicuous chief. They were also known, and are often so designated at the present time, as Tartars, while their ancestors appear to have been known to the ancients as Scythians. It is possible that these races had a certain ethnic unity and they

certainly made use of a speech that was widely understood
among them. Before the time of Mohammed these peoples
migrated from the barren tablelands of Mongolia and spread
over the steppes of Turkestan, and appeared upon the banks
of the Oxus. At a subsequent date they came into contact
with Mohammedanism in Persia and gradually embraced
Islam, entering into the services of the Caliph of Bagdad.
They called themselves Turkomans. The Suljukians, who
settled in Khorasan, Persia, were the first Turks to become
conspicuous in history. They increased in number and power
until they ruled Persia, Armenia and Syria, the greater part of
Asia Minor with the country from the Oxus to beyond the
Jaxartes, reaching from the Mediterranean to the borders of
China.

The Suljukians surpassed all other Moslems of their age
in fierce intolerance, and thus it was that the crusades were
provoked, producing a unique event in the history of the relations of Christianity to Islam.

About the middle of the 13th century, a tribe of Turks,
not Suljukian, were driven by Mongol invaders from Khorasan
into Armenia in search of pasturage for their flocks. Out of
these came Ertogrul, who turned westward and sought settlement in Asia Minor. He came into Phrygia and Bithynia,
and there his son Othman, or Osman, was reared, who became
the founder of the Ottoman Empire.

Othman became head of his tribe and was a loyal subject
to the Sultan of Iconium, who did not interfere with his
freedom to prey upon his neighbors. In 1299 he began a
more independent career, which to his death in 1326 was
marked by gradual conquest, until, with his capital at Brousa,
he ruled over Phrygia, Galatia and Bithynia.

Thus began the long line of Turkish Sultans whose sway
was gradually extended over all Asia Minor, Armenia, Syria,
Arabia, Egypt and Tripoli in Africa, and Thrace, Macedonia,
Greece, Albania, Montenegro, Bosnia, Herzegovina, Servia,

Bulgaria, Roumania in Europe, until even the walls of Vienna were besieged by the armies of the Ottoman Sultan seeking to break through the barriers into the heart of Europe and to carry Islam to the North Sea. Thus the rise and spread of Mohammedanism in the Near East is briefly recorded. At the height of its power all Europe stood aghast at the threatened possibility of universal Moslem conquest. The Pope of Rome is said to have declared that he feared the Sultan of Turkey more than he feared the devil himself.

That part of the third division of our topic, dealing with the Wahabi revival and Dervish movements, we will consider under another heading. We will here but refer to the decline in this period of Moslem national supremacy.

The decline of Mohammedanism as a political power in the last century has been almost as rapid as its rise was under Abu Bekr and his successors in the first period, and the Ottomans, and the Mogul Emperor in the second period. Much of the quick rise of different Moslem leaders, eventuating in the creation of an Empire, can be accounted for in part by the peculiar conditions that seemed especially to favor the rapid advance of an intrepid leader backed by a horde of followers inspired by the belief that, through war, they were rendering a service to God and that the booty thus secured was theirs by divine right. To this is to be added the belief that death in battle insured an immediate entrance into the most entrancing joys of paradise. There is no doubt that Islam was able to inspire its votaries with a sense of unity wholly lacking in its opponents.

On two notable historic occasions, unbelieving barbarians have conquered the followers of Mohammed, the Suljuk Turks in the 11th century, and the Mongols in the 13th, and in each case the conquered have forced their religion upon their conquerors.

In addition to the so-called Moslem lands and countries that contain large numbers of Mohammedans, like China and

Russia, there are scattered Moslem populations surrounded by unbelievers. Among these are the Polish-speaking Moslems, of Tartar origin, in Lithuania, who inhabit the districts of Kovno, Vilna and Grodno; the Dutch-speaking Moslems of Cape Colony, and the Indian Coolies that have carried their faith to the West Indies and to British and Dutch Guiana.

As we trace the decline of Moslem power, we note the early dissensions in the territory invaded by Jenghiz Khan, requiring a second victory by his descendant Tamerlane. Next we note the Mogul Emperors in India flashing across history with all the brilliancy of a fabulously wealthy eastern court, remaining for a brief period like a dream or vision of a glorious past, and then disappearing, except for the broken monuments of their former supremacy. The regions ruled by this series of brilliant Moslem emperors passed under the government of a Christian queen.

We turn then to the rule of the Saracens in Spain, who aspired to invade northern Europe, but who were compelled to withdraw to Africa, and Spain passed again under a Christian government.

The Ottoman Empire that once held sway over the country stretching from Persia and India to the Adriatic, including vast areas in Europe and the entire southern littoral of the Mediterranean, now possesses no territory upon the southern shores of the Mediterranean and has but a slight hold upon Europe. Morocco, Algeria, Tunis, Tripoli and Egypt have all passed from Moslem rule to government by Christian powers. Persia, once proud of her position among the Mohammedan nations, is now but a vassal of a Christian state. The fact is almost startling, that, whereas, a few centuries ago, Mohammedan kingdoms and empires were the most powerful and dreaded governments upon the face of all the earth, now not one remains with even a semblance of independent power possessing the elements of continuity. Islam as a national force in the world has ceased to be, and so the dream of Mohammed of a mighty theocracy under the control of the Caliph of Islam has passed from earth without the possibility of return.

It is a question worthy at least of speculation, if the loss of political and national power has not tended to drive Moslems back to the contemplation of things spiritual. As hopes of conquest have been destroyed, devout Moslems have sought spiritual victories over themselves and others, as is manifested in some of the more modern mystical developments. These are questions worthy of serious consideration.

CHAPTER III

SOME STRUGGLES OF ISLAM AND CHRISTIANITY

Islam has throughout its history been a militant religion. Between it and Christianity there have been several conflicts when one or the other religion seemed to hang in the balance. A consideration of some of these turning-points of history may throw into clearer relief the problem of the evangelization of Islam. Before considering these it may be of interest to recall one of the fierce battles of the infancy of Islam — a battle in which Christians were in no way involved — during which the life of the infant religion was nearly extinguished. The battle in question is known as the battle of Ohod, and the contending parties were, on the one hand, Mohammed's enemies from Mecca, and, on the other, the Mohammedans of Medina led by the prophet himself.

In 625 A.D., during the third year of Mohammed's residence at Medina, and twelve months after the battle of Bedr, in which the forces of Mohammed had routed the Koreish warriors of Mecca, the war clouds gathered again about the adopted home of the Prophet of Islam. Word was brought to Medina that an avenging army from Mecca was on its way, nearly 3,000 strong, to break the power of Mohammed and at the same time to regain the plunder that was captured in the previous battle. Of these 3,000 troops, 700 were clad in mail, 200 were mounted on horses, and 2,100 rode on camels. In order to inspire the soldiers to greater effort, 15 women were added to the train who, with timbrels and songs of wild cadence for kinsmen slain at Bedr, incited them to their mightiest endeavor. The battle was fought on the fertile plain of Ohod, near the city of Medina. The army of Mohammed was only 1,000 strong, as it set out to engage in

battle, and before the battle began, 300 of his followers
deserted, leaving only 700 to match the 3,000 of the enemy,
and of these 700, only 100 were clad in mail and only two
mounted on horses. The conflict seemed a most unequal
one, the invading army numbering fully four to one to the
army of defense.

The battle opened on January 26, and it seemed at the
outset that victory must be with the Koreish army, because
of their overwhelming numbers and vastly superior equipment. Mohammed himself, having donned a coat of mail
and a helmet, with a sword hanging from his girdle, occupied
an eminence in the rear of his troops, where he might watch
and direct the battle. The Moslems fought with great desperation and effectiveness, and for a time seemed to be gaining
ground. At first their fierce ardor carried all before it. They
showed the same contempt of danger that they revealed at
the battle of Bedr twelve months before, but they were not
able to keep up the unequal contest. Finally their ranks
were broken, and quick discomfiture followed. The standard-
bearer was slain and his banner disappeared. The Moslems
broke at every point and fled for refuge to the overhanging
rocks of Ohod.

It was a moment of extreme peril for Mohammed, who was
still in the rear watching the conflict and endeavoring to check
the flight of his followers by calling upon them to return, and
shouting: "The apostle of God is here. Come back."
But still they fled. The enemy bore down upon him, while
there rallied about him a small party of devoted followers.
Stones and arrows flew thick around him; he was struck in
the face by one of the missiles and a tooth was broken; his
helmet was crushed in and two of the rings were driven into
his cheek; a gash was made in his forehead. A warrior of
the attacking army suddenly appeared, and with drawn sword
was about to cleave the head of the prophet. Just at that
moment one of Mohammed's followers threw up his arm and

received the blow, which nearly severed his arm from his body, but which at the same time saved the life of Moham- med. Stunned, he was seized by some of his men and carried into a cave in the vicinity, where relief was given to him in his distress. In the meantime, the word had gone forth among the enemy that Mohammed had been slain, upon which their pursuit ceased and the invading army gave their attention to the booty. Mohammed was taken from his hiding-place and returned to Medina, while the hostile army went back to Mecca.

The battle of Ohod has not generally been referred to, to my knowledge, as one of the decisive battles of the world. Creasy, in his classic work on the " Decisive Battles of the World," makes no allusion to it. But it seems to me that few, if any, battles have ever been fought upon whose outcome so much depended as upon the battle of Ohod. True, the prophet was defeated, but not disastrously.

But let us imagine for a moment what would have been the result had the faithful defender of Mohammed not been at hand, or had he been but a few feet farther away when the sword of the avenging army was about to fall upon the head of the prophet Mohammed. Had Mohammed been slain in that battle, there is no doubt that we should never have heard of him or of his religion. His hold upon Medina was at that time so slight that his directions with reference to this battle were disobeyed. He planned to fight the battle about the walls of Medina and so gave orders, but the army decided to fight it on the plains of Ohod and overruled their commander. Up to that time the Koran had been by no means completed; Medina itself had not been fully won; Mecca was in open and violent hostility; Mohammed was known more as a leader of an army whose principal object was the plundering of passing caravans than as the founder of a religion. There can be little doubt that had he fallen in that battle in January, 625 A.D., we should have never known his name or heard of the religion that he established. It requires but a slight stretch of imagination to see what mighty interests turned upon a single moment at the crucial point in that decisive battle.

The first of the critical struggles between Islam and Christianity is known as the battle of the Yarmuk. It occurred in the year 634 A.D. in the caliphate of Abu Bekr, only two years after Mohammed had died. Before Mohammed died he had so overawed the various tribes of the Arabian peninsula that they accorded him a nominal suzerainty and professed Islam. When, however, it was known that he was dead and that the aged Abu Bekr ruled in his stead, these tribes, always restive under control, threw off their allegiance. The first year of Abu Bekr's caliphate was occupied in wars directed to resubduing the Arabs to Islam. In this struggle his most successful general was Kalid. When Arabia was once more conquered, the aged caliph dispatched his armies to spread the faith of Islam in other parts and to win rich booty for the ruling congregation at Medina. In the practice of Mohammedanism these two ideals have from the beginning gone hand in hand.

The brilliant Kalid led the attack on the Persians in Mesopotamia, where he maintained his reputation as a general by achieving several victories and winning considerable territory. Meanwhile another army under a less distinguished general marched northward to make an attack on Palestine. At that time Heraclius was emperor of the Romans. He was a man who had reason to be proud of his military deeds. Although in the early part of his reign he had steadily suffered defeat at the hands of the Persian king, Chosroes II, so that in 617 Chosroes captured Chalcedon opposite Constantinople, yet in the years that followed he had as steadily defeated Chosroes and by 628 had regained the territories of Asia Minor, Syria, Palestine and Egypt, which the Persian had wrested from him.

Proud in the memory of these signal victories over one of the greatest military powers of the age, Heraclius looked with disdain on the rough, untutored Arabian hordes which came against him. Perhaps rumors of Abu Bekr's successes made him anxious, for he collected a large army which is said to have numbered ninety thousand men. The Arabian forces were massed on the banks of the Yarmuk to the eastward of the Sea of Galilee. The Yarmuk is a deep gorge, at the bottom of which runs a stream. It is the most northerly of the three deep gorges that cut deep into the trans-Jordanic territory, dividing it into four parts. The ancient Jabbok and Arnon are the other two. All three are deep and difficult for an army to cross. Heraclius, when he approached with his army, had incautiously encamped on the plain of Wacusa. The plain was formed by a great bend in the Yarmuk. It was bounded on three sides by steep precipices and on the fourth by a ravine. The Romans thought that it was a camping ground easy to defend, but the Arabs soon gained command of the ravine by which it was approached, and there the two armies lay through the long summer. Several skirmishes were fought, but nothing decisive was accomplished. At this juncture Kalid was recalled from Mesopotamia. He hastily crossed the desert and arrived at Wacusa in September of the year 634. In the battle that followed it seemed at first that the Romans would overwhelm the Arabs, but the Romans were unable, because of the formation of the ground, to make their superiority in numbers tell. The Arabs fought with their usual desperation, and at last the Romans were forced to yield. Many of them were pushed over the edge of the gorge and perished. The rest were taken prisoners. On the next day Kalid took possession of the tent of the Roman commander. Thus in the first clash of arms between Islam and Christian forces the Mohammedans were triumphant.

The battle of the Yarmuk was a decisive battle. It laid

A Moslem Arab Gentleman

all Syria and Palestine open to the armies of the Caliph, and, although other engagements took place — engagements which gained for the Moslems such cities as Damascus and Jerusalem — the battle of the Yarmuk set the standard which prevailed. In less than ten years Egypt had also yielded and some of the fairest provinces of the Christian empire of Byzantium, which still called itself Roman, were lost forever.

The second battle of Islam with Christian forces is commonly known as the battle of Tours, in which the Arab army, pushing north across the Pyrenees, sought to conquer France and open the way for the conquest of Christian Europe. Just a century after the death of Mohammed, when the Saracens had gained complete control of Spain and their armies were massed on the southern border of the Pyrenees, their great military leader, the head of the Saracen Government in Spain, Abderrahman, whose skill and prowess as a general had already signalized his conquests in Africa and Spain, conceived the idea of overrunning France and establishing Mohammedanism as the religion of Western Europe.

It must be borne in mind that, up to this time, the conquering Arabs had met with no defeat or even setback, as they pushed their forces across North Africa and won the complete subjugation of Spain. Charles Martel, the son of Pepin Heristal, already engaged in his endeavor to unify the divergent forces under his rule, commanded the areas invaded by the Moslem hosts. The Mohammedan forces are reported to have greatly exceeded in numbers the Christian forces sent against them. The universally victorious advance of Mohammedanism naturally inspired the Christian forces of France with genuine terror. The Mohammedans came to the attack with their women and children in camp, in a multitude which the record of the monks referred to as " beyond the power of man to number." They came with the fixed purpose of establishing their homes in France, their mind harboring no thought of possible defeat. Thus they pierced through the mountains, spread over the level territory at the north, plundering the country and smiting all with the sword.

One of the fullest reports of this great battle, referred to as the battle of Tours, is taken from the records of an Arabian chronicler. He reports the battle as lasting seven days, at the end of which time, through a combination of events, the great general, Abderrahman, was slain. Consternation spread through the ranks of the Mohammedans, and the tide of the first great battle won by the Christians was turned and the Christian army remained master of the field. One chronicler puts the loss of the Arabs at 375,000 men, and the loss of the Christians at only 1,000, but this statement is manifestly not reliable. The details of the battle are meagre, but the Arabian historian speaks of the complete overthrow of the Moslem forces and the withdrawal of the remnant of the army into Spain.

Thus the movement of the Mohammedan hordes into Western Europe was checked, and later Spain was able to free herself from the Saracen hosts and return again to the ranks of Christian countries. Quite beyond the saving of Europe from Saracen invasion remains the importance of the fact that here, for the first time, Christian forces successfully met and turned back the tide of Moslem invasion. It did much to put heart into the Christians and to convince the Moslems that they were not invincible. This battle, which rescued Christendom from Islam, took place in 732.

A third decisive conflict between Islam and Christianity was the siege of Constantinople which resulted in its capture in 1453. This was the result of a long series of triumphs on the part of the Turkish Mohammedans. The Turks had first entered Europe in 1356, when the forces of the Sultan Orkhan occupied the towns of Tzympe and Gallipoli. Between 1359 and 1402 the Sultans Murad I and Bayezid had conquered most of ancient Thrace and modern Rumelia. Then came Timur-leng or Tamerlane who overran the Asiatic dominions of Bayezid in 1402, and took Bayezid captive. Tamerlane died however in 1405. During the reigns of Mohammed I and Murad II (1405–1451) the struggle for the Balkan countries was renewed and the Turkish conquests were pushed up to the borders of Hungary. By 1451 the dominions of the once proud Cæsars had dwindled to the city of Constantinople and a small territory around it.

At this juncture Murad II died and was succeeded by his son, Mohammed II, then a youth of but twenty-one years. Constantine XI, who had been crowned emperor at Constantinople three years before, was led to underestimate the character of Mohammed by the fact that while Mohammed was in his teens Murad II had tried in vain to associate Mohammed with him in the government, and Mohammed had betrayed such a distaste for national affairs that he was released from these burdensome duties. Constantine, accordingly, demanded the augmentation of a certain stipend which the former Sultan had paid him for keeping a possible rival a virtual prisoner at Constantinople. Mohammed, who was occupied at the moment with other enterprises, replied courteously. But a little later, having made a truce of three years with Hungary, he unceremoniously drove away the messengers of Constantine and set about preparations for the conquest of Constantinople. He began to construct a fortress on the European side of the Bosphorus about five miles above Constantinople, where the channel is narrowest. On the opposite shore there stood a similar fortress built by a former Sultan. Constantine remonstrated, but in vain. It became evident that a decisive struggle was inevitable.

During the winter of 1452–3 both sides were busy with preparations. Mohammed collected a large army and gave personal attention not only to its equipment but to the plans of attack. He was constantly discussing them with any one whose opinion of such matters he valued. Firearms had been employed for some time by both Christians and Moham-

medans, and Mohammed employed a Hungarian named
Urban, who cast for the Turks a monster cannon that was a
terror to Christians and Turks alike. He also collected
a fleet of three hundred and twenty vessels with which to
besiege the city by water.

Constantine on his part was not idle, but his resources
were far inferior. He had previously sought to bring the
Byzantine church into closer harmony with Rome in order to
unite Christendom against the Turks — an act which alien-
ated many of his own subjects. The Grand Duke Notoras
declared that he would rather see the turban of the Sultan
than the tiara of the Pope in Constantinople. In the end
Islam triumphed because of the division of Christendom.
Only six thousand Greeks out of a population of one hundred
thousand took part in the defense of the city. The Pope sent
Cardinal Isadore with a small body of veteran troops and some
financial aid. The Venetians and Spaniards also sent some
aid. Constantine had, however, but 9,000 men with which to
defend walls fourteen miles in circumference. He had but
fourteen ships, though these were larger than the ships of the
Turks. The Turkish troops employed are variously estimated at from 70,000 to 250,000. The siege began on April
6th and was by the bravery of Constantine and the Venetian
commander Guistiniani prolonged until May 20th. During
this time the Christians performed many gallant deeds both
on the water and within the walls. Finally, however, on May
29th the Turks broke through at the gate of St. Romanus, and
after fierce fighting in the city, during which Constantine
was killed, Constantinople capitulated on May 30th, 1453.
Thus Islam by the hands of the Turk extinguished the last
long lingering remnant of the once proud empire of Rome,
and took as hers the capital chosen by the first Christian
emperor.

When Constantinople was taken by the Turks, many
Christians fled to Italy, carrying with them precious manu-

scripts of Biblical and Christian books as well as of classic authors in Greek, of which the West had long been ignorant. In due time the study of these books led to that revival of learning which we call the Renaissance, the ferment of which produced the Reformation.

The fourth great conflict between Islam and Christianity occurred in 1529. Suleiman the Magnificent, who was Sultan of Turkey from 1520 to 1566, brought the Ottoman rule to the zenith of its power and glory. His ever victorious armies pushed their triumphant way to the North and West, conquering everything before them. In 1529 he entered Hungary, alarming Ferdinand to such an extent that he sent an emissary to Constantinople to negotiate peace, at least to obtain a truce. Though this seemed momentarily successful, it was soon broken, and in May of that year Suleiman left Constantinople with an army of 250,000 men and 300 cannon, with the avowed purpose of driving Ferdinand from his kingdom. The army of Ferdinand was overcome, and the Sultan advanced as far as the walls of Vienna. The city was nearly surrounded, and the entire country west of the Danube was white with the tents of the invading Moslems. Four hundred Turkish vessels, well manned and commanded, floated on the Danube, watching the city by water. Inside the city was a troop of only about 16,000 men; the fortifications of the city were incomplete, with only 72 guns, an ineffective wall and an undisciplined army. In October of that year the Turks assailed the city with their accustomed desperation. They were repulsed. Provisions were scarce, and the weather became severe; the army was discouraged. One more charge was made against the city, but without success, and the veteran troops refused to respond to the call for advance. A retreat followed, and Vienna was saved for Christian Europe.

The fifth decisive conflict in the attempt of Islam to win world supremacy took place in 1683. The Mohammedans were not satisfied with their previous failure in the attempt to penetrate Europe through the valley of the Danube, and although the Ottoman Empire had lost not a little of its prestige by the failure of Suleiman to capture the city of Vienna, another attempt was made in 1682, under Mohammed IV, who ruled in Turkey from 1648 to 1687, to push his army through Vienna into the heart of Europe. This enterprise was inaugurated under the leadership of Kara Mustapha, inspired by the revolt of the Hungarians against Austria. In 1683 munitions were collected at Adrianople, on a scale scarcely approached, never surpassed, by the Moslem forces. The muster roll amounted to 275,000 men, besides camp followers and irregular troops. It is estimated that an army of not less than half a million was thus brought to bear upon this border Christian city. The Poles came to the aid of the Austrian Emperor Leopold with 58,000 men. The city of Vienna was garrisoned by only 11,000 men. The second siege of Vienna lasted from July 15th to September 12th, 1683. Historians report that had Kara Mustapha, the Grand Vizier, been willing to lead his troops in a general attack against the city, there were various periods within the dates above given when the city could easily have been taken by the Ottoman forces; but he, hoping to secure the surrender of the city and thus himself to become the master of the situation and the controller of all its vast wealth, kept his troops back from the charge, until reinforcements came to the city, and a direct attack was made by a flanking movement upon the massed Ottoman forces. Under the personal leadership of King Sobieski of Poland, the Ottoman army broke and fled in hopeless rout. Janizaries were cut to pieces, the entire camp, artillery and military stores were captured by the conquerors, and the defeat was complete. Kara Mustapha retired in disgrace, and the second and last attempt of Moslem forces to conquer Europe was thwarted. This success put heart into Christian Europe, and from that time even to the present hour the Christian forces have gradually taken possession of Ottoman territory, until now the remnant existing as the Turkish Empire is struggling for its life.

Each one of these five significant conflicts between Mohammedans and Christians must stand as among the great battles of history upon the issues of which mighty interests hung. These interests were not wholly religious, since Mohammedanism was vastly more than a religion. It stood for a civilization, a condition of society, an intellectual bias, a religious theocracy, that put its stamp and seal upon every race and country it dominated. Had Islam prevail.d in all of its five great conflicts with Christianity, a wholly different civilization would have succeeded the Christian order overthrown, and a new history of the world would have been written.

We are now witnessing the sixth and probably the last of the national and international conflicts of Islam. Although only a small part of the Mohammedans of the world are actually engaged in this contest, as indeed was the case at the battles of Tours and Vienna, the entrance of the Ottoman Empire into the world war as an ally of the central powers and under the other prevailing conditions precipitated a conflict which must necessarily be determinative of the question whether or not there shall continue to be anywhere upon earth a Mohammedan Empire upon whose throne shall sit the Caliph of Islam.

The conflict now waging, unlike those that preceded, is both religious and political. Lines of religious cleavage are running up and down, back and forth, across the faith, practices and religious thinking of Moslems, appearing in various mystical movements and indicating a religious unrest and dissatisfaction never before experienced. The centralized government upon the Bosphorus has hitherto been able to exercise a measure of restraint and direction that has prevented radical disruption and has maintained a degree of at least outward amity. Recent events at Constantinople have brought down upon the Ottoman leaders the severest condemnation of devout and able Mohammedans, not only in Turkey, but in all of the other Moslem countries. Dissatisfaction with present religious practices and conditions is outspoken and unequivocal. This has not all arisen from the war, but the war intensified what already existed and gave the Moslem leaders a boldness of critical utterance unknown a few years ago, but now proclaimed unhindered in every land where Moslems dwell. There is today waging among Mohammedans a battle of religious and social ideas, revolutionary in their nature, and destined radically to change the thinking, belief and practices of the followers of the prophet.

The failure of the national conflict and its consequences are easier to understand. For 400 years the Ottoman Empire has stood as the religious center of the Mohammedan world. It has been the dream and expectation of loyal Moslems that the influence and power of that Empire would increase until it became the dominant national force to which all other nations would be subject. This is but an essential part of the Mohammedan belief that God is the God of the Moslems and to them rightfully belong the kingdoms of the world. Conviction of the truth of this doctrine has brought comfort in the face of the national defeats and humiliations of the past 350 years. So long as the Ottoman Empire persisted and the Caliph sat upon the throne and the Sheik-ul-Islam authoritatively interpreted the sacred law to the faithful, trusting in the omnipotent strength of Allah, they entertained the hope that some day that power would manifest itself and Islam would prevail. These have observed their Caliph and the Sheik-ul-Islam with all solemnity call in vain upon the faithful to give their lives to a holy war. Instead of a loyal response, condemnation of the act has arisen from Egypt, India, North Africa and other Moslem centers. They see their Caliph impotent, almost a prisoner in his own palace, with no prospect of another to take his place in the sacred office. They see the once proud Ottoman Empire allied with two so-called Christian nations in a war with other Christian nations and with Moslems arrayed against them in alliance with their Christian enemies. They note the rapid encroachment of Russia and Great Britain upon the sacred Moslem territory,[1] while Constantinople has already passed almost wholly under the control of Germany with an economic crisis never before experienced threatening her entire domains.

To give the crowning blow to the prestige of the Ottoman Caliph, Arabia arrayed herself upon the side of the Christian allies, seized the sacred shrines of Islam at Mecca and Medina and repudiated the Moslem ruler upon the Bosphorus, while Persia holds a position of armed hostility to Turkey. Thus the Caliph, whose sacred duty is to guard the shrines and relics of Mohammedanism, is powerless to protect, much less to perform, the ordinary functions of his high office.

Whatever is the final outcome of the war, it is clear to all Mohammedans as it is to the world that there can never again be an Ottoman Empire over which a Sultan, the Caliph of Islam, will maintain control as an independent sovereign. This war has already broken the solidarity of the Moslem world and given to the 230,000,000 followers of the prophet of Arabia a new freedom from centralized religious authority and temporal control.

An unprecedented liberty has come to the Moslems of all countries to think and believe as their consciences dictate. The organized religious system has broken down and for the first time since Mohammed, his followers are becoming free from political terrorism. The consequences growing out of this last decisive conflict of Islam are of surpassing importance to both the Christian and the Moslem world.

[1] Since the above was written Russia has through internal dissensions fallen out of the conflict, but Great Britain, having conquered Bagdad and Mosul, is pushing on westward. In Palestine she has taken Gaza, Jaffa, Bir-saba, Hebron, Bethlehem and Jerusalem, and is pushing northward toward Nablus.

CHAPTER IV

THE STRENGTH OF ISLAM

Whatever may be our opinion about Mohammedanism, we lose by attempting to ignore the elements of strength possessed by it. No religion has ever taken a strong hold upon any people that did not have within it many elements of power. No religion has existed for any period and influenced the lives of any considerable number of people, that did not command fundamental truths, both religious and psychological. The secret of strength in Islam is found in the truths which it contains and the correct principles which it inculcates; or, to put it in another form, it is strong in proportion to the thoroughness with which it has answered and answers today the most pressing questions that crowd upon human life and that make religious belief practical to the life of him who accepts it. A religion which professes to come from God and to reveal God to men and to afford a way of salvation from the sin and burden of the life that now is, must secure a hearing and command a following. If we add to these fundamental truths, ability to answer in part the religious inquiry of the human heart and a certain pomp and show and promise and forecast of power, then that religion will possess a basis of appeal which to some people and in some countries becomes irresistible. It is our task at this point to inquire into some of the elements of strength which have revealed themselves in Mohammedanism from the beginning. We achieve nothing by closing our eyes to these historic facts of the religion with which we stand face to face and to which it is our mission to present the gospel of Jesus Christ. We mention some of these elements of strength, most of which appear upon the surface. Our enumeration is not by any means exhaustive but sufficiently so perhaps to bring before us that which Christianity must fairly meet if it would win the Moslem world.

1. One cannot escape from the fact that a religion which has won and holds the allegiance of one-seventh of the world's population must have in it many elements of strength. The very fact of the number of those who profess Islam as their religion is in itself an element of power, to the Mohammedan believer as well as to the one outside the fold who contemplates this great religious body, second in number only to the followers of Jesus Christ. A religion that receives the allegiance of the majority of the populations of all the states of North Africa, of the Turkish Empire, Persia, Afghanistan, Turkestan, Bokhara, Arabia, Syria, the Malay Archipelago and Peninsula, making rapid progress in its extension south into the Sudan in Africa, and numbering nearly seventy millions in India with many millions in China and Russia, is in itself an indication of religious strength and force that must be seriously reckoned with. When they tell us that this religion is making rapid progress among some of the wilder tribes of Russia today, that it is getting a foothold in both East and West Africa south of the Sudan, that it already has its mosques in Natal and is reaching out and making converts in still other countries, — we need no further arguments to convince us that the force of Mohammedanism is not dead, but that it is a religion alive, active and powerful.

2. As one studies the history of Islam from the days of Mohammed to comparatively recent times, he cannot fail to be impressed with the surpassing pomp and grandeur of many of the Mohammedan states. Books have been written upon the wealth, display, and power of the Mogul emperors of India. It is no wonder that the Mohammedans point with great pride to the achievements of these emperors as they mastered the most fertile part of India and ruled with a brilliancy and glory hardly equalled, never surpassed, in the

history of world rulers. The story of the rise and power of this series of brilliant emperors reads like a romance, although it is in itself but the true history of an epoch in the life of India and of Mohammedan supremacy. Although the empire has fallen, Mohammedanism, as a religion, has remained with an increasing number of followers. The same is true, although in a lesser measure, of the Caliphate that centered in Bagdad, covering a series of centuries following the death of Mohammed.

The rise and development of the Ottoman Empire, beginning with Othman and reaching its supremacy and power in Suleiman the Magnificent, tells a story of national development hardly second to that of the Mogul Emperors themselves. The story is one of which every Mohammedan may well be proud, especially when he realizes that at the height of the supremacy of the Ottoman Empire under Suleiman and his immediate successor it held in its absolute sway more territory than was ever held by the Empire of Rome, and was then the most powerful empire on the face of the earth.

The Mohammedans also have reason to look back with pride upon the conquests of Islam during the first century of its history after the death of its prophet. What Moslem heart would not naturally swell as he realizes the fact that within a hundred years from the death of his honored leader, Mohammedanism had conquered a large proportion of the then known world. Beginning without organization or wealth or leadership, with a little handful of followers of the dead prophet, in the city of Medina, they had raised up, equipped, and sent into the field victorious armies before whose conquering tread tribe after tribe, nation after nation had fallen, until Western Asia to the borders of India and nearly the entire country about the Mediterranean, including Spain and a part of France, acknowledged the supreme power and sway of Mohammed as the prophet of God and the head of the new theocracy.

3. Every Mohammedan must be ready under the call of the Caliph to respond with the offering of himself and his life in the defence of his faith. In the earlier days of Mohammedanism, many tribes as well as individuals made permanent their allegiance to Mohammed and Allah by taking the sword and joining the Mohammedan forces in a battle of conquest or of defence. Many of these entered into the new faith with little knowledge and no spirit of allegiance, but after participating in an extended campaign of conquest in which booty was freely distributed, their loyalty became permanent. While there has never been, with one exception, since the days of Mohammed a call for a general holy war, yet the fact that every Moslem is expected to volunteer whenever such a call should come, has tended to create a permanent reserve army of the able-bodied men in Islam whose first duty is to respond without hesitation. This has helped strengthen and deepen the sense of brotherhood and of common responsibility. It has helped build into a unity the followers of Mohammed and to strengthen the bands that bind them together into a great organization fundamentally military.

It is but natural, therefore, that a people thus taught should love war and with a cruel fanaticism revel in it. Even before the death of the prophet the fighting spirit raged throughout Arabia and war seemed to be the chief purpose in the life of all Mohammedans. It was an accepted doctrine of that religion that the sword was the key of Heaven and of Hell and that a drop of blood shed for God, or a night spent in arms, was of more avail than months spent in fasting and prayer.

4. Mohammedanism is the most democratic of the great non-Christian religions. It was a revolt from the ecclesiasticism of the time and from the control of the church by the priesthood. Islam is fundamentally a religion without a priest, in which every believer deals directly with his God. Theoretically, at least, every Mohammedan has equal voice

with every other Mohammedan in the control of religious matters. There is no caste, no hierarchy, the humblest believer worships side by side and with equal rights with the loftiest ruler. It is possible under Mohammedan rule and practice for the beggar to rise to the highest position in the Mohammedan state and in the Mohammedan religious order. This presented from the beginning strong attractions to the humble members of the Arabian tribes, and it has been one of the features of strength of Islam even to the present time. Among the Sunis the Caliph of Islam himself receives his authority and power from the voice of the people. When Adbul Hamid II was deposed and Mohammed V was appointed his successor, there was a form of election by which Mohammed was given authority and power as the head of the Ottoman Empire, and thus was made, in the judgment of the people of Turkey at least, the Caliph of Islam and the Protector of its Holy Shrines.

5. We are liable to lose sight of the fact that Mohammedanism is not only a religion but it is a form of government. It is only when Mohammedans live under Christian or other governments that they are unable to put into practice this principle of their religion. As established by Mohammed, if not prevented by some other form of national administration, all Mohammedans would now be under a Moslem government in which the laws of the country are the laws laid down by Mohammed in the Koran interpreted by precedent and tradition. The idea which has been held before Mohammedans of all time, and forward to which they have looked with eager anticipation, is that of Mohammedan rule not only for all Moslems but for all the world, under whose sway Christians and pagans would be swept into the Moslem fold. The national idea of Mohammedanism has had more to do with its extension in the world than the religious idea. The spur of conquest, the force of arms, the triumphant victories won in the name of Mohammed have sprung from the theocratic

conception of religion. This has made Mohammedanism the physical power which it has been in all its history. When Islam is bereft of its dreamed-of Mohammedan rule, it will have lost a large measure of its victorious and inspirational power.

6. The astuteness of Mohammed is demonstrated by the simplicity of his creed and the exactions with which certain observances are demanded. There is much of permanent psychological value in the exactions required of all Mohammedans in the practice of their religion, in that by such repeated acts of devotion or worship the believer becomes more fully committed. In the earlier days many Moslems requested release from the five prayers, but Mohammed was inexorable in his demand that five times a day the faithful Moslem should engage in prayer. The other exactions that are demanded from all the faithful, such as fasting, pilgrimages, almsgiving, etc., all have their place in centering the thought of the Mohammedan on his religion and in binding him more fully to it as a part of his daily life. The strongest features of Mohammedanism which have given it a firm hold upon all followers of the Prophet to the ends of the earth are the daily exactions enforced upon all loyal Mohammedans. The strictness with which multitudes observe these demands, together with the pressure which they bring upon others to hold them to the prescribed observances of the faith, constitute a permanent force. While these demands have repelled some, undoubtedly they have bound with unbreakable bands others who at first were weak in the faith but who, through the practices of Islam, became strong and aggressive promoters.

The same astuteness is shown in the clearness and definiteness of the demands made. No Mohammedan is left in doubt as to what his duties are day by day and hour by hour. He knows just when and how he should pray, just when and how alms should be given and pilgrimages made and fasts observed. He exercises no independent religious judgment;

that has already been done for him, and all that is required of him is obedience not only to God but to the precedents, practices, and exactions of his religion. And these are within the range of his possibilities.

7. Outside of the Bible no religious book has played so conspicuous a part in the propagation of a faith as the book of Mohammed. The lofty style in which it is written, the character of the Arabic language used throughout, the high-sounding phrases so sweet to the ear of one who speaks and knows the Arabic tongue, have given it a lasting hold upon the religious thinking of the great multitude of Arabian followers of the Mohammedan creed. But even beyond the bounds of those who know Arabic, the rotund phrases in which the Koran abounds when read, chanted or repeated in their religious services, take a deep and mystical hold upon the hearts of the followers of Mohammed. The Koran contains in itself many of the permanent elements of poetic beauty and, in its ritualistic uses, takes the place of various forms so widely used in Christian worship and satisfies, to a considerable degree, the longing of the heart for the mysterious and exalted.

8. Mohammedanism has experienced a great advantage in the simplicity of its credal statements. It requires no long explanation. The necessary period of instruction for even a savage to grasp the idea of God as one and almighty and of Mohammed as his prophet is comparatively brief. This expresses the length and breadth of the Mohammedan confession of faith. In the face of the diversity of creeds and declarations put forth by Christians, Mohammedanism has a great advantage, of which Mohammedans are well aware. However much of tradition may have grown up around this credal statement, and however varied may be the interpretation thereof, the whole Mohammedan world is united and absolutely agreed upon this single declaration of faith. The one who accepts it is not expected to understand it in all its length and breadth, neither is he required to make explanation,

he simply repeats it and becomes a Moslem. Nothing further is required in the way of credal statement or declaration of belief.

9. It was a wise and far-sighted provision of Mohammed to make, for the chief condition of entrance into his fellowship, absolute submission to the law of God as revealed through Mohammed. The very name Islam signifies submission to the will of God. A man to become a follower of Mohammed must resign his will to God's will and find his highest and most complete happiness in that act. That is the Mohammedan's life, the sum total of his existence, whatever follows must grow as a corollary out of his complete obedience to God as revealed through his holy religion. While this principle was not new, being but a gross form of what was already taught by Jesus Christ, nevertheless, as presented by Mohammed, in its simplicity and bluntness, it had and yet has a permanent power over the lives of all whom it dominates. There is no other single principle of Islam which takes such a strong hold upon its followers and binds them together so completely with a bond of common fellowship and common service under the hand of a common deity as this fundamental doctrine. All Mohammedans become brothers in service to one commonly recognized God to whom they submit their wills and commit their lives.

10. Of the five demands which Mohammedanism places upon all its followers no one is of greater worth to the Mohammedan institution as a whole than that of the pilgrimage to the sacred shrines of Islam demanded of every true and loyal Mohammedan. This custom, so faithfully followed, has been the great unifying power during the last ten centuries to the varied Mohammedan peoples and races scattered as they have been in the different countries, speaking different languages, and following different customs. It is at Mecca upon these sacred pilgrimages that the assembled Mohammedans become conscious of the unity and solidarity of their faith.

Their performance of ceremonies there together impresses them with the wide extent of Mohammedanism, and sends them back to their homes firmly fixed in their belief and unalterably convinced of the strength of Islam. The pilgrimage has been of untold value in cementing Mohammedans together into a unity and in promoting the solidarity of the millions of Moslems scattered throughout the world.

11. The foundation of the Moslem faith rests upon a rockbound theory of deity. The Mohammedan begins with God and ends with Mohammed. His conception of Allah is exalted and fundamental. The first Sura in the Koran on this subject reads as follows:

" The Merciful One is firmly seated upon the throne. To Him belongs whatever is in the Heavens and whatever is in the earth and whatever is between them both and whatever is under the earth. And if thou speakest aloud with thy voice then indeed He knoweth the secret and what is most hidden. God, there is no God but He, to Him belong the most excellent names."

One verse in the second Sura of the Koran reads:

" There is no God but He, the Living, the Eternal. Slumber seizeth Him not nor sleep. To Him belongeth whatever there is in the Heavens and what is in the earth. Who is it that intercedeth with Him except by His permission? He knoweth what was before them and what will be after them, nor shall they combine any portion of His knowledge except what He hath hidden. His throne encompasseth the Heavens and the earth, nor doth guardianship of both burden Him. And He is the exalted, the Mighty One."

The first Sura of the Koran is used among the Mohammedans somewhat as the Lord's Prayer is used among Christians. One of the religious acts of the Mohammedan by which eternal credit is acquired is the repetition of the ninety-nine names or titles of deity, all of them of an exalted character.

However much may be said as to the God of the Mohammedans being not the same as the God of the Christians, and there is ground for the declaration that He is widely different, nevertheless, all must agree that the Mohammedan's conception of deity has been fundamentally exalted from the days of Mohammed.

12. Mohammedan teachings of the future life have had tremendous influence even over the wilder and less civilized races, and today they hold the Moslem devotee in a grip which leads him to face death for his religion without flinching, since by so doing he is sure of an immediate entrance into the highest Heaven of the Moslem's Paradise. There is an unalterable belief in a hereafter, and in fact in two hereafters, one in the Paradise of the faithful and the other in the depth of Hades. To the true Mohammedan the future life is a real paradise according to the ideals of his life and practices on earth. Immediately upon the resurrection he passes into the presence of the angels, who welcome him to the delights of paradise, there to dwell forever in the enjoyments of carnal pleasures.

On the other hand, those who are unfaithful, and especially all who refuse to believe that Mohammed is the only prophet of God, enter into the eternal tortures of Hell.

The Mohammedan's wonderful abode of the faithful is at some point off the earth and of a size that no human standards of measurement can approximately give. The righteous, soon after entering paradise, are invited by Allah to sup with Him at His table, after which they are escorted to the mansion prepared for them where throughout all eternity they will enjoy such bliss as was never dreamed of in the wildest fancy of imagination. Women have their place in this abode of the faithful according to the teaching of Mohammed. Perpetual youth is enjoyed there by all. In his conception and his description of the future joy of the true believer, Mohammed has evidently sought to please all the senses and faculties of men.

13. The inevitable conclusion of the Moslem conception

of the surpassing power of Allah is that man is nothing in the hands of the All-Mighty who knows the end from the beginning, and therefore man is powerless to do anything that will change the final results of his life. This theory is inconsistent, as are many of the doctrines of Mohammedanism, with their theory of sin, but inconsistency is not one of the things that trouble Mohammedans. It is probably true that fatalism is especially suited to the character and disposition of those who dwell in the tropics. It is an easy matter to throw off responsibility upon an all-merciful God and to leave oneself in his hands. The common expression of fatalism is " God is merciful." This doctrine probably does not have the same hold upon the Mohammedan of the temperate zone, where thought is more exact and penetrating, but with the easy-going man of the tropics who does not like to trouble himself about the future and who has an unshaken belief in the almighty power of the over ruler, it is natural for him to assume and to act upon the assumption that the end has already been determined, quite irrespective of his own character and deeds. This paralyzing conception of man's relation to God is attractive to people of this type and has unquestionably been one of the sources of strength and power in the extension of Mohammedanism.

14. While the Mohammedan doctrine of sin differs widely from the Christian doctrine, it has in it elements of great attractiveness to the Mohammedan. As is stated elsewhere, sin to the Mohammedan is a failure to accomplish all that is commanded by the law, rules, precedents, and regulations of Mohammed. Every such violation is charged up against the believer in the accounts of Heaven. In order to free himself from those condemnatory accounts and appear, after his resurrection, with credits sufficient to turn the balance upon the right side, he performs certain acts like prayer, alms, pilgrimages, fasts, etc., for each of which varying credits are due him. Sin to him is not a perversity of character but a

perversity of deeds, and the remedy is not through any system of atonement but by the fulfilling of the demands of his religion sufficiently to secure a cancellation of his debits in the books of eternity. This conception of sin and its remedy makes it possible for every Mohammedan to accumulate sufficient merit to insure him free entrance into Paradise.

15. The doctrine of sin and the method of cancellation together with the belief in fatalism have led in actual practice among large bodies of Mohammedans to indulgences for the commitment of acts which their religion condemns. If by the saying of a certain number of prayers, or the making of a pilgrimage, or by the unusually strict observance of a fast, a believer can wipe away a great number of sins, a large part of the restraint of the commands of his religion is lost. While this is one of the radical defects of Mohammedanism, it is one of the features that appeals strongly to many of the followers of Mohammed. In other words, its demands are not so exacting and difficult of fulfillment that the Mohammedan cannot take upon himself the obligations of his religion without greatly interfering with his daily life except for the necessity of doing certain religious acts for the removal of the penalty. This has made it possible to enlarge its borders and to include among its members many who recognize themselves as unworthy followers of the prophet, but who believe that through their performance of pious ceremonies they will be fully admitted into the Moslem's Paradise.

16. It is almost a necessary corollary of the Moslem's conception of deity that they with equal force repudiate and condemn idolatry. In Mohammed's time much that he saw in the worship of the Christians of Arabia and Syria impressed him as being largely the worship of images. He reacted from that form of idolatry and made doubly strong his definition and characterization of God and multiplied prohibitions against the worship or adoration of any other being or beings. He opposed polytheism in any and every form, and Islam

has been iconoclastic of all appearances of idol worship, removing from the churches which they capture pictures and images and chiselling out, when cut in stone, representations of the Cross. The Mohammedan places of worship are notoriously free from pictures or images of animal or person, geometrical figures and designs being used for ornamental purposes. Monotheism has been one of the sources of their bitter opposition to the Trinity and to recognition of the divinity of Jesus Christ.

17. There are a large number of rules and regulations in Islam that have at least the appearance of morality. Some of these are highly worthy as practiced by Moslems and are frequently cited when comparison with the practice of Christians is drawn. We can here mention but three of these, although the list might be considerably lengthened.

(1) In the second Sura of the Koran the following statement occurs, " They who devour usury shall not arise from the dead but as he riseth whom Satan infecteth by a touch. . . . God hath permitted selling and forbidden usury. . . . Who so returneth to usury for them shall be the continuance of Hell-fire, for they shall continue therein forever." While Moslems as a whole have not held absolutely to this most commendable and highly moral injunction, the taking of usury has been almost universally condemned, and in Moslem countries the money-lenders and usury-takers are almost invariably other than Moslems. In Turkey they are usually from the Christian population. The general sentiment of the Mohammedans is against the taking of usury.

(2) Whatever may be the motive which prompts, the Mohammedan is liberal in the giving of money for the support of the poor and for helping his fellow believers in time of distress. Very seldom does the spirit of giving lead the Mohammedan to contribute to the support of those who are not Mohammedans, but within his own circle and among his own people he has a reputation for liberality and hospital-

ity. The guest of the Moslem need not necessarily be a Mohammedan to receive of his best. The giving of alms is one of the five great fundamental demands put upon all Mohammedans by the prophet himself. This brings a large return for the support of Moslem institutions, for the erection of fountains by the roadside in dry and desert countries, and manifests itself in many other ways. One cannot escape from the fact that the Mohammedan expects, through his liberality, to gain credits in the accounts of Paradise. Yet the fact remains that every Mohammedan is taught that almsgiving is a vital part of his religious life.

(3) Although the subject does not bulk large in the Koran, Mohammedans generally take a firm position against drunkenness. Tradition says that Mohammed set his face strongly against the use of wine and sought to discourage the drinking habits of his country, claiming that intoxicating drink was not only injurious to themselves but displeasing to God. Tradition reports that during Mohammed's life a group of his followers at an entertainment became so intoxicated that when the hour of evening prayer arrived few of them could properly attend to their devotions. When this fact came to the ears of Mohammed, he with indignation spoke words of sharp reproof and wrote in one of the Suras of the Koran, " But true believers, come not to prayers when ye are drunk." As the Mohammedan prayers occur five times in the twenty-four hours, there is no space between the hours for stated prayers when the Mohammedan can indulge largely in intoxicating liquors and expect to be in proper prayer attitude at the allotted time. Mohammedans throughout the world have a reputation for temperance, although this is sometimes exaggerated, since occasionally a Mohammedan claims that Mohammed forbade the use of wine but said nothing about brandy and whiskey. On the whole Moslem influence against the use of intoxicating drink has been wholesome.

CHAPTER V

ISLAM AND THE OTTOMAN EMPIRE

There is special reason for giving unusual space to the discussion of the rise, growth, and supremacy of Islam in Turkey. In the first place, the sacred shrines of Islam as well as of Christianity are within the Ottoman Empire. The geographical reason alone is sufficient, since not only did Mohammed live and die in what was, until 1916, Turkish territory, but the same is true of Jesus Christ. Not only does Turkey now contain the places from which these two great missionary religions sprang, but the first conquests of each were in that same country. Islam won Arabia, and Christianity conquered Asia Minor, while both made signal conquests in North Africa.

In addition, the head of the Turkish Empire has for 400 years been regarded, by many, if not all, Moslems, as the Caliph of Islam. Abdul Hamid II did more to establish himself as the Caliph than any of his immediate predecessors. and he was measurably successful in calling the attention of the Moslems of the Islands, India, Russia, China, and Africa to himself and in encouraging journeys to Constantinople upon the part of pilgrims to Mecca that he might have audience with them and send them back to their homes with presents and instructions as to the unity of the faith in and through himself. Until the great war, Turkey was rapidly becoming the religious center of the faith. It is at Constantinople that the Sheik-ul-Islam, the official interpreter of the Koran, sometimes referred to as the High Priest of Islam, resides. Under the hand of the reigning Sultan are held the sacred relics of Mohammed, such as his war flag and one or more of his garments. He was also the protector of the sacred shrines at Mecca and Medina, annually providing the expensive hangings for the Kaaba.

Turkey was also the only independent Mohammedan Government or Empire remaining from the long list of Empires that have sprung into existence, continued for a period, and passed into history. We need but to mention the Saracen rule in Spain, the Mogul Empire of India, the modern Persian Empire at the zenith of its glory, and others. While the Mogul Empire may have been more brilliant in its setting, none of these equalled in strength, aggressive force and significance that of the Ottoman Empire at the height of its supremacy. To it the Christian world looked with anxious solicitude, and for 400 years Turkey has figured conspicuously in nearly every European question and for centuries has constituted a problem, to the solution of which the nations of Europe have bent their best energies.

Again, Turkey, more than almost any other country for 400 years, maintained the supremacy of its Mohammedan Government, although a large portion of its population, not the majority, were non-Moslems, mostly Christians. Here has been wrought out and tested the ability or lack of ability of Moslems to rule over non-Moslems and to give them a safe and just government while according them liberty of conscience. Turkey has furnished the most open and varied field for the study of the relations of a Mohammedan government to non-Moslem races. The fact that a part of Turkey is in Europe and the remainder bordering upon European waters, has brought the subject to the attention of the West, if not of the entire Christian world. In fact, multitudes understand Islam only as it presents itself in Turkey and they interpret it as it manifests itself in dealing with and ruling over non-Moslem peoples. To these, the *Mohammedan* is the *Turk*, and Mohammedanism is the Turk in action.

Turkey commanded the attention of the world because of its relations to the great European struggle. All are watching with solicitous interest the Turkish end of the conflict and are wondering how the outcome will affect Ottoman supremacy and Moslem prestige. For instance, already there is much discussion regarding the future Caliph, if Mohammedanism is to be able to have one at all. The Caliph, by Mohammedan tradition if not by law, must be the ruler of an independent Moslem state. This at once excludes India, Persia and Egypt, while Afghanistan and Turkestan are too insignificant to presume to hold such an honor. Turkey, while the outcome of the war is yet in the balance, is the only Moslem state that can qualify, and Moslems as a whole are loth to recognize the successors of Abdul Hamid II as holding that high and sacred office.

Mohammedanism exhibited within the bounds of the Turkish Empire, including Arabia, is the purest that exists anywhere today. The fact that Constantinople was the city of the Caliph, and that the shrines of Mohammedanism are in Arabia, and that Arabia has been so little influenced by great Western movements like modern education and modern scientific discoveries, must account for this conservatism.

The Azhar University in Cairo is on the border line between the old and the new with discussion rife, the conservative element holding to the old with a characteristic tenacity, while modern ideas and especially modern education seem to be working their way into the thinking of some of the students and a smaller number of the teachers; questions bearing upon this important subject are under constant discussion, both in the Moslem press and in private.

Constantinople has been the center of contention and strife, not only national and international, but also intellectual and religious. The political questions gathering about the Balkans and the Near East have had their headquarters on the Bosphorus. The Governments of Europe have sent as their representatives some of their best and most astute diplomats to the Porte in order that they might hold their own in the political discussions and possible political conflicts that there constantly arise. At the same time Constantinople has been the battle-ground of the conservatism of the East in open and direct conflict with the progressive spirit of the West. Conservative Mohammedans have resisted the encroachment of Western ideas, while the more liberal Moslems, many of whom received their education in Europe, pressed for liberalism both in the matter of modern education and of religious belief.

For years the battle has been fought around the question of education. The moderns won in this conflict, and Constantinople has boasted the best modern schools to be found anywhere under a Mohammedan government. At the same time these even have not been wholly liberal, but have been more or less permeated by traditional conservatism. The conflict over modern education carried on in Constantinople has been reflected in the larger cities in the interior of Turkey and the Balkans, until, throughout the Ottoman Empire, the more conservative and the most liberal in matters of education have lived and worked side by side, without open conflict, but with no little spirit of rivalry and even heart-burning within. The conservative Mohammedans have been eager to have everything modern and Western driven from their educational system, in order that they might return to the idea of a Moslem school whose chief education should be reading the Koran and the commentaries thereon in Arabic, and the discussion of questions of Moslem theology and scholasticism; while those who supported the opposite side of the question were eager to have schools introduced by the Government that should teach modern science and languages, history and geography, as they are taught in the schools of Europe. Constantinople papers have repeatedly published articles by leading Mohammedans declaring that the absence of such schools, under the control and direction of the Government, was driving Mohammedans to send their children to avowedly Christian institutions in order to secure for them an adequate modern education. Some of the institutions to which they have sent their children have been in Europe, where the Mohammedan youth was wholly separated from the teachings and practice of his religion, and surrounded by influences which were decidedly non-Mohammedan, if not actually anti-Mohammedan. If, instead of going to Europe, the Mohammedan children were sent to a Christian school within the bounds of the Empire, they did not become so widely separated from the practice of Mohammedanism, but, while in the school, they were in an atmosphere that was decidedly Christian, and so for the period of education, they lost positive instruction in Mohammedanism and were thrown under the influence of Christianity.

These two forces, one working for the retention of the old conservatism, and the other contending for a more liberal treatment of modern questions, have been in conflict in Turkey more especially during the last twenty-five or thirty years. The influence of Abdul Hamid was cast decidedly against the introduction of modern ideas and ideals into the Empire. But, in spite of his influence and attitude, the process has continued, receiving an unusual impulse at the time of the re-establishment of the Constitution in 1908, and especially under the Young Turk Party which succeeded to power, although the influence of the Sultan himself, Mohammed V, so far as he had any influence at all upon the Government, has been in favor of conservatism.

What has been said with reference to the introduction of modern education bears also directly upon the subject of the religious establishment. It will be difficult to make this thoroughly understood by one who is not familiar with the Turkish method of thought. To the Turk, his entire life and even his surroundings become a part of his religion, and he looks upon all questions from a religious point of view. It would be impossible for him to understand how one could be educated in modern schools and not be directly affected in his religious belief. In this latter supposition Mohammedanism is not so far wrong, because it usually follows that a liberal education leads directly to liberal Mohammedanism.

It is stated on good authority that the Young Turk Party that led Turkey into the war was controlled by a group of men numbering less than fifty, and that not one of that group was a strong believer in traditional Mohammedanism, while most of them were practically without religion. The three men, members of the larger group, who for years controlled the destinies of the Turkish Empire, were atheists, although they were careful to conceal this fact, lest they lose the backing and support of the rank and file of the Mohammedans of the country. Their interests were not for the perpetuation of Mohammedanism, its beliefs or its institutions, except as they could thus strengthen their own position. They were more successful than one would naturally expect, although their acts were widely criticized by the conservative Moslems, to such an extent that statements were publicly made denouncing Turkey and its leadership as no longer Moslem but primarily European and Christian. This criticism was not allayed by the alliance formed between Turkey and Christian Germany and Austria, and later with Bulgaria.

The Grand Vizier and the Sultan himself no longer exercised dominant control in the affairs of the Empire. After Turkey entered the war, and even previous to that date, these men were but figureheads in the government, and were allowed to retain their official position only with the understanding that they were not to interfere in the administration of national affairs. The real governors were Talaat Bey, in 1917 made Grand Vizier but formerly the Minister of the Interior, and at times holding other portfolios in the Cabinet, Enver Pasha, the Minister of War, with other portfolios to his credit, and Bedri Bey, the chief of police of the city of Constantinople. These were the men who made no claim of allegiance to religion, but who seemed to hold in their bloody hands the destinies of the Ottoman Empire.

Another feature entering into Mohammedanism in the Turkish Empire, and one that must needs have consideration, is the fact of the great number of races that make up the population of the country. This condition is not often recognized, but it is one of the chief elements requiring consideration when studying this subject.

Arabia is inhabited almost wholly by Arabs, and the population of North Africa is comparatively homogeneous. This is also true of Persia. But when we turn to the Turkish Empire, we find the population consisting of many different nationalities often in conflict with each other, with separate traditions and maintaining their separate existence, although dwelling side by side for generations. We sometimes speak of America as the great melting-pot of separate and divergent nationalities. The word " melting-pot " has never been applied to Turkey, since there is no tendency to amalgamate or blend these nationalities, but each remains distinct from all other races, with only slightly blending features.

This has a direct effect also upon the Mohammedanism of Turkey, since the followers of Islam in that country are not all of one race or of one people by any means, but are divided among various peoples and various races. There are several of these Mohammedan races.

1. *The Turks.* The name " Turk " is a word that is wholly void of any real significance. They themselves apply the name to all Mohammedans who dwell in Asia Minor, without reference to their race or origin. Whenever any one in Turkey changes his religion, as for instance, an Armenian or a Greek, and becomes a Mohammedan, he is announced in the language of the country as having become a " Turk," and ever thereafter is called a " Turk."

The Mohammedans, therefore, in Asiatic Turkey, pass under the general name of Turk, as the Mohammedans in

Russia pass under the general name of Tartar. This perhaps grows out of the fact that the Turks were the Mohammedan conquerors of the country, and have given their name to all people who follow their religion. The Suljukian Turks were the first to come into prominence and domination in Asiatic Turkey, followed by the Ottoman Turks, who later swept down across the country from the Northeast. Genghis Khan and Timur, who appeared upon the scene, gained their strength, not from the forces they brought with them, but from kindred groups whom they encountered in their migrations. The founders of the present Turkish dynasty came later, adding to their numbers from the peoples whom they found in the country conquered.

Thus, during the centuries of their control, covering the period of their great supremacy and later decline, they have drawn upon other races, upon almost every family of the Caucasus, Western Asia, and the countries of the Balkan peninsula, so that today the Turk no longer represents any particular race, but is an intermixture of peoples and races, but with a Tartar name.

As to his religion, the Turk took upon himself the ideals of Arabia, adopting the Arabic language as his religious tongue, although retaining something of his Tartar vernacular and Persian style, but greatly changed and worked over through the use of the Arabic. It is reported that at least seventy per cent of the words in any Turkish paper are Arabic, practically in their original purity. The Tartar words and sounds are few, thus revealing the fact that the Turk himself has been Arabicized to the extent that he has lost his language and his Tartar ideas and has become in these respects essentially Arabic.

There is probably another point in which the old Tartar spirit remained, that is, in the underlying, inherent cruelty of the Turk as displayed in his modern treatment of the non-Moslem races of his country. There is no other way by which the massacres characterizing the administrative methods of the Turkish Government can be adequately explained than by the fact that, while the Turcoman and the Tartar of the Middle Ages, in contact to a degree with Western civilization, have taken on some of the outward appearance of that civilization, he still retains his old savagery of heart. This, under provocation, has come to the surface repeatedly in the massacres that have so characterized the government of Turkey now for nearly, if not quite, a century, breaking out sometimes in one part of the empire, sometimes in another, but always with the same characteristic, unfeeling savagery. This has been demonstrated more fully during the period of the war in the atrocities which the Government perpetrated upon the Armenians and Syrians in the East, and upon the Greeks in the West. This savagery is not a direct outgrowth of Mohammedanism, because many devout Mohammedans have protested with great vigor against the practices of fiendish cruelty in which so many of the Turkish leaders seemed to take keen delight. One could almost imagine that, in their fanaticism, excited by the wars in Europe first, and afterwards by their own entrance into the European conflict, the old spirit of Genghis Khan and Tamerlaine has re-appeared in all its heartless fury, demonstrating to the world how far the Turk actually is from modern civilization, and how much of the brute still remains in his heart, though for a time hidden from view.

Those who have been familiar with the Turks for the last half century, and have met them in social intercourse as friends and neighbors, both in the capital and in the interior cities, have been free to speak of their admiration for the gentlemanly, hospitable Turk, and there have been reasons for thus speaking. No one who has had these experiences has failed to recognize the marvelous hospitality of the Turkish gentleman, and the more one is brought into contact with him, under normal conditions, the more he is impressed with his politeness and apparent kindliness of heart and readiness to fraternize. But, just as soon as the old latent passion is aroused, stimulated by a sense of fear, or possibly inspired by a suppressed race hatred, then the old Tartar spirit bursts forth with all its fury, and our polite, hospitable Turkish gentleman may become the despot of the Middle Ages, killing without compunction, spreading sorrow and untold suffering far and wide, with apparent glee. Mohammedanism has seemed to exercise little restraint over him, and has even been called into requisition by him as an excuse and defense of his acts of violence. This is the Turk, the ruler of the Turkish Empire, dwelling throughout Asia Minor and Eastern Turkey, and reaching down toward Arabia.

2. *The Shiahs.* In Turkey, one of the tribes of Kurds, called the Kuzzlebash, is quite separate from that of the Turk. Their religious sympathies are affiliated with the Mohammedans of Persia, as they are Shiahs, belonging to the sect of Ali, and having little in common with the Turkish Mohammedans of the Ottoman empire. They do not possess in anywhere near the same degree the spirit of cruelty of the Turks. They are looked upon by Mohammedans generally as of doubtful orthodoxy, so far as their religion is concerned. Their language is Koordish and Turkish; they are largely tillers of the soil, are generally submissive to authority, frugal and industrious.

In some regions, like the upper waters of the Tigris River, there is much evidence that some of these tribes of Shiahs had a Christian ancestry, as there are occasionally found among them Christian books, the ruins of Christian churches, and the remnants of Christian names. They generally live on good terms with their Christian neighbors, and have repeatedly declared that their sympathies are with the Christians rather than with the Mohammedans. Their divergence in belief from the Mohammedans is so great that the Turks often hold them in open contempt. They may be called the most liberal among all the Mohammedans of Turkey. They do not keep the fasts; they allow their women to go about unveiled, and practice certain rites, such as the breaking of bread and the distribution of wine on certain religious occasions. They have also among them fragmentary survivals of pagan observances which appear in some of their forms of worship. They belong to one of the Mohammedan fraternities, the Bektash, which was once a powerful Islamic organization.

The Shiahs of Turkey add little if anything to the strength of Mohammedanism, and offer a large field for Christian approach, because of their predilections in favor of Christianity. In the recent persecutions of Armenians these Shiah Kurds have nobly come to their aid.

3. *The Kurds.* While the Kuzzlebash tribe is sometimes classed as one of the Kurdish tribes, its members are quite distinct from the main body of the Kurds, a powerful race found in largest numbers in the Eastern section of the Turkish Empire, in Southwestern Caucusus and in Western Persia. The history of the Kurds is shrouded in mystery. Many of the Kurdish tribes in the regions described have not yet been completely subjugated by Turkish authority. It is only within the last century that they were brought under any real semblance of governmental control. They are semi-nomadic, seeking the cool uplands during the summer months, and coming down with their flocks and herds into the warmer valleys in the winter period. Unquestionably they are of Eastern ancestry, with Aryan roots forming the framework of their language, although the language has many mixtures from the Turkish, Arabic, Armenian and Persian. They are classed as Mohammedans, but the various tribes have different phases of belief, and they show composite character as a race. Some of them are Sunnis. They are given much to robbery and have a vein of cruelty running through their history, although their cruelty is not to be compared with that of the

Turk when aroused. They are great lovers of booty, and have frequently been used by the Turks in inaugurating and carrying on massacres among the Armenians and Syrians because of the booty offered them if they would carry out certain programs of killing.

The Kurd is not a source of strength to Mohammedanism in Turkey, and is more easily approached by one who is not a Mohammedan than the Turk himself. He has many characteristics which are admirable. He is usually true to his promises. He will give himself to the defense of a man whose bread and hospitality he has shared, and even when he meets a stranger upon the highway, if he returns his salutation, the stranger has nothing to fear from his hand. If friendly he is as hospitable as the Arab.

4. *The Druzes.* Tribes of these people are met in the Southern Lebanon and anti-Lebanon ranges, in the hinterland of the Beirut coast. They are a people of war-like disposition, but numerically inferior to the Christian populations of the districts in which they dwell. However, through their bellicose propensity, they have gained a predominance in central Syria. They are pure monotheists, with a high standard of morality, calling themselves Mohammedans, but they maintain no mosques and rarely practice polygamy. The orthodox Moslems practically repudiate them, since their interpretation of the Koran differs so widely from the orthodox interpretation. Often, when with Christians, they do not hesitate to declare their sympathy with and even belief in Christianity. They have little in common with the tribesmen of the plain, and are in doctrine at least estranged from the surrounding Semitism. Some have traced the special tenets of their religion back to the Persians. More probably it is an infiltration of foreign ideals and ideas in a region that is largely cut off from intercourse with the lowlands.

5. *Mohammedan Immigrants.* Since the Turkish authority was firmly established in Western Asia, the Sultans have

endeavored to bring Mohammedan settlements from other countries to occupy the unpopulated districts of Turkey. This has been particularly true at the end of unsuccessful wars, when Moslem inhabitants of lost provinces have been urged and aided to move into what still remained of Turkish territory. In order to aid these, often they were exempted from taxation, and every facility offered for transportation and the establishment of their residence.

This was the case in recent years with the Caucasus provinces. When several of the Turkish provinces passed from Turkish control to Russia, large bodies of Circassians came over and spread themselves quite widely over Eastern and Central Asia Minor. These seem to be a rather mixed people, who worship in mosques, but some of whom bear Christian names. They have a standard of living above that of the ordinary Turk, and wherever they settle they live in a degree of comfort unknown to the Turkish peasants. Prosperous farming communities have grown up around their villages, and in cities they seem to possess a natural aptitude for commerce; some of them have made able government officials. It is thought that no less than 500,000 Circassians occupy different sections of Asiatic Turkey.

In addition to these, without dwelling at length upon the various races, there were colonies of the Noghai Tartars, who came over into Turkey after the Crimean war. And now, since the Balkan wars, large numbers of Mohammedans have come into the Empire from the territory in the Balkans that fell to Greece, Servia and Bulgaria. Many of these Mohammedan refugees have been brought over by the Turkish Government and colonized in different parts of Western Asia Minor.

6. *Christian Populations.* The Christian populations, also occupying different sections of Asiatic Turkey, have maintained their separate national existence through centuries of Mohammedan rule. We will not dwell upon these at length,

but it is especially important that we mention the Armenians, who have for more than 2,500 years occupied as their capital and center the high tablelands of Eastern Turkey. They represent the most historic race in the Turkish Empire today. Their own history goes back several hundred years before Christ, and their traditions even to Mount Ararat, which until taken, within the last fifty years, by Russia, was in the Turkish Empire and a part of ancient Armenia.

The Armenians were the first nation to adopt Christianity as a national religion. This occurred in the beginning of the 4th century A.D. They have had a varied history as a people, always centering around the plains of Van and Moush. Between the 10th and 9th centuries B.C. the Vanic people became the nucleus of a confederacy of mountain tribes forming the kingdom of Urartu. The cuneiform inscriptions found in that general region at the present time, as well as the Babylonian records, show that they were a strong and warlike people. The boundaries of the Urartu or Armenian state were well established 800 years B. C.

The history of the Armenians is more or less closely related to the history of the Hittites, as the representatives of this Vanic kingdom waged war with the Hittites farther West, in the 6th and 7th centuries B.C. Some have suggested that they may have had a common origin with the Hittites. There is little doubt that the Armenians of the present day are direct descendants from these ancient Urartu peoples. The mountainous and inaccessible condition of the country which they occupy may account in a large measure for the purity of the race, which has preserved an Armenian physical type. They are proud of their ancestry, calling themselves *Haik*, and their country *Haiasdan*, after one of their ancient and noble leaders. They have never called themselves Armenians, that name having been given them by their neighbors, deriving it from Aram, one of their later and famous kings.

The location of Armenia was unfortunate in that it occupied

the battle-ground of Western Asia, Persia, and the regions later occupied by the Turcoman tribes upon the East and Northeast; while the Mohammedan forces from the South and the Turkish hordes of the West met upon the highlands of Armenia, century after century, as a common battle-ground.

The Armenians are a hardy, industrious, intelligent, progressive race, developed by centuries of conflict with neighbors, and in a region where the climate is severe and where a living is obtained from the soil with the greatest of difficulty. To these things must be attributed, in a large degree, the fact that the race has persisted through the centuries of conflict, persecution and war that have swept over their fair land. As has already been stated, they became a Christian people in the 4th century, and have held to their Christianity through the existence of a National Church with a persistence worthy of their ancient history.

In view of their industry and tendency to increase in numbers and to prosper in the face of the greatest difficulty, they have attracted to themselves during the last century the jealousy and suspicion of the Turks, their over-lords. Not allowed to carry arms, restricted in their movements, subject to severe taxation and oppression, with a degree of religious persecution, the race has continued to increase in numbers and in prosperity. It was one of the first races of the Turkish empire to welcome the idea of modern education and to make great sacrifice for its promotion. Their young men and young women were among the first to avail themselves of the mission schools and to adopt the new ideas that came in through the missionaries and their institutions from the Western world. Armenian young men, who from the remote parts of Eastern Turkey turned their faces to Europe and America, both for study and for commercial and industrial purposes, have revealed a spirit of enterprise and a consequent prosperity far surpassing that of any of the Moslem races in Turkey.

Owing to this great prosperity, Abdul Hamid began a system of persecution, culminating from time to time in open massacre, which had for its end two purposes; the securing of the wealth which the Armenians had so industriously earned; and the reduction and consequent weakening of the race.

It was inevitable that a people of this character, who have dreamed of a restoration of their ancient kingdom and glory, should long for a time when there should be an independent or autonomous Armenia.

The massacres of 1895–96, in which tens of thousands of the wage-earners of that historic race were put to death, need not be dwelt upon here. The massacre in Adana in 1990, inaugurated by Abdul Hamid following the restoration of the Constitution, was unquestionably planned at Constantinople to weaken the Armenians in Cilicia, whom the massacre of 1896 did not touch.

The late atrocities committed upon the Armenian people are too recent to require general description. This is the most severe attack ever made upon the race, with the one avowed purpose of eliminating the Armenians from the Turkish question and of making a future independent or autonomous Armenia an impossibility. This undoubtedly was instigated through the fear on the part of the Turkish Government of the strength of a people superior in natural qualifications, although unarmed and greatly inferior in numbers. The venom of the attack is revealed by the fact that not only were the men seized and in large measure put out of the way, but the women and children were treated with an atrocity surpassing that recorded in history since Tamerlane. Germany cannot free herself from guilt in this, one of the greatest crimes of the 20th century.

Undoubtedly this attack upon the Armenians was regarded by many of the Turks as a part of the holy war, in which the Mohammedans were called upon to eliminate the infidels in their midst and to restore Turkey to its rightful Mohammedan lords. The statement has been made by Turkish officials that the plan of elimination of non-Moslems includes not only the Armenians but the Greeks, against whom many atrocities in Western Turkey have been perpetrated since the Balkan wars, and after that the Jews, who, although they have been quiet and loyal citizens of Turkey, are regarded by the Mohammedans as a foreign element.

The mixed character of the Mohammedan peoples of Turkey, together with their contact with three leading Christian races, namely, the Armenians, the Syrians and the Greeks, has tended to a modified Mohammedanism, giving it certain characteristics which it does not possess in other countries. It has developed and perpetuated a spirit of opposition and of religious hatred that one does not find in India or even in North Africa. The fear of the supremacy of these more prosperous, enterprising and enlightened Christian races has seemed to call out the worst to be found in the Turkish races. This applies more especially to the Turks, who are the real rulers of the country, than to some other Mohammedan peoples above mentioned. The Turks, recognizing their own physical and mental inferiority, have sought to make up therefor by the ferocity with which they have dealt with their Christian subjects and the severity of the rules and laws imposed upon them.

The policy of suppression has been adopted and put into operation for the last half century, which has resulted in developing these persecuted races along hardy and aggressive lines. They have all shown great recuperative power, so that, following each outbreak, there has been a brief but rapid period of reconstruction and reorganization, the success of which has surprised the outside world. We may expect that, in the present instance, after peace has been restored in Turkey, these Christian races, and especially the Armenians, will reveal their power to rise from the ashes of the fire of their

KING AND QUEEN OF ALBANIA

ENVER PASHA
Former Minister of War in Turkey

A KOORDISH CHIEF

own destruction and demonstrate to the world their inherent ability.

The character of the Mohammedans in Turkey, to which only the briefest reference has been made above, presents an unusual field for the Christian approach. The Turks themselves are not a unit. In the terrible persecution of the Armenians carried on during 1915, 1916 and 1917, there have been strong protests from within the Turkish ranks and from high official circles, but beyond this, among the different tribes of Kurds and Circassians, a sympathy has been shown toward the persecuted which reveals a spirit of brotherhood that can be made use of in all future endeavor to bring to these people the knowledge of the true Christ.

We may sum up the situation in Turkey, so far as it relates to the Christianization of Islam, as follows:

(1) Recent events in Turkey have demonstrated, both to the Mohammedans and to the world, that Mohammedan solidarity has been severely shaken if not absolutely broken. The call for a holy war, issued with all solemnity and ceremony, proved a failure so far as it sought to produce a unified Mohammedanism against the non-Moslem world. The Caliph of Islam has lost his leadership, so that today there is no generally acknowledged Caliph. In the mosques of Egypt, prayer is offered for the Khedive of Egypt and not for the Caliph.

This fact is so widely recognized by the Mohammedans of Turkey that they have repeatedly spoken to the American missionaries of their sense of discouragement about the superiority and supremacy of their religion and its capacity to meet the needs of their country. At the same time they are in despair with reference to their country itself, freely declaring their disapproval of the treatment of the Armenians, pronouncing it un-Mohammedan.

The fact that there are Mohammedans engaged upon both sides of this great conflict, those of Egypt and India fighting against the forces of Turkey, is to them a constant demonstration that the unity of Mohammedanism is broken and that the dream of a united Mohammedan world has vanished. The same spirit prevails in a measure in Persia, and the Mohammedans of these two countries are rapidly coming to the conclusion that they can build no hope for the future upon the unity and solidarity of those who believe in Mohammed.

(2) It is a fact of no little significance that, during the last few years, the work of the Bible Societies in Turkey has been marked by an unusual sale of New Testaments in the Arabic and Turkish languages. Hundreds of thousands of copies of these books, in whole or in part, in the five years before the war were sold to Mohammedans. When a Mohammedan has once bought a book, it will not be easily destroyed; in fact, the feeling prevails that if a book is purchased it must be read in order to get back the value of the purchase money. But added to this is another fact, that the Moslem does not lightly destroy any printed paper upon which the name of Allah appears. We can well believe, therefore, that these sacred books are for the most part intact, and that they are being read and are exerting their revolutionizing influence upon the thinking of the owners.

Repeatedly there comes to the surface evidence of a widespread custom among Mohammedans of meeting in secret places, and there, in groups, reading the New Testament and discussing the teachings of Christ. Occasionally we learn of particular groups in which Mohammedans themselves report that the discussion is always favorable, and that not infrequently prayer is offered to Jesus Christ during these sessions. The Mohammedans in Turkey, to an unusual degree, are studying the content of Christianity.

(3) We have already spoken of the interest which Mohammedans of Turkey are taking in the importance and value of Western education. Therefore we need not here dwell upon

this fact except to report it as one of the encouraging features of the present situation in Turkey. Christian schools, in which Mohammedans in unprecedentedly large numbers are studying, report not a few inquirers among the open-minded Mohammedan youth, with some conversions even during the period of the upheaval of the war. A few years ago parents were persecuted severely by their Moslem neighbors and officials for permitting their children to attend mission schools; that persecution is slight today, and in many places seems to have wholly disappeared.

(4) The manner in which the Christian Armenians met this terrible onslaught upon them at the hands of the Turk, both as individuals and as a race, made a deep impression upon a multitude of Moslems. The Armenians have usually been given the privilege of accepting Islam and remaining at their homes. It is true that a few have done this, but, taken as a whole, the Armenian race remained true to its belief in Jesus Christ, and they refused to deny Him in order to save their lives. This was a mighty object lesson to their persecutors and made a profound impression upon the Mohammedans who witnessed this loyalty. Tens of thousands of Moslems, officials and others, who saw this readiness to face persecution, every kind of suffering, and ultimate death, rather than give up their belief in Christ, will talk to their children of what they saw, and the testimony will be passed on to the third generation. Masses of Christians, with cheerful courage, singing hymns and with prayer, left their homes and started out upon their journey toward the desert and to almost inevitable death, as true martyrs to their faith as the Middle Ages ever witnessed.

That the missionaries remained in Turkey when they might have left the country and retired to places of comfort and safety, choosing of their own volition to stay with the people who needed their help and to die with them if necessary, as many did, made also a lasting impression of the power of the Gospel of Christ to hold men true in the face of threatening death.

This period of stress and strain in Turkey afforded an unusual opportunity for presenting to the Mohammedans the fundamental truths of the Gospel of Christ as revealed in Christian service and Christian loyalty. The Mohammedans have had a demonstration of the truth of Christianity greater than that which could possibly be given by any spoken word or any printed volume.

(5) One other point bearing upon the situation is the fact that so many Christian young women from among the Armenians, young women who had been trained in the mission schools, strong of mind and of faith, were forcibly taken into Mohammedan harems. The whole world stands aghast at the cruelty and horror of this treatment. Undoubtedly many of these, when the war is over, will be restored to their friends, but unquestionably many will remain throughout their lives in a Moslem home. It is inevitable that into that home these women will carry the leaven of their Christian training, thinking, and living. Christian truth cannot be thus suppressed, but will necessarily work its way out through the fabric of the society into which these women are thrust so much against their will, and will appear, in its beauty and in its power, in those homes, as it manifests itself in the thinking and the life of the children. These spiritual forces will never be dissipated; the seed of the Gospel of Christ, sown in the hearts of these young women, will unquestionably bear fruit in the years to come. We have every reason to believe that this terrible disaster to a Christian race, one of the most terrible in modern history, under the hand of God will prove to be one of the divine means for implanting the spirit of Christ in the strongholds of Islam.

There is every reason to believe that the events of these years, so deplorable in themselves, will eventuate in opening Turkey to the approach of the Gospel, as we have never dared, in all the history of modern missions, to pray that it might be opened. Surely the Lord's ways are not our ways; but there is every evidence that He is laying before the Christian world an opportunity to reach Mohammedanism through its inner citadel.

During the last generation the Mohammedans of all countries have been taught to look toward Turkey as their political and religious, if not their intellectual center. Many pilgrims who have gone to Mecca have also proceeded to Constantinople to have audience with the Caliph and to receive instruction from him to take back to their people. Proclamations from Abdul Hamid were repeatedly issued from Constantinople to the Mohammedans of the world, until there had grown up a feeling among many, a conviction with some, — that Constantinople was the capital of Mohammedanism and the center of its influence and power. With this preparation, which may be compared to the preparation of the Roman Empire for the coming of Christ, the way is opened to begin at Constantinople and in the Turkish Empire a direct and aggressive plan for reaching the Mohammedans, not only of Turkey, but of the whole Moslem world.

CHAPTER VI

PAN–ISLAMISM

The tendency of Mohammedanism was to break up into sects often openly antagonistic to each other. Since the followers of the Prophet lived under so many different governments, spoke such a variety of tongues and represented so many divergent interests, it was but natural that even with the common creed and ritual and the pilgrimage to Mecca, there should be a tendency to draw apart. The ideal Moslem state was a theocracy in which the leader was both civil and religious head. So long as Mohammed lived, and until Islam had extended beyond the borders of the caliphate, a unity was maintained through the state. This was not difficult while wars of conquest were waged and the entire Moslem body was called upon to fight the battles of their faith. When, however, allegiance to different and even hostile chiefs was demanded, and the Caliph no longer ruled over all Moslems, the traditional unity was broken in upon. When to this we add the fact of some 150 different sects, we have a heterogeneous mass of religionists whose chief unity lies in the name, the repetition of the creed, the fast of Ramazan, the Book, and the pilgrimage to Mecca.

Then there were the diversified races. Dr. Wilson gives the number of these as follows:

80,000,000 Caucasian
70,000,000 Mongol-Turks
44,000,000 Malay Dravidians
36,000,000 Negroes and Negroids

The Arabs, Kurds, Turks, Mongols and Albanians have also their racial antagonisms. A general Jihad could no longer be expected, as in the earlier days of conquest.

Pan-Islamism came in as an endeavor to unite divergent elements and cement Islam into a more compact mass of believers. It did not begin its endeavor by formulating a new creed or introducing some new form of worship but simply by declaring and attempting to practice the unity of all Mohammedans. It remained for Sultan Abdul Hamid II of Turkey to conceive the idea of uniting the discordant and heterogeneous elements in Islam and of welding them into a united whole. While he ruled over but a mere fraction of the great body of Moslems in the world, he was the Sultan of Turkey, in direct succession from four centuries of Sultans who claimed to hold the high office of Caliph and who had been so recognized in varying degrees of devotion by Mohammedans of many other countries. His assumed title was "Commander of the Faithful, Imam of Moslems, Refuge of the World, Shadow of God, King of Kings, Arbiter of the World's Destinies, Lord of the Two Continents and Two Seas, and Sovereign of the East and West." This title contained enough high-sounding terms to give prestige among peoples who were inclined to honor display and presumption. He had also been invested with the insignia of his office, the sword of the Caliph Omar and the standard and cloak of Mohammed.

Mohammedans do not imagine the Caliph as a pope, " but as a supreme ruler; above all as the *amir-al-mu'-minin*, commander of the legions of Islam, which sometime would make the whole world bend to its power."

Among the great mass of ignorant followers in all parts of the world, the Sultan of Turkey, invested with so much authority and power, could not but command a dominating influence. Not a few of these believed literally in the reality of his titles, while the presence of foreign Ambassadors at the Porte was interpreted to mean the visible token of the submission of the countries from which they came. Abdul Hamid was not slow in disseminating among the Moslems of his own dominions and especially among those of other countries the information that he was the Caliph of every country and race of Mohammedans as well as the one by whose authority all kings and emperors held their thrones.

Through the agency of different sheiks and dervish orders, his agents, widely sent upon secret missions, were supplied with funds under directions to use these liberally, everywhere, with influential leaders and at popular shrines. It is said that Abdul Hamid spent half his revenues in this way. These trained envoys, or messengers, were preachers of a great and overmastering Islam that was destined to wax stronger and stronger as it extended its borders, until the entire world should be won. Also the faithful were promised unusual rewards for robbing Christians of their property and even of their lives. The press was requisitioned and periodicals took up the subject, while books proclaimed the merit of disloyalty to Christian rule and the triumph of the crescent.

Children were brought to Turkey from Java, Sumatra and India, to be there trained in loyalty to the Sultan. Special effort was made to win the Persian Shiahs to the plan of a united Mohammedanism. To them was sent one of the most powerful of envoys, who had established at Mecca a Pan-Islamic Society, besides serving as a bold propagator of the idea in Egypt and India. His declaration was, " If all the Moslems would unite, all the nations on earth could not resist them." The Shah did not yield to this scheme, although many Persians did.

As an aid to winning Arabia to his plan the Hajaz railway was planned and built as far as Medina. The Shah of Persia, the Khedive of Egypt and the Mohammedans of India contributed several million dollars to the enterprise. The Arabs were inclined to be favorable. The propaganda was pushed at Mecca among the 100,000 pilgrims who came annually to kiss the black stone of the Kaaba and so insure for themselves happy entrance into paradise. This was one of the most widespread and rewarding methods of disseminating the idea that Islam was to triumph over Christianity and become speedily the one supreme and ruling religion.

The movement was preeminently anti-Christian and had as its goal the triumph of Islam over Christianity both as a personal and a national religion. A policy of repression followed in Turkey, manifested in the tightening of restrictions against Christian schools, the Christian press and the freedom of the exercise of what had heretofore been regarded as Christian rights. Persia followed with the same plan of repression.

There can be little doubt that the frequent massacres of Christians that took place in Turkey under Abdul Hamid were but a part of the general plan of repression. These were always accompanied by wholesale and forcible conversions to Islam and the appropriation for the use of Moslems of the property of non-Moslems, and especially that of the Christians. It is true that there were massacres of Christians in Turkey before the days of Hamid, but it remained for Hamid so to organize and systematize massacre and forcible conversion as to make it almost a science of murder and propagandism.

No one would attempt to predict the end of this widespread and carefully directed movement to unite the Moslem world against Christendom, had nothing interfered to interrupt the propaganda. It received a new and almost startling impulse upon the visit of the Emperor of Germany to Constantinople in 1898, following a tour in Palestine. Whatever may have been the purpose of the visit, the Moslems in Turkey received the impression that Emperor William was the friend of Islam and that his influence and endeavor would be in the interests of the triumph of the crescent. Among Moslems his coming with presents was taken as open acknowledgment of the superiority of their Caliph, and his cordial expressions of admiration for Mohammedanism made them believe him to be at heart a Moslem.

Soon after Turkey entered the recent war, thus becoming an ally of Germany, Turkish papers in Constantinople printed the statement that when the Kaiser visited the Sultan and the Holy Land he became a Mohammedan and really went on to Mecca and so became a Hadji. The story ran that he kept his conversion to himself, but that quietly his court and the court of Austria, and finally the people of both countries, became Moslem. The Kaiser's conscience would not permit him longer to keep silent respecting his new-found faith, and towards the last of July, 1914, he made known to the world the fact. Immediately the Christian nations inaugurated a holy war, making simultaneous attack upon these two Moslem states.

In order to prove the truth of this story, pictures of some of the ruined churches and cathedrals in Belgium and Flanders were shown, with the declaration that these were destroyed by the Kaiser's army, which of course they would never have done but for the fact that they were no longer Christian. In the mosques of Turkey prayer was offered for Hadji Wilhelm, to whom the Moslems of Turkey pinned their faith and upon whom they relied to save Islam to the world.

The uprising of the Young Turks and the restoration of the Constitution in 1908 was not a part of the program of Abdul Hamid in his Pan-Islamic propaganda. The massacre he carried through at Adana was his last endeavor to put Islam upon the throne and to send Christianity bleeding to its destruction. It looks as if the hopes of a united and victorious Mohammedanism are not in a way to be realized. The Mohammedans in India and Egypt have demonstrated their absolute loyalty to England, the political enemy of Turkey. The relations between the Moslems and the Germans in Turkey are becoming daily more strained, as belief in Germany's power or even purpose to save Mohammedanism weakens.

The present rulers of Turkey not only are not actuated by any real zeal for Islam but they are devoid of a religious motive in the present struggle. They are out for personal triumph and not to propagate a religion. Of course it is understood that Sultan Mohammed V was but a figurehead, who had no voice in leading Turkey into the war and no power to avert the impending disaster. The sudden abrogation of the capitulations, under which representatives of Christian nations have lived and carried on business in Turkey for a century and more, might seem to indicate religious zeal, but this act will not bear such an interpretation. The motive was to secure to Turkey governmental and national privileges and prerogatives of which the capitulations deprived her. The act had no religious significance, and is as strongly resisted by Austria and Germany as by England, Russia, Italy and the United States.

A supreme and perhaps final effort to unite Mohammedanism in a deadly struggle with Christianity was made in the fall of 1914, when a holy war was proclaimed with all the ceremony and solemnity of which the government was capable.

Pan-Islamism seems to be doomed to eternal disappointment. No longer is the Caliph at Constantinople recognized as the successor of Mohammed, the Shadow of God on earth. In Egypt, in the mosques, the name of the Khedive has been substituted for the Caliph. Moslem circles are seriously discussing the question of the future head of the Moslems of the world. No Moslem country presents itself as fulfilling the requirements of the Koran and tradition. Is Pan-Islamism possible with no Caliph and without even a country that is independent of domination by a non-Moslem power? It would seem that the deep-laid, far-visioned plans of Abdul Hamid are to end in overwhelming disaster to the country that, in his dreams, he saw ruling the Moslem nations and dictating to all others.

Abdul Hamid lost no opportunity to impress upon the chancellories of Europe that, in case the Christian nations of Europe thwarted his purposes, he might not be able to suppress the forces of Islam, all of which were ready to leap to his assistance and defense against Christian aggression. The 67,000,000 Mohammedans in India have been free to send their warnings to England that Mohammedanism is a unit, not only in India but in the world, and that in case of adequate provocation the Moslem forces of the world might unite against all the forces of Christendom. These threats have been repeated at different times, and have occasionally changed England's contemplated attitude toward the Mohammedans in India.

Then, too, the Senousi in North Africa, an order of dervishes that has sprung up in the last generation, has as one of its objects the mobilizing of the forces of Mohammedanism in order to fight a holy war at the call of the Sultan of Turkey. Many stories have been reported of their extensive preparations and of their wide following in every Moslem country, with fanciful pictures of what would be the result should the Sultan of Turkey declare a deadly conflict between Mohammedans and non-Mohammedans.

Much has been said of the increasing sense of unity among the Mohammedans and of the secret preparations going on among them for a great contest of strength, should adequate provocation arise. At the same time, it is widely known that the Sultan of Turkey is the possessor of the flag which Mohammed himself is alleged to have carried in his battles of conquest at Medina, and Mohammedans have not been backward in stating that, should the Sultan of Turkey take the flag to the mosque of Mohammed the Conqueror in Constantinople and there proclaim a holy war, millions of Moslems, if not the entire Moslem body of the world, quite irrespective of the governments under which they lived, would rise as one man, and the world would be bathed in blood.

Within two months after Turkey had entered the European conflict as the ally of Germany and Austria, it seemed wise to the Sultan and his advisers to precipitate the crisis and to involve the entire world in a universal Jihad. With that end in view, in the mosque of Mohammed the Conqueror, the leading Moslems of Constantinople were assembled, and the Sheik ul Islam, in the most solemn form and in accordance with the conditions laid down for such act, called upon the Moslems of Turkey and the world to rise against the forces of Christianity that were attempting to crush out Mohammedanism, to throw off the yoke of oppression and to declare their freedom. On the next day the Sultan, the Caliph, issued a proclamation to the " Soldiers of Islam," calling upon them everywhere to offer and if necessary to lay down their lives for the defense of their faith. The place was auspicious, since it was the mosque that commemorates the greatest victory of the Turks over Christianity, the conquest of Constantinople in 1453. Prayers followed the declaration, long speeches were made, and there was great jubilation. A procession was formed, which passed through the main part of the city, waited upon the Grand Vizier, and also assembled in front of the German and Austrian Embassies. The German and Austrian Ambassadors were complimented by public addresses from the leaders of the Jihad, and both Ambassadors replied in terms that were interpreted by the Mohammedans as of the most hearty approval. The German Ambassador spoke of the long-standing friendship between Germany and Turkey, and of their common struggle for the welfare of the Mohammedan world, announcing that before both Germans and the adherents of Islam there would lie a glorious future as soon as German and Turkish arms had won the victory. The Austrian Ambassador with more caution referred to the holy war which the Emperor of Austria was waging, together with Turkey, and of the sympathy that bound the two countries together. Whatever may have been the intention of the German and Austrian representatives, the Mohammedans took these utterances as positive evidence that those two countries were bound together with Turkey in the one purpose of waging a holy war, first against Russia, France and England (Italy had not then entered the war), and secondly, against all Christian nations that did not recognize the supremacy of Islam and give it free hand in development.

This demonstration, spectacular in the extreme, did not seem to call out an enthusiastic response even from the Mohammedans within the borders of the Turkish Empire. The first mobilization had been practically completed, but the desertion of Moslem troops, in every part of the empire, was almost unprecedented. There was no general enthusiasm. The call for a holy war did not seem to bring out any special volunteers for military service, even in Turkey, and in India and Egypt, the two countries that were expected to be most affected, there appears to have been no response at all. Mohammedan troops from India joined the British forces in Flanders. The Mohammedan soldiers in Egypt organized for the defense of Egypt against the Senousi of the West and against attacks from the Turkish forces on the East; while the Mohammedans in India, at the beginning of the war and before the call for a Jihad, asked England, in case Turkey should be involved, to use her influence to see that Turkish territory was not violated. Later, after the call had been issued, the Mohammedan forces of both Egypt and India seemed to rally wholly to the support of England as against the Central Powers and against Turkey.

Thus the first and most solemn endeavor of Islam to mass its forces against unbelievers throughout the world proved to be a failure. The outcome was that Turkey herself became involved in the conflict on the side of Germany and Austria against three Christian powers, while the Mohammedan forces of Egypt and of India arrayed themselves in opposition, and Mohammedanism was torn asunder by this supreme and what will probably be final endeavor to array the Moslem world against all non-Moslems.

We can reveal the true spirit of the militant Moslems of Turkey in no more vivid way than by quoting from a sermon delivered in Saint Sophia, Constantinople, by Oubeid Ullah Effendi, in August, 1914. It was the purpose of the preacher to arouse the fighting spirit of his hearers and prepare them for the formal call for a Jihad that was soon to follow. Sermons of this character were preached in many different parts of the country during the summer and autumn of 1914, revealing a deliberate and carefully organized plan to strike a crushing blow when the hour arrived. We can make but brief extracts from this characteristic address, delivered with great unction, and calculated to appeal to the religious and patriotic spirit of his hearers.

" O Moslem people, I gather you here at the beginning of the holy Ramazan to call you to an external holy war (Jihad), — a war against atheist (giaour) Europe. Perhaps some of you think it is not proper for me to preach about politics under this sacred dome, but I tell you the Mohammedan religion is a political religion, and the most important problem about which one can ever preach in this sacred place is politics. Real politics is to defend the nation against internal and external enemies; so I come to declare to you, O ye Moslem people, to get ready for a holy war. We are at the beginning of the holy Bairam; I bring you good tidings, this is the dawn of a victory. . . .

" Some time ago I read in a prophetic book that when the name of the ruler of the Turkish Empire is Mohammed and also the Grand Vizier is Mohammed, then the time of blessing, victory and prosperity has come for the Moslem world. Now listen! Our king is Mohammed Reshad, and our Grand Vizer's name is Mohammed Said Pasha. Praise God, cheer up (Inshalla)! The year 1914 will be a year of prosperity and victory for the Moslem nation. Get ready for the holy war. The Islam world has reached the end of its humiliation. Let us be sincere and enthusiastic

Moslems, — real Moslems renew and strengthen their faith." . . .

"There is not a single Moslem in the world whose heart does not burn from the oppression, cruelty, and persecution of the foreigners, and everybody was pleading with God for better days, for victory. Now I say to you, praise God, our victory is near! But if we wish that this religion shall be victorious and reign over the world we have to be willing to sacrifice everything."

"Come, let us pray to our God and say, O Lord, we repent at this Bairam for all our deeds which were contrary to Thy will, and we are willing to do everything, to give everything for the victory of the religion. Let us say so and do so. If you want to be acceptable to God be ready for the holy war."

"I bring you good news. There is general war reigning all over Europe. Perhaps some will say, 'Is this good news? Is not general war a disaster rather than something to delight in?' We have so often prayed saying, O Lord, let these giaours (infidels) quarrel with each other, and now God has listened to our prayers. . . . Be glad! Twenty millions of giaours are killing each other with most devilish instruments. May God make it more!" (The people said "Amen.")

"We have not to watch these things with a cold indifference. We have also to march. We have responsibilities. All the Islam world is blaming us. Last year I went to Tripoli. There the people asked me, 'Why are you not declaring holy war?' This year I went to Arabia. There our poor co-religionists were anxiously asking, 'Has God given you the sword in vain? You have been subject to every kind of disaster, you have been deprived of many sacred rights. Why do you wait then? Let the Calipha bid us to rise and we are ready.'"

"There are three hundred millions of Moslems over the world and we are only one tenth of them. All the rest is under the slavery of the giaour world. It is our duty to save them from this humiliation. Rise now, it is time to make them free. . . .

"Be glad! Thirty millions of giaours are eating each other's flesh, destroying each other's cities. Yes, they will destroy, they will slaughter, they will break, they will be broken. May God make it more!" (All the people said "Amen.") . . .

"God has commanded men to make war. War is legal, because if men do not kill each other the world will soon be filled with men and it will be a bad place. Do not say a civilized man should not think so. Civilization is hypocrisy. What benefits do we have from the civilized world?" . . .

"Be not afraid of death. Do not spare your lives or your money. If you do not give your money in this world, in the world to come your gold will be taken from you and after being heated in the fires of hell will be bound on your foreheads and on your loins.

"Let us close by saying again, be ready for the holy war."

It does not require a great stretch of the imagination to detect a strong parallel between Pan-Islamism and Pan-Germanism. It is not merely the existence of two forces, the one politico-religious and the other purely political bolstered up by a form of religion, aspiring to world conquest, but we have the spectacle of the political power attempting so to dominate the Moslem theocracy that it shall be identified with and even become a part of the German scheme of conquest. It was by encouraging the Pan-Islamic idea in the Turks that Germany hoped to appropriate to her own selfish uses the fanatical zeal and religious ambitions of the Moslem world.

CHAPTER VII

THE GREAT WAR AND ISLAM

Whatever final effect the war may have upon the national life of the world and whatever revision of geography it may demand, there is little doubt that the story of its influence on two great religions will record its most fundamental results. This is the first war in which the question has been raised as to why Christianity did not prevent it. Never before has Christianity been recognized as possessing power capable of preventing any war, and now thousands asked why it did not exercise the power it possesses and make impossible such a conflict. In a word, the war brought to the front the great fundamental truths of Christianity which are recognized as capable of exerting an influence over the national life of the world that would prevent international wars. It is upon Mohammedanism, however, that the most startling effect is produced, and the influence here is quite different from that upon Christianity. The war called out some of the greatest and most fundamental principles of Christianity, while it shattered hitherto unassailable doctrines and beliefs of Mohammedanism.

While aware of the fact that Islam is not a race or an ethnic religion, nevertheless the relation between Mohammedanism and races both in numbers and nomenclature has been from the beginning unusually close. The followers of Mohammed have been through all history and are today classified in terms which belong only to races. The word Arab, while characterizing a race has, in a widely increasing circle in Africa as well as in other countries, come to mean a Mohammedan. The crusades were an attack of Christian Europe upon the " Saracens " of the Holy Land and the Mohammedans who occupied Spain during the period of Islam's supremacy there bore the name Saracens. The Mohammedans in Russia are called Tartars, and the great Mohammedan empire in India was called the Mongol or Mogul Empire, while even today in Turkey, no matter to what race they may belong, Mohammedans are called Turks. The modern Mohammedan problem is therefore, in appearance at least, a race problem.

We must bear in mind that from the time of Mohammed, Islam has aimed at a theocracy. Mohammed was the religious as well as the civil and military head of his followers. The same was true of the Caliphs that succeeded him; the greatest Mohammedan Caliphs of history have been not only religious leaders but great civil rulers and have commanded large military forces used for defence and conquest. One of the boasted elements of strength in Mohammedanism has been the expectation of ultimate control as a religion and as a political power of all the nations of the world. In presenting Islam to those not followers of the prophet the ideal has always been held up that Islam was one day to conquer, through divine intervention, all the races of the earth and that upon the throne of the nations was to sit the supreme, unconquerable, all-powerful Caliph of Islam. The humblest negro of Central Africa who has become a Mohammedan has been taught to think of himself as an integral member of a great conquering world power.

In addition to the expectation of world conquest is added the boast of unity. Mohammedans have looked upon Christians with contempt because of their divisions. They have observed the gulf between Roman Catholics and Protestants, followed by the breaking up of Protestants into many different sects, and have contrasted the divided state of Christendom with the boasted unity of Islam. They have instanced their one simple creed, their one universally accepted authoritative book, their one acknowledged prophet, and have been able to maintain that Mohammedanism is a united body. They have claimed that not only are they able to live together in harmony, but that they are ready to join forces in the resistance of any common enemy, and, if need be, to die to the last man for the defence of their faith.

It is true this unity has never been fully realized even under the great Sulliman the Magnificent when the Ottoman Empire became the greatest and most mighty empire on earth. Under Abdul Hamid II a supreme effort was made to weld together the different Mohammedan elements and races into not only a moral, but even into an organic unity. Pilgrimage to Mecca and Constantinople was conspicuously encouraged and the pilgrims returned to their homes with royal presents to preach the magnificence of the Turkish Empire and especially of Abdul Hamid, as well as to proclaim the unity of Mohammedanism. Royal exhortations in the interest of unity were sent to the remotest Moslem centers and every endeavor was made to impress upon all the followers of Mohammed the essential oneness of their religion and its ultimate triumph. As an illustration of the success of this endeavor of Abdul Hamid, we have but to refer to the fact that when the United States was negotiating with the Mohammedan Moros of the Philippine Islands, the negotiations were carried on at Constantinople by the United States Ambassador with Abdul Hamid II, and the arrangements were there completed by which the Moros recognized the suzerainty of the United States. These efforts at Moslem centralization led to the use of the expression Pan-Islamism, causing no little alarm in the chancellories of Europe because of the fear that united Islam would become an open menace to civilization. England was especially alarmed because of her ninety millions of Mohammedans in India, Egypt, and other British dependencies.

Hitherto the great decisive battles of Islam have been those which Mohammedans have fought with Christians.

The Battle of Tours, when the Saracens of Spain crossed the Pyrenees and attempted to conquer the capitals of Europe in the name of the prophet, marked the first reverse of Islam in its triumphal march to victory. The forces of Charles Martel were able to turn back the Moslem tide from permanently holding territory north of the Pyrenees. Centuries later, in 1492, this reverse was followed by withdrawal of the Saracens from Spain. In 1529, Sulliman the Conqueror, who brought the Ottoman rule to the zenith of its power, led his triumphant army to the north and west until they confronted the walls of Vienna. Driven back by the Christian forces in defeat, the attempt was repeated in 1693 under Mohammed IV, who made the last great attack upon the citadels of Christendom and the heart of Europe. As Vienna resisted and drove back the would-be Moslem conquerors, the rising tide of Islam was turned. Gradually and one by one the conquered provinces of Hungary were restored to Christian government. Later Roumania, Greece, Servia, Bulgaria, Bosnia, and Herzogovina were released from the power of the Turk. North Africa, country by country, was freed, Persia no longer remained an independent Mohammedan power, and last of all Macedonia and Egypt threw off completely the yoke of Turkey and came under Christian rule.

Nevertheless the imperial spirit of the Mohammedan was not broken. He still dreamed of the day when under some intervention of Allah the Christians would be punished for their resistance and Moslem sway would be reestablished not only over the lost provinces of Islam but over the entire world.

Turkey entered into the great European War under the leadership of the central powers. While this step called out protests from many leading Mohammedans in Turkey, as well as in India and Egypt, it did not cause an immediate disruption, although Mohammedans from India, from Egypt, and from Morocco were fighting shoulder to shoulder on the plains of France with the enemies of Turkey and against

Turkey's Christian allies. This was the first time in history that Turkey had been involved in a great international war as an ally of so-called Christian nations. The Mohammedans in Russia showed sympathy with Russia, an enemy of Turkey.

A decision was made under the leadership of Germany to put to test the supreme and final resort of Islam. In November, 1914, most solemnly and formally, first under the direction of the Sheik-ul-Islam, and then by the Caliph of Islam himself, a call directly to the Moslems of Turkey, and indirectly to the Moslems of the world was issued for a holy war against all enemies of Mohammedanism. There has long been a general fear among the nations of all Europe especially, and even beyond, which in the history of Islam has never been tested, that whenever such a call should go forth, there would be a general response among the 230,000,000 of Mohammedans in the world. According to the belief and teachings of Islam, it would be impossible for a genuine Mohammedan to fail to respond and still retain his position as a true believer.

The fetwa calling the Jihad or holy war was issued in the Mosque of the Conqueror at Constantinople and was accompanied by all the official solemnity possible, to impress upon the Mohammedans of Constantinople, of Turkey and of the world, the seriousness of this great supreme attempt to unite in a holy and deadly conflict all Mohammedans against all non-Mohammedans and especially against the open enemies of Turkey. Quite contrary to expectation there was no unusual agitation even in Constantinople. From many parts of Turkey strong protests even were directed against what was called the unholy alliance between the Government of the Caliph and Christian nations. The grounds of these protests were that Turkey was not attacked and that there appeared no possibility of gain on the part of the Ottoman Government, but rather every possibility of serious loss. The Mohammedans of India held mass meetings of protest and these protests were voiced in long telegraphic messages to the

Sultan of Turkey. At the same time messages of loyalty to Great Britain were also sent. Similar protests arose from Egypt, from Abyssinia, from Morocco, until the evidence was complete that the only call for a general holy war ever issued by the highest authority in Islam had utterly failed of its purpose and had resulted in a hopeless division among Mohammedans. Persia showed marks of disloyalty, and as a final proof of the seriousness of the rupture, leading tribes of Arabia united in open rebellion against the boasted Caliph at Constantinople. They took possession of the sacred shrines of Islam which, through all Moslem history, have been under the special care and protection of the Caliph. In a message sent to the Sultan of Turkey the Arabian forces repudiated him as the Caliph, congratulating the Mohammedans of the world upon the restoration of the control of Mecca and Medina to their rightful protectors, namely, the successors of the Koreish tribes from which Mohammed sprang.

In Turkey itself it was reported, upon what seems to be unquestioned authority, that not more than 20 per cent. of the Mohammedans were in sympathy with the administration, while the remaining large body of Moslems deprecated the entrance of Turkey into the war, and the formation of an alliance that has caused irreparable disaster to their holy religion, to say nothing of the physical ruin it has brought upon their country.

There is today no central Mohammedan power, there is no recognized Caliph of Islam. The cherished hope of the ultimate triumph of Mohammedanism as the ruling religious and physical force in the world is rapidly disappearing. Belief in Mohammedanism as representing an adequate force for world government is losing its place in Mohammedan thinking. The boasted solidarity of Islam no longer exists in anywhere near the same measure that it prevailed even a decade ago; and there is no possibility of a return even to the former sense of unity.

The last great Moslem power, the Ottoman Empire, as a result of this European war has already lost its national significance and the Mohammedan world is casting about for a new Caliph. There is no evidence that one can be found who can be at all generally recognized. The Caliph must be, according to Mohammedan law, the ruler of an independent Mohammedan country which today hardly exists. And if, by agreement of the European powers, the Hejaz in Arabia, in which the holy places of Islam are located, should be set aside for Arabian self-government and allowed for the time being to control these sacred shrines, there is no evidence that the Mohammedans of the rest of the world would recognize the ruler of that small territory as the universal Caliph. One-seventh of the population of the world is vitally affected by the outcome of the war. The breaking up of the unity and solidarity of Mohammedanism is of tremendous significance to the entire Christian world.

The effect of the present war upon Islam, and especially the alliance of Turkey with two Christian nations, cannot now be adequately estimated, but it is possible to trace some significant tendencies. The attitude of Germany in general toward Mohammedanism before the outbreak of this war is clearly expressed in action taken at the German Colonial Congress held in Hamburg in 1910, in which the Moslem peril in East Africa was discussed. As the outgrowth of that Congress the following resolution was adopted:

" Since the progress of Islam in our colonies is accompanied by grave perils, this Colonial Congress recommends a thorough study of Moslem propagandism. The Congress is thoroughly convinced that everything which favors the progress of Islam and hinders the progress of Christianity should be avoided, and especially commends the cultural efforts of missionary education and hospital work, to the support of the Colonial Government. We also recognize in the Moslem peril an urgent challenge to German Christianity to occupy the regions threatened by Islam with missionary effort."

In this Congress were Protestant, Roman Catholic and Socialistic leaders.

Those who have kept careful record of the public utterances of the Kaiser since 1898, when he made his famous speech at the grave of Saladin, announcing that Germany was the natural protector of Mohammedanism the world around, report that in none of these utterances has anything been said to which a Mohammedan could take exception. The Kaiser has carefully avoided reference to the church or to Jesus Christ. He has repeatedly and constantly used the name of God, but in this use he has apparently taken pains to avoid anything that could in any way give offence to the most devoted and pious Moslem.

At the outbreak of the war there were many indications that Germany placed great reliance upon her alliance with Turkey as a central Mohammedan power. A telegram from the Turkish capital at Constantinople, sent after the call for a Holy War, was in terms as follows:

" The outbreak of hostilities in Afghanistan is expected in the course of the next few days. A rebellion in India should then follow. The full effect of the Holy War already finds expression among the Senousi and all the tribes of the southern Sudan, as well as in Persia, which is in a state of war."

All this shows how much Germany depended upon the uprising of the Mohammedans in the various countries governed by the enemy to aid German arms in this great world conflict.

In another chapter we have referred to the attempt of Germany to embroil the entire Mohammedan world in a conflict with Germany's enemies under the form of a call for a Holy War, so that this need not be discussed here. The alliance of Germany with the greatest and only really Mohammedan country in the world had marked influence over the thinking of many Germans and has led to most searching discussion on the part of German missionary leaders, as to what effect this alliance with a Mohammedan power must have upon the attitude of the Church and mission organizations in Germany toward Mohammedans and Mohammedan countries.

Prof. Friedrich Delitzsch of Berlin, during the first year of the war, declared in an address delivered to a large audience in Berlin, as reported in the *Christian World* of April 29, 1915, that Islam, so far from being a barren and retrogressive faith, leaves the door wide open to religious, moral and social progress, and that therefore no German Christian need be ashamed of an alliance which, begun in time of war, will be cemented and bear worthy fruit in times of peace. This statement of Professor Delitzsch does not harmonize well with the utterances of the German Colonial Congress held five years before, but the circumstances were different.

Prof. Wilhelm Hermann, of Marburg, in a lecture which was reported in the *Christliche Welt* of March 18, 1915, said:

" We must be convinced that they (the Turks) understand us and we them. Were this not the case our alliance would be a false and unworthy one. . . . As Christians we can understand and reverence their religious convictions, and our future lies along the same road as theirs."

Professor Troeltsch, in the *Evangelisches Missions-Magazin* of June, 1915, after discussing the alliance of Germany with Islam, said:

" Islam is thereby recognized as one of the great acknowledged religious world powers which can no longer be a missionary objective but must be left, just as in the Christian world, to its own inner religious development. It is unlikely that this result will ever be reversed, and it will affect the treatment of the Moslem problem in our Colonial possessions. For all that, Christianity is of course not invalidated in the territories occupied by the white race (to which, apart from the Christian communities in our Colonies, it seems bound to confine itself), though it is limited as regards its world mission. It seems to be conclusively established that humanity is distributed into distinct spheres of religious life, free henceforth to stimulate one another religiously, but each bound to fulfil its own destiny.

This will astonish or alarm no one who has already come to this conviction on general principles from a study of the history of religion, but it is now beginning to be universally evident from the course of historical events."

The statements of these learned professors here quoted did not at that time represent the sentiment of all the Christian people of Germany, although it was a live question among them how far, in the face of the political alliance with Turkey, German Christians and German missionary societies could put to the front the question of missionary work among the Mohammedans.

Three months before Professor Troeltsch's article was printed, there appeared in the *Missions-Magazin*, Herr Würz editor, an editorial to which Professor Troeltsch's statement may have been a reply:

" The most important future issue for Christian missions is, how far their inward participation in the present world conflict, as denoted by the summons to a Holy War, will influence Moslems in their attitude toward Western culture, and above all as regards receptivity toward the Gospel of Christ. Little can as yet be said on the matter, although we are not without hope. Moreover, our duty at the moment is not to make conjecture as to the future but so to live in the present, with every sense alert, that we shall be ready for the tasks that lie before us."

It is an interesting fact, worthy of note here, that Herr Würz is the Chairman of the Sub-Committee of the Continuation Committee of the Edinburgh Conference on the subject of Christian work for Mohammedans. It is a subject to which he has given much time and thought, and one in which he is profoundly interested.

In reply to Prof. Troeltsch's article, Herr Würz wrote as follows:

" The problem of our present relation with Islam could not be more cogently presented than it is here, and, therefore, we too are grateful for Professor Troeltsch's article. What seems to him the verdict of history upon the age-long yet false claims of Christianity, is in fact one of the greatest dangers of the present hour. True, we need have no fear for the world-wide validity of the Gospel of Christ; humanity will need it as much as ever in the future and it will prove as effectual as it ever has been. But our own share in that Gospel may well be at stake, if, in the political alliance with the Mohammedan world, we lightly esteem the incomparable treasure with which we have been endowed by God. That would mean, not the end of the world mission of Christianity, but certainly the end of our world mission on behalf of Christianity. It may be difficult for us when, as a natural consequence of political alliance, the consensus of public opinion is friendly towards Islam, to maintain our clear Christian consciousness with regard to that faith. But if we do, we may bring blessing to that Mohammedan world with which we are now outwardly so closely associated."

Prof. Julius Richter, editor of the *Allgemeine Missions-Zeitschrift*, printed editorially in his magazine of December, 1914, a statement, written before the call for a Holy War had been issued, from which the following quotation is made:

" Will Turkey unfurl the green flag of the Prophet, and with the war-cry, ' Islam at stake,' let loose the jihad? And will such a summons find a hearing and response in the Moslem world? That Germany and Austria will thus be forced into something like a brotherhood of arms with Turks, Persians, Afghans, and perhaps other Moslem peoples, is an uncomfortable thought. There is, however, a community of interests which is too far-reaching. Unless one were absolutely convinced that Moslem lands are hopelessly incapable of reform, one could hardly, from a higher level of human development, stigmatise as an outrage any attempt on the part of a Moslem people to save their existence and perhaps regain a portion of their power by means of a war in a political combination which at last may be favorable to them."

This subject was taken up in the German magazines and became a matter of much discussion and heart-searching. There are many German Christian leaders who do not feel comfortable at the thought that Germany has formed an alliance with Mohammedanism making missionary work among Mohammedans forever impossible.

In 1916, representatives of Missions connected with the

German Evangelical Missionary Committee assembled to discuss this important question. Every Society was represented. Bishop Hennig, a member of the Continuation Committee of the Edinburgh Missionary Conference, was the presiding officer. One of the most important questions brought forward for consideration was what missions may do in order to protect the home churches from a wrong valuation of Islam and to bring them to a proper valuation of it. Mr. Schlunk, of Hamburg, in reporting this Conference in the *Evangelisches Missions-Magazin* of June, 1916, said:

" Wide circles of the German people not only stand in actual danger of placing an incorrect valuation upon the religion of Mohammed but they have already fundamentally fallen prey to this danger. Through a determined admiration of Islam they become equally determined to forget their own Christian position, and believe, that if possible they are in this way fulfilling their obligation to the German cause. . . . If one has expressly demanded, however, that the Ottoman Kingdom should be absolutely excluded from the sphere of missions, he therefore has sought also thereby to cut the vital nerve of all missionary work and to bring into question the essential superiority of all Christianity to the non-Christian religions. Should this become a chronic situation, it might have serious consequences. It might even lead to an obscuring of the fact that we are a Christian nation and that we must be loyal in all our actions to the standpoint of Christianity. . . . We look rather helplessly upon the tendency, and it is good that we are able to have confident faith that our God will lead us also out of this difficulty. We must make practical comparisons of religions from a decidedly Christian standpoint and encourage such comparisons. In this we have no ground for remaining silent over the vital forces of the non-Christian religions. . . . Primarily, however, we must bring the will of the Christian portion of the nation to our side and fundamentally change our relationship to the world of Islam. Here it is a question not of expediency but of duty, not of temporary friendly contact but of lasting ethical and religious responsibility."

We will close these quotations by again quoting from an article on this general subject by Herr Friedrich Würz, published in his magazine:

" One hears a great deal said now-a-days about Germany's alliance with Islam. It is difficult to discover the true significance of the phrase. Indeed no alliance can be made with a religion. It is a fundamental power, and though people can perhaps take advantage of it for a definite object, through the able influence of its followers, it, however, obeys exclusively its own indwelling precepts. First of all, this statement means merely that since the Sultan as caliph proclaimed the Holy War, Germany has the power of the Islam spirit of unity and with it the sympathy of the entire Mohammedan world on her side. This has already been discussed. There is, however, in the statement, perhaps without intent, a compliment to Islam itself. It is represented as a power worthy of alliance with Christianity and as something essentially of equal rank with Christianity — perhaps even worthy of cultivation — but in no wise as something which must first be overcome or lifted up out of itself, through the higher Christian virtues. People urge two reasons why Christianity's claim of superiority over Islam must be relinquished. The one lies in the bitterness which is being caused by this war among the Christian peoples; the other in the sovereign independence with which Islam in present historical events places itself beside Christianity (meaning the alliance of Germany with Islam). There are, as is obvious, just now many reasons against Christian missions among Moslems. We are accustomed to having all sorts of objections raised against us — be it in the name of learning or be it in the interest of politics. Perhaps we have become so very much accustomed to them, that it will do us good if, because of the vigorous objections, we are forced to earnestly analyze them. This is not a question of the opposition of non-Christian adversaries on the mission field, which to a certain extent is responsible for the enduring worth of missions, and which in Christ's name can be subdued and transformed. Here we encounter to a greater extent the opposition of our own nation — and such threatens to slowly cripple the cause of missions, since the missionary enterprise has not been occupied fundamentally with such opposition, and has not, through earnest spiritual work, overcome it. People should not accuse us of being blind to the strength and good which in some way Islam or other non-Christian religions may possess. It is not necessary to fasten our cause to an untrue balance. Therefore, every honest critic will find us always ready for an honest setting forth of the facts.

Is it not now unpatriotic for German Christians still to regard the Mohammedan world as an object of missionary endeavor and Islam as an obstacle to combat? This is the warning question we hear arising from these objections when they are raised within the political circle. This question may also find an echo with many a friend of missions. However, we have face to face with it, a good conscience, because we German mission sympathizers, as heretofore in colonial questions, so now in the great decisive hour stand true to our Fatherland. Only we must remember that our duties toward the Mohammedan world can only adjust themselves for us according to the essentials of the Christian belief. If we are obedient to these, then in the end it will be best for our Fatherland.

Under present circumstances, whatever has to do with both these arguments for the equal rank of Islam makes the bitterness more keen, and its pernicious effects on the Mohammedan world have already been covered. If we had to turn to the Moslems merely as missionaries of the Christian civilization, it might perhaps discourage us. However, the political rôle, which the leading power of the Mohammedan world is now playing (" Our alliance with Islam"), I admit, can perhaps alter our disposition toward the Mohammedans, but in no case can it change our severe opinion of Islam, to say nothing of confirming its equality with Christianity. These could only rest upon an inherent equivalence of both religions, considering their historical foundations and their effects upon mankind. At this point our own observations, as also those of missionaries to the Mohammedans, and the testimony of converted Moslems, do not correspond with the views of our critics. We have not yet learned to know Islam as disclosed by its documents and as exemplified in life, as something of such merit that we should lack courage to contrast it with the Gospel.

However, the matter is not settled with this negative judgment. We must have a compelling argument why we cannot withdraw from the battle against the Mohammedan world, and it is well that the opposition in the home land forces us to a renewed and earnest examination of this cause. It has already been demonstrated with great force in the circle of Mohammedan missionaries that the one power by which the struggle against Islam can be successfully undertaken is the personally proved Gospel; only when the missionary possesses this, has he a prospect of victory. What is of value to a missionary is of value to a mission community. Therefore, the essential question, the answer of which will settle our entire relation to Islam, becomes removed to the sphere of personal experience. Here we must decide whether we have faith to believe that the power of the Gospel can overcome even so gigantic a force as Islam, and at the same time, whether it exerts such an influence in our lives as to make its power manifest to the Moslems through us. We are led now to a similar train of thought as Paul expresses it in Romans 1 : 13–17, when he explained to the Romans whence came to him the inward constraint and courage to proclaim the Gospel of Christ in the great and important city, in spite of their powerful resistance. To him it was the revealed truth of the word of Christ and His cross. Today only this can give us the right and the courage to overcome the intellectual and moral opposition of Islam, though in quite a different way. Our self-examination on this point is the first step in our new survey of Islam. From this point on we win a great liberty on all sides. First of all, as concerns our own countrymen, if we have the painful duty of following for the time being an unpopular course, we are indeed obeying clearer directions."

Perhaps undue space has been given to the effect of this war upon the relation of the Christians of Germany to Mohammedanism, but the question is unique and will probably be discussed more at length in the readjustments that follow the war. Outside of Germany there has been no such revulsion of feeling, neither has there been discussion of the same character or import. Mohammedans have joined with the Allies shoulder to shoulder in this conflict, but there has been no unusual alliance calling for any religious readjustment, while on the other hand the attitude taken by Turkey in the treatment of her non-Moslem subjects has tended to turn the sympathy of the Christians of the world against Mohammedanism as an effective religion by which a government may be administered. Certainly the war has not developed any new features of attraction or revealed any new evidence of inner strength in Mohammedanism. Nothing has occurred that could possibly give the impression that Mohammedans are not the legitimate object of missionary endeavor, while the reverse is distinctly true.

The Revolt of Mecca from Turkey and the Establishment of the Independence of Hejaz (West Arabia) is of such importance that special consideration must be given to the event.

On June 22, 1916, dispatches from Cairo, Egypt, reported that the Grand Shereef of Mecca had come out in open revolt against the Turkish Khalifate. Soon thereafter the entire proclamation of the Shereef, upon which this report was based, was published, and we are able to weigh in a measure the importance of the step taken which separates the Sultan of Turkey as Khalif from the direction and control of the sacred shrines of Islam.

It must be borne in mind that Mecca was the birthplace of Mohammed and not the center from which he extended his sovereignty over the greater part of Arabia and across North Africa. The capital of his realm was Medina, a ten days' caravan journey away and to the north. As has already been shown, it was from Medina that Mecca was captured and made the sacred place of Islam. The residence of the Khalif was in Mecca until it was removed to Damascus and later to Bagdad, thence to Cairo and finally to Constantinople. For five centuries it was located at Bagdad, for nearly three at Cairo, and for four in the Ottoman Empire. In spite of this fact, however, the Arabian Peninsula has retained its prestige in the Moslem world as the birthplace of the Prophet and as the holy land of Islam. Under the general disorganized condition of the entire country, the Mohammedan Empire fell asunder and violent contentions sprang up between many states, thus weakening the central authority of the Khalif. The Hejaz was perhaps one of the most poorly governed regions of the whole Mohammedan world, given over to confusion and plunder. It was out of this condition that the Shereefate of Mecca emerged.

There were many descendants of Mohammed, especially from the marriage of his daughter Fatima with his cousin Ali, and many settled in Arabia either as agriculturists or as heads of wandering Bedouin tribes or as pious collectors of toll from Mohammedan pilgrims. Somewhere about 1000 A.D. certain leaders of Mohammed's descendants were able to gather about them powerful followers, until two hundred years later one of these descendants of Ali, named Katada, succeeded in establishing for himself a real supremacy in Mecca. To this chief the name Shereef, "The Noble," was applied, and so the word came to mean the head of the reigning family in Mecca, the direct descendant of Mohammed. His chief authority was in Mecca itself, but from generation to generation the extent of the territory governed by the Shereef depended upon his energy and the following he was able to command. Sometimes these Shereefs were pitiless robbers, levying unwilling tribute from pilgrims visiting the holy shrines. They regarded this as their privilege by right. Gradually the Shereef came to cover in his territory the city of Taif, from two to three days' journey east of Mecca, and to Jidda, the port of Mecca on the Red Sea two days to the west. The authority of the Shereefs was very little questioned and was taken for granted, although they were not officially recognized by the Khalif or by the leading Moslems, and yet it came to be a common matter of belief that the holy city belonged rightfully to the Shereef, unquestionably representing a branch of the holy family.

When Egypt was conquered by Sultan Selim of Turkey in 1517, the protectorate of the holy land of Islam was taken over, the Sultan styling himself the servant of both holy cities. From that time on the name of the Sultan preceded that of the Grand Shereef in the official prayers, but when the Sultan of Turkey assumed the title Khalif the name of the Grand Shereef was dropped. For three centuries the Shereef held unquestioned a varying amount of control and prestige in the holy cities of Islam. At the beginning of the present century the Wahabis of central Arabia set out upon a campaign of reform in a holy war directed primarily against the Turkish domination. They obtained possession of the holy cities, forcing the Shereef to recognize their authority. These were expelled at considerable cost by Mohammed Ali of Egypt. The Shereef was punished for his inefficiency in protecting the holy city from the Wahabis and he, with several members of his family, was banished, but the head of another branch was appointed to his vacant post.

At that time there was no suggestion of an attempt to abolish the Shereefate. The relations between the Shereef at Mecca and the Sultan at Constantinople were never cordial. The Shereefs were looked upon as a necessary evil which pre-

HUSSAIN THE FIRST, KING OF THE HEDJAZ AND GRAND SHEREEF AND EMIR OF MECCA

vented the Hejaz from being constituted a regular vilayet of the Empire, although the Sultan of Turkey had military and civil officials but with functions subordinate to the power of the Shereef.

During the Turko-Italian war Turkish authority in Arabia, especially in the southern part, was contested, and the Turkish Government asked Shereef Hussein to aid in relieving the besieged Turkish garrison at Obhar in the rebellious territory. Hussein with his irregular army entered upon a campaign which assisted the safe retreat of the beleaguered Turkish garrison. Possibly this put into the mind of the Shereef a consciousness that Turkish authority was weakening, while he gained an undue sense of his own ability and power.

It must be borne in mind that there has always been more or less question in many quarters as to the authority of the Sultan of Turkey to claim the title of Khalif. For more than nine centuries the Moslem world had regarded it as obligatory upon the Khalif to be able to trace his descent from the Arabic line of Koreish from which Mohammed sprang. The question had never been taken up and forced to an issue. In the face of these questions, it is not strange that the Shereef of Mecca, after his experience in aiding the Turkish garrison to escape, conceived the idea that he himself might become a real rival of the Sultan of Turkey, a pretender to the Khalifate. So far as is known, this idea had never been broached in the Moslem world, but not infrequently European writers on Islam had made a suggestion that the Shereef of Mecca might be the Khalif. At the same time, it has been evident that in Arabia the Turks have made little or no attempt to affiliate with the Arabic people; the Turk is decidedly unpopular there. The Committee of Union and Progress that has ruled in Turkey since 1908 has not won favor in that part of the Turkish domain. Pilgrims from Constantinople to Mecca have reported scandalous proceedings on the part of the Young Turk leaders. The falling off of pilgrims to Mecca and therefore the decrease of the revenue obtained from this source of income has not tended to warm the Arabian heart toward the Turkish rule on the Bosphorus. The despotic methods used by Abdul Hamid and the final participation of Turkey in the European war have been looked upon by the people of Mecca as against their holy religion. Even Western Arabia, which had formerly accepted Turkish sovereignty, now turned against the present Turkish régime. It was under these circumstances and surrounded by these conditions that on the 25th of the month Shaaban, 1334, Shereef Hussein, Emir of Mecca, issued his proclamation of independence.

PART II
MOHAMMEDANISM AS A RELIGION

CHAPTER VIII

FOUNDATIONS OF BELIEF AND PRACTICE

Mohammedanism takes its authority from two sources, the Koran and tradition. While these two sources are distinct, widely separated and sometimes apparently contradictory, if either one should fail, Islam would suffer serious loss. Both are held in sacred deference and wield transcendent power in the control of Mohammedans in all parts of the world and in unifying their belief and practices. Both of these sources must needs be studied by all who would understand the followers of the prophet and especially by those who would attempt to present to Moslems the truths of Christianity.

When Mohammed died, his revelation existed only in fragments in the hands of the people and written upon all sorts of materials. We will not pause to consider whether these were penned in whole or in part by Mohammed himself. It is sufficient for our study to know that soon after his death the Caliph, Abu Bekr, at the suggestion of Omar set out to assemble these scattered fragments into a continuous and authoritative canon of Islam. This process of collection began the year after Mohammed died and, under the hand of Zeid, the chief secretary of Mohammed, was soon completed. One of Mohammed's wives had kept important passages in a chest, while others were still in the hands of scribes and secretaries who first wrote them down from the lips of the prophet. Some were written upon palm leaves, on fragments of parchment, on stones and bones and in the memories of men. The compiler industriously sought to secure from written statements and from those who had committed to memory the spoken words of their revered leader, everything that had been spoken or written by him or at his dictation. These chapters or suras were assembled into a book that made only a rude attempt at order in arrangement of chapters with reference to chronological sequence, context or subject.

This collection was copied widely and distributed in distant countries. It afterwards came to the attention of Othman, fifteen years after Mohammed's death, that these copies varied greatly from one another. They were all called in and destroyed and an authoritative text was issued, copies of which were deposited in the leading Moslem cities. This became the standard version that has been enforced by law; thus the Koran has maintained a remarkable uniformity of readings throughout the entire Moslem period. The book is one over which there has been little discussion as to the true text, since that question was authoritatively settled within two decades of the death of their prophet. Uniformity of text did not prevent widely divergent and contradictory statements appearing in different parts of the book. These show the absence of a system in the mind of Mohammed as well as radical change of opinion in different periods of his ministry.

Whenever these amount to irreconcilable contradictions, the theologians hold that the passage last revealed should take precedence over all others. Even here there is much ground for controversy owing to the fact that in every case the chronological order of the utterance is difficult to determine since some of the suras are made up of earlier and later revelations. Without regard for the order of writing, the longer suras or chapters are put first in the canon and the shorter ones last. Since the later suras were generally the longest, there is almost a reversal of the natural order, and consequent confusion.

In spite of these defects, the Koran is held by Moslems in great veneration and as the word of God delivered to men through the mouth of his holy prophet. It is the absolute guide for all Mohammedans, both in religious and in secular affairs. It is the sacred law for the Moslem courts as well as the last court of appeal for the state. After the promulgation of the constitution in Turkey in 1908 and the assembly of the two houses of parliament at Constantinople, reports of the proceedings of parliament frequently contained the statement that a measure proposed for action was referred to the Sheik-ul-Islam for report thereon as to whether it were in accord with the sacred law of the Koran. If the report were unfavorable, the measure was dropped or so modified as to put it into harmony. No matter with how many variations the meaning of the text may be interpreted, its authority is never questioned.

This gives to the Moslems a book bearing the unquestioned stamp of Mohammed, believed to be the prophet of God who revealed the contents of the Koran to his chosen prophet; thus the Koran becomes to all Moslems the very word of God, the source and fountain-head of their sacred religion.

In addition to the Koran and of secondary importance come the teachings of Mohammed. This includes whatever he is reported to have said as well as the things he is reported to have done. In the endeavor to interpret the Koran, recourse was had to reports of what the prophet had said or done during his life. At the same time, long discussions were held as to what the prophet would have done under certain actual or hypothetical circumstances. Out of these sayings and discussions there has grown up a vast body of traditions embodying statements or reported habits or practices of Mohammed, all of which serve to supplement the Koran in matters of faith and practice. These traditions have varying shades of authority according to the character of the line of witnesses through which the tradition has been preserved. Hundreds of thousands of these sayings or reported acts have been handed down, at first orally, but later committed to writing. Upon these, various schools of theology have grown up, and many sects, often differing widely from each other in their religious practices.

We may compare these Moslem traditions to the creeds, doctrines and discussions of the early Christian Church that have been handed down to us and that so frequently are given equal or even greater weight in Christian discussion than the direct teaching of Christ and the Apostles. There are some who put more emphasis upon the findings of a church council than upon the words of Paul, and who hold a historic creed in equal or even greater respect than the direct command of Christ.

The Moslem traditions have been carefully collected and preserved. Dr. Zwemer states that there are 1465 such collections in existence, but that only six of these are classed as standard by the orthodox school. This collection furnishes a field for the work of the higher critic surpassing anything to be found in our own Christian records. Let no one think that criticism was born with the critics of our own Scriptural records. Mohammedanism has had them for more than ten centuries, though they work on the traditions, not on the Koran.

One of the critics of Islam's traditions, Abu Dawud as-Sijistani, declares in his work upon the subject, that, out of 500,000 traditions he examined, he recognized as trustworthy only 4800, and yet he states that, among the 4800, he had included some that, in his judgment, were " nearly authentic."

The great variety and number of traditions which shape the daily practices of the follower of Mohammed and the uncertainty as to who are orthodox and who are not, has opened a wide field for difference of practice among Moslems. These variations occur more frequently in practice than in fundamental belief, although, in some cases, like that of the difference between the Shiahs and Sunnis, they include matters of supreme importance, even though both parties accept the Koran without dissent.

The value of a tradition depends upon the trustworthiness of the parties responsible for the transmission of the story, as nearly all for some two centuries were handed down orally. Owing to the phenomenal memories of men of that period and country, when writing was little used and the memory was trusted to carry even long poems and important historical records, undoubtedly these traditions give us much accurate knowledge of the life and teachings of Mohammed. The point we need to keep in mind is that in the Koran we have but a fraction of the teachings and practices of Mohammedanism. No Moslem sect bases its belief and practices upon the Koran alone. Scholars err in assuming that when they have mastered the Koran they have mastered Islam. The traditions bear as important a part as the Koran itself.

Whatever else may be said, Islam is the religion of Mohammed. In the belief of Moslems the Koran came through him alone and the traditions that have followed are all connected with his person and his life. He shares with no one else the honors of Islam. All who have contributed to the success and progress of Islam in the world have done so because they were true to their leader, to them the prophet of God.

When Mohammed appeared in Mecca the inhabitants of Arabia were broken up into a great number of tribes or clans. The Arabs and the Jews had little in common and Christians were apart from all others. Blood relationship was the dominant bond, uniting peoples for enjoyment, protection or aggression. While Christianity had introduced the idea of fraternity through religion, it had not become associated with the ideas of government or of Christian armies for purposes of conquest. It remained for Mohammed to bring to the scattered tribes of Arabia and through them to other tribes and races, the idea of a religious bond that took precedence over the ties of race or tribe. He taught that difference of belief is what divides men and not difference of blood, and this new principle became the basis of organization for world conquest.

The Koran was written in Arabic, since that was the language spoken by Mohammed and his followers and was the only language with which they were familiar.

It is evident that Moslems have misinterpreted the utterance of their prophet upon the subject of the language of the Koran.   Mohammed said:

XLIII.   " Verily we have made it an Arabic Koran that ye may haply understand."

XLI.   " And if we had made it in a foreign tongue, they had surely said, ' Unless its verses be clearly explained, etc.' "

XXXIX.   " An Arabic Koran, free from tortuous wording, that haply they may fear God."

There are other quotations of a similar import.

Tradition has seemed to make these declarations mean that the Koran was written in Arabic because it was a sacred tongue and therefore it must not be put into any other language. Unquestionably it was the purpose of Mohammed to reach the people of Arabia through the medium of the language there spoken, and had he lived to propagate his gospel among people of other languages, he probably would have advocated putting the Koran into that language also.   The above quotations from the Koran seem to warrant that supposition.   It is reasonable to assume that the preaching of Mohammedan missionaries would have been more efficacious had they been able to present the Koran in the vernacular of the persons addressed.

To three-fourths of the Moslem world Arabic is a dead language.   It is however the sacred language of Islam which is not to be lightly regarded nor taught to unbelievers, according to the Mohammedan commentaries.   It is the language in which the Koran was handed down to earth, and, according to the strict interpretation of Mohammedanism, the language in which it must eternally remain.

In the earlier days no attempt was made to translate the Koran into other languages, because the followers of Mohammed understood Arabic.   Later, however, when Mohammedanism spread to Persia, India, among the Turcomans, as well as among other races, in order to prevent those people from losing their hold upon Mohammedanism, certain translations were either permitted or looked upon with indifference. At the same time Moslems were conscious of the fact that the Bible, and especially the New Testament, was being translated into languages read and understood by Mohammedans, and particularly by those who did not read and understand the Arabic. This necessarily led to a recognition of the fact that Mohammedanism in such cases was at a disadvantage, and, in order to defend their own religion, versions in other tongues seemed to be essential.

The first translation of the Koran into any other language was into Latin in 1143; this translation was not discovered, however, until 1543, when it was published in Basle. This was afterward rendered into German, Italian and Dutch. A second Latin translation was made in 1698, followed by some others.

The first French translation was printed in Paris in 1647, and better ones followed. One Sura was translated into Spanish in the 13th century, but so far as is known there has never been a complete Spanish version.

There was probably an early Hebrew translation of the Koran, because fragments have been discovered. In the 17th century there was a translation into Hebrew, and in 1857 a full Hebrew translation of the Koran was printed in Leipzig.

The first German translation was made from the Latin in the 17th century, followed by others. A Dutch translation was printed in 1641. A Russian version appeared in St. Petersburg in 1776; an Italian version in 1547.

There was a polyglot edition of the Koran printed in Berlin in 1701, that gives the Koran in Arabic, Persian, Turkish and Latin.

There have been many English versions. The first was Ross' translation from the French in the latter part of the

17th century. Sale's translation, appearing in 1734, has passed through many editions and is widely known today. In 1861 a new translation was made by Mr. Rodwell, with the Suras or chapters arranged chronologically. Dr. Margoliouth regards this as one of the best produced. Edward Henry Palmer made a translation in 1880. There are two English translations by Moslems, one that appeared in 1905, another in 1911.

One of the earliest versions for the use of Moslems was made into the Urdu language by a Mohammedan Sheik in 1790; this has gone through several editions. An Arabic-Persian interlinear edition was published in Calcutta in 1791; there is also a Persian translation of the Koran.

In more recent years there has been unusual activity in translating the Koran into vernacular tongues used by Mohammedans who are not able to read the Arabic.

To sum up: The Koran has been translated into twelve European languages, not counting the polyglot editions, and in these languages, thirty-four versions, not less than eight in the English language alone. In Oriental languages there are some ten versions.

From the missionary standpoint, this is an advantage, since he can induce Mohammedan readers of the Koran in their native tongues to compare its teachings with that of the Bible, and so secure a more intelligent hearing; thus they will be able to reach a more intelligent conclusion. It is understood, however, that these versions of the Koran have not yet had wide circulation, and the Mohammedan leaders at centers like Cairo and Constantinople have discouraged the translation of their holy book into any vulgar tongue.

A Moslem lawyer in Lahore, India, recently, in protesting against the mistaken policy of not allowing Moslems to have the Koran in their native tongue, said: " The reason why Christians succeed is because everywhere they have the Bible and say their prayers in their mother tongue; whereas we have wrapped up our religion in an Arabic dress. We should give the people the Koran and let them say their prayers in their own language."

It is reported that this statement was met by an orthodox Mohammedan with the counter-statement, " Thou art thyself an unbeliever to say such things." [1]

The *Egyptian Gazette* states that there is to be issued shortly, under the auspices of the Moslem community of England, an authorized English translation of the Koran. For three centuries there have been in existence English translations of the Koran, but none of which were issued under Moslem auspices. The translator of this new version is an English and Arabic scholar who has devoted six years to the task of translation. Not only does the issuance of an authorized translation of the Koran indicate a wide departure from the teaching and practice of Islam for 1200 years, but they go even farther than this and are to make special terms for the purchase of the book by non-Moslems. The old idea that " None shall touch the book but the purified," and that infidels must not be permitted to purchase the Koran, is thus set aside and a new era begins.

The extreme fatalism so often attributed to Mohammed is hard to reconcile with the emphasis he puts on prayer, fasting, alms-giving and the pilgrimage. He calls prayer the Pillar of Religion, and the key of paradise, and yet if all Moslems are destined to be saved, why the need of prayer?

In actual practice, Moslems do not differ so much after all from the multitude of Calvinists who find themselves unable to limit the fore-knowledge and the power of God, while at the same time conscious of self-determining faculties. The Mohammedan finds no difficulty in acknowledging the supreme fore-knowledge of his God and in praying to him for favor. In actual practice, however, Moslems are decidedly fatalists.

[1] For a full statement on this point we would refer to the *Moslem World* for July, 1915, pp. 244-261.

This is one of the chief reasons for the rapid spread among them of epidemic and contagious diseases. They will not apply preventive measures, as Allah already knows what the end is to be. Dr. Cyrus Hamlin tells of an old Turk in Constantinople who, in the midst of a cholera scourge in the city, was eating a green cucumber, skin and all, bought from the open market. The doctor warned him of his peril and advised him to throw away the remainder of his meal. The Moslem replied, " If I was born to die of cholera I will die of cholera when the time comes, no matter what I eat or where I eat it." He proved that he had been destined to die of cholera that night.

The backwardness of Moslems in education, enterprise, inventiveness, and along all lines of progress so characteristic of the West, has been attributed to the strong element of fatalism that is interwoven with Moslem thinking, and relates to so many of the acts of their daily life. To the Moslem his future is assured by the fact that he is a Moslem. Over him Allah watches as a great Master above his own. Why should he, a mere man, exert himself in a fruitless attempt to alter the fixed order of the universe? It is the line of least resistance to let God have his own way, both in the direction and control of the world without as well as of the life within.

From early in the Medina period Mohammedans have observed Friday as a day of special worship in the mosques or places of common prayer. It makes little difference as to how the day came to be chosen; the fact remains that to a degree Friday is to the Moslem what Saturday is to the Jews and Sunday to the Christians.

The Moslems do not regard Friday as a day in which no secular work shall be performed, but its primary significance lies in the instructions of the prophet that upon Friday all true believers assemble in their places of worship and engage in united prayer and listen to religious instruction. Mosques are used on other days for prayer and often for group prayers and for preaching, but unusual significance is given to Fridays, when religious addresses or sermons upon a variety of topics may or may not be given by a recognized leader. The mosque service upon Friday, requiring no address, is not as fixed in its form as is the worship of most Christian bodies, where the sermon figures so conspicuously. Friday is the day usually chosen for the announcement to Moslems, of any great event like a call to a holy war and for inciting to any concerted action.

A devout Moslem is not left in doubt as to his obligations to his religion. The instructions to all Mohammedans are so explicit as to his duties as a Mussulman, and these duties are so few in number and so within his powers of performance, that a new convert can be quickly introduced to all the mysteries of his religion and instructed in the new ritualistic duties he has assumed.

The first obligation is to learn the creed or confession of Faith. As it is the shortest confession of Faith of any religion or even of any sect, committing it to memory imposes no severe task even upon the most illiterate. The creed is, " There is no God but God, Mohammed is the Prophet of God."

This is constantly repeated by the believer and may be called the battle cry, the watchword of Islam. Tradition reports that Mohammed once said that " Whoever repeats this creed shall receive rewards equal to the emancipation of ten slaves and shall have 100 good deeds put to his account and 100 sins blotted out, and that the formula will be a protection from the power of the devil."

Wherever Moslems are found, this creed is the conspicuous sign and seal of their faith. It is inscribed upon banners, and door posts, engraved upon coins, printed upon public documents, repeated in prayer, used as an exclamation of surprise, as a defence in danger, and as an expression of joy. As a sign and seal of conversion to Islam, the repetition of this formula aloud and before witnesses is all that is required, although it is expected its meaning will later be explained and that the believer will believe it in his heart.

The second required act of Islam is Prayer. This does not mean a spirit of devotion that pours itself out in praise and petition to God, but simply the committing to memory of the stipulated prayers of the faith and the utterance of the same at the times fixed and in the way prescribed. These prayers are all in Arabic and can be offered in no other language. One who does not know Arabic is forced to learn a series of expressions conveying to him no meaning, but which he must repeat at stated intervals and under certain conditions to meet the prayer exactions of his religion.

The first condition of prayer is that it shall be offered five times each twenty-four hours, at stated intervals, wherever the believer may be at that time, and in whatever situation he may find himself. The second condition requires that it be addressed towards the Kaaba in Mecca. Private houses and all public places of worship are so constructed that the worshiper will meet with no difficulty in determining the proper direction for his prayers. Another, and one of the most exacting preparations for Moslem prayer, is legal purification. Upon this there is no little difference of opinion, and books have been written explaining and describing the value, effect and efficacy of purification by water, or, if water is not available, by sand, in preparation for prayer. These instructions as to method often go into the most puerile and even disgusting details. While this ceremonial purification was undoubtedly inaugurated as a sign and seal of inner purity, and is even mentioned as such in theory, this is not alluded to either in the Koran or in the more elaborate directions regarding prayer preparation.

The posture in prayer is of great significance, beyond the point of compass to which it is directed. It consists of a series of hand and arm motions, genuflections and prostrations at certain fixed points in the wording of the prayer itself. Any departure from the letter of the instructions nullifies all that has preceded and the whole formula must be repeated. The prayer consists of quotations of phrases and even chapters from the Koran, which include expressions of praise, confession of sin, and petitions for guidance and help.

The true Moslem is enjoined to pray at dawn, just after noon, two hours before sunset, at sunset, and two hours later. The first prayer must be offered before the sun has risen. These hours of prayer are all preceded by the call to prayer from the minaret, given in a clear, penetrating and far-carrying voice and in the Arabic language. The new convert to Islam is carefully and minutely instructed as to what is expected of him in the matter of prayer.

The third demand of the Moslem is that of fasting. Every Moslem is expected to observe the month of Ramazan, or Ramadan, the ninth month of the Moslem lunar year. This is the chief and by far the most important fast. Tradition speaks of fasting as for God alone Who will give the reward. It says, " Every good act that a man performs shall receive from 10 to 700 rewards but the rewards of fasting are beyond reason." During this month of fasting from sunrise to sunset, not a drop of water or a morsel of food is to pass the lips. Even smoking is forbidden. There are exemptions for travelers, invalids, infants, etc. The severity of this fast, especially when it comes in the period of long days, is alleviated by turning night into day, so that much of the period of fasting is spent in sleep. Among the especially pious, voluntary fasting is not uncommon. Mohammed said, " He who forsakes the fast of Ramazan becomes an infidel, whom to deprive of his property and his life is lawful." This accounts in part for the care with which this fast is guarded.

Every Moslem is expected to give alms. This pillar of Islam rests upon tradition and is based upon the reported example of the Prophet. The word used is " Zakat," which means purification, and is applied to legal alms or the poor fund. This is called purification, because the theory is that the gift of a part of one's possessions or income purifies or sanctifies what remains. Under Moslem rule, alms were collected by the pious tax-collector, but under Christian governments they are voluntary. The recipient of the alms may be any one of the following, the poor, the homeless, the tax-collector, slaves, debtors, those fighting for Islam, and travelers. It is deeply ingrained in the Moslem mind and belief that credits from giving alms, even the granting of hospitality, will greatly accrue to his advantage in paradise. They look upon Zakat as an investment in futures which is sure to yield large and lucrative returns.

The last demand upon the Moslem is the Pilgrimage to Mecca. This is incumbent upon every free Moslem who is of age and has sufficient means for the journey. All who make the pilgrimage are highly honored throughout the Moslem world. They are taught to believe that special favors from God, both for this world and for the world to come, can be purchased by such a pilgrimage. If, for any reason, one cannot personally make the journey, he is at liberty to engage a substitute to go for him. Incidentally the pilgrimage has played an important part in solidifying Mohammedanism and impressing upon Moslems the reality and the unity of their religion.

Other practices, like circumcision, and various fasts and festivals, have played a large part in the administration of Islam. Circumcision is not mentioned in the Koran, but has become the initiative rite among Moslems throughout the world. This is based wholly upon tradition.

The above five pillars of the faith of Islam comprise the substance and practices of the faith, to which a convert can readily conform, and by conforming he becomes a Moslem in good and regular standing. While some of the exactions are severe, and none of them especially easy, they present to the convert a clear and precise program of procedure which leads him into the holy of holies of the religion of the Prophet. No independent thought or judgment is required, or even permitted, only obedient submission and an unquestioned compliance with the precepts and traditions of the faith. The simplicity and clearness of the demands as well as the self-surrender required, all add to the strength of Islam and have a tendency to bind to each other and to their religion all followers of Mohammed.

Mohammed established a religious state founded upon military principles. The two conceptions were inseparably associated.[2] " That he who possesses material power should also dominate the mind is accepted as a matter of course; the possibility that adherents of different religions could live together as citizens of the same state and with equal rights is excluded."

Margoliouth sees in the five daily prayers a military drill, and in the fasting month a test of endurance, and in the claim of being the leading religious caste on earth with the right of all that was outside, an enthusiasm provoking force. It was in this last feature that warriors conceived themselves as fighting for God to win the world to him. Under this theory the Moslem world became a mighty military camp, daily disciplined for service and ready always for aggressive action.

To this should be added the idea of the equality of all true believers, which was a fundamental doctrine with the prophet and probably intended to be without exception. There was no hierarchy of officials. He made no permanent appointments, not even his successor. The officials he appointed were for local or temporary purposes. This equality of believers became attractive to the tribes of Arabia, especially those that had not succeeded in acquiring wealth or power. The democracy of Islam has been a source of strength in the appeal it made to those who admired the power of a triumphant

[2] Dr. C. Snouck Hurgronje.

leader, with whom the humblest believer might be upon terms of equality. To the lower classes, the suppressed and the helpless, Islam came with a message of uplift and cheer, and inspired a hope of altered conditions.

In later years, permanent officers and a certain amount of rank and title have crept in. This was probably necessary for the organization and control of the Moslem state. But one cannot fail to note that wherever this has been done, as in Persia and Turkey, conversions to Islam have been nil except through the employment of external force. Wherever Isalm is making headway among pagan tribes and peoples, the doctrines preached are those that won in the first century after the death of Mohammed.

Mohammed made no claim to pre-existence, and the strictly orthodox Moslems deny his pre-existence, his power of intercession, and that his person and tomb should be reverenced. But the Sunnis as well as the Shiahs are accepting traditions that declare his preexistence even before the creation of the world in the form of " the Light of Mohammed." It is but the Sufi doctrine of the Primal Will and the Arian doctrine of Christ. This has inevitably led to the idealizing of his earthly life, not entirely dissimilar to that of Confucius by his followers in China. The sinlessness of Mohammed is proclaimed, and the pronunciation of his name is vested with delivering power and saving grace.

The strict unitarianism of Mohammed can hardly be said to exist today in the face of the general practice of Mohammedans to deify their Prophet. This is a direct, and, to the orthodox, an embarrassing, innovation, which seems to be upon the increase.

To the deification of Mohammed is added the prevalence of saint worship, or at least of sacred veneration. Some of the sects, like the Shiahs, venerate the Imams as manifestations of God and sometimes as very God. Many of these are credited with divine powers, even to the performance of miracles.

Thus the dwelling place of the dervish and the tomb of the venerated Sheikh become shrines to which the devout make pilgrimages and from which supernatural aid is invoked.

This veneration of saints is carried to absurd extremes in Persia especially, and among the Shiahs everywhere, but also in other parts of the Moslem world. Such beliefs and acts are unauthorized by the Koran. This movement appears to have grown out of the desire upon the part of Moslems to discover a mediator between God and man. Islam offers no relief, and so almost by instinct Mohammedans have first ascribed this office to their Prophet and then to conspicuous religious leaders.

CHAPTER IX

MOHAMMEDAN AND CHRISTIAN CONCEPTIONS OF GOD

A fundamental requisite for the evangelization of Islam is an understanding of the Mohammedan idea of God on the one hand and the Christian idea on the other. This is necessary in order that the Christian may know the basic elements of religion that Mohammedans already possess, and may know what he himself has of value to add.

Foremost among the features of the Moslem conception of God is his unity and aloneness. This was a fundamental doctrine with Mohammed. It is asserted in the Koran often and in many ways. The 112th Sura is called the Sura of the Unity. It reads:

> In the name of the merciful and compassionate God.
> Say, He is God alone!
> God the Eternal!
> He begets not and is not begotten!
> Nor is there like unto him any one!

The aloneness and eternity of Allah could not be more forcibly stated. The sura is probably an early one. The statement " he begets not and is not begotten " was probably addressed in part to the heathen Koraish of Mecca, as sura 53 shows, but it was also directed in part against the Christians. Mohammed was strongly prejudiced against the Christian doctrine of the Trinity and the Christian beliefs about the divinity of Christ; he did not understand them. Some other statements of the oneness, aloneness, and supremacy of Allah are the following:

132

Your God is one God; there is no God but he, the merciful and compassionate. (Sura 2¹⁶⁷)

Verily Allah is mighty over all. (2¹⁴⁸)

Power is altogether Allah's. (2¹⁶⁰)

Allah bears witness that there is no god but he, and the angels and those possessed of knowledge standing up for justice. There is no God but he, the mighty and wise. (3¹⁶)

Were it necessary such quotations could be greatly multiplied, for the assertion of the aloneness and supremacy of Allah was often on the lips of the Prophet. But it is superfluous to assemble proof-texts, when Mohammed made the confession, which constitutes one a believer and also forms the beginning of the call to prayer which rings out from every minaret in the Moslem world five times every day, the assertion: "There is no God but Allah and Mohammed is his prophet." In the face of evidence so patent and so well known it needs no demonstration to prove that Islam, like Judaism, Zoroastrianism, and Christianity is a monotheistic religion. It only remains to inquire into the character of its monotheism.

The name Allah does not help us much. It is made up of the definite article *al* and the root *'ilh* " god," derived from the same root as the Hebrew *'eloah*, sometimes employed in Hebrew poetry for " God," the plural of which, *'elohim*, is the most common general designation of deity in the Old Testament. Etymologists sometimes debate whether *'ilah* may not be derived from the verb *'ilaha*, which means " to fear," " be perplexed," " to adore." In all probability the root was at first the name of deity, signifying " the terrible one," and the verb was derived from the noun. All this, however, lay far back in Semitic heathenism. In the Old Testament *Elohim* means " God " (sometimes " gods ") and in Moslem parlance *Al-lah* simply means " the God," i. e., " the One True God."

Later Mohammedan tradition recognized ninety-nine names for Allah. These names are descriptive epithets, but by no means all of them are found in the Koran. Of those that go back to the Prophet the two most frequently employed are " the Merciful " and " the Compassionate." From these we should infer that one attribute of God as Mohammed knew him was mercy. We should err, however, if we supposed that Allah's mercy was akin to the graciousness of the Christian God. It is rather compassion or an indulgent pity for the shortcomings and foibles of men. When put thus, the statement is only a misleading half truth. To obtain Mohammed's idea of God's mercy and compassion, one must inquire toward whom these qualities were exercised and whether they were offset by opposite attributes. Light is thrown on this in Sura 2^{203} where we read " Allah is compassionate to his servants." It would appear from this that in order to experience his mercy one must be his servant. This is in reality the teaching of Islam. Allah showers his favors upon those who believe. Thus Sura 23^1 begins:

Prosperous are the believers who in their prayers are humble, and who from vain talk turn aside, and who in almsgiving are active.

Again, Sura $3^{13,14}$ declares:

For those who fear are gardens with their lord, beneath which rivers flow; they shall dwell therein for aye, and pure wives and grace from Allah; the Lord looks on his servants who say " Lord, we believe; pardon our sins and keep us from the torment of the fire."

Towards those who do not believe Allah exercises no mercy. For them are prepared the lurid torments of the Moslem hell. Thus in Sura 22^{55} we find:

For those who do not believe is shameful woe.

And in verse 71:

> The fire Allah has promised to those who do not believe.

Similarly, in Sura 39[33]:

> Is there not a hell for the unbelievers?

The nature of the punishment which is inflicted in hell for this heinous sin of unbelief is set forth in Sura 22[20]:

> Those who are unbelievers, for them are cut out garments of fire, there shall be poured over their heads boiling water, wherewith what is in their bellies shall be dissolved and their skins too, and for them are maces of iron. Whenever they desire to come forth therefrom through pain, they are sent back into it: " and taste ye the torment of the burning."

Allah, then, was believed to possess such a character that for the mere intellectual defect of unbelief he would subject men to such barbaric torture. It ill becomes Christians to speak harshly of Mohammed for thus conceiving God, for the conception entertained of him by some theologians bears a strong family resemblance to that of Mohammed, but it must be said that in Christianity such conceptions form no large part of the New Testament teaching, while in Islam the Koran itself iterates them again and again. Indeed it was with such terrifying threats of barbaric visitation of the divine displeasure upon unbelievers that Mohammed sought to bear down all opposition to his mission. In Islam, therefore, God is conceived as not primarily interested in the conduct of men, but in their attitude of belief or unbelief towards him and his Apostle. His mercy is limited to those who believe. It is to them only that he is indulgent. Thus in Sura 39[54] we find:

> Say, O my servants, who have been extravagant against their own souls, be not in despair of the mercy of Allah; verily Allah forgives sins, all of them; verily Allah is forgiving, merciful.

It appears from the evidence here adduced that according to the Mohammedan conception Allah is not bound by any standard of justice. Rather he forgives and indulges those who, by accepting without question the Mohammedan teachings, flatter him. It is not strange that, as Mohammed conceived God thus, he should not think of him as a loving Being. One who is so self-centered as to be always thinking of the attitude of men toward himself, not as a test of moral qualities, but as a recognition or non-recognition of his own power, has no place in his heart for love. There are but two or three passages in the Koran where the love of God is spoken of. One of them is Sura 5⁵⁹. It runs:

> O ye who believe! whoso is turned away from his religion.—Allah will bring instead a people whom he loves and who love him, lowly to believers, lofty to unbelievers, strenuous in the way of God, fearing not the blame of him who blames.

It seems that here God is not really said to love men, but to love certain qualities of some men.

In Sura 3¹⁴⁰ Allah is said to love those who are patient. Also in 3¹⁵³ we read:

> As for what thou hast resolved, rely upon Allah; verily Allah loves those who do rely.

Finally in 3²⁹ occurs the following:

> Say, If ye would love Allah, then follow me and Allah will love you and forgive you your sins, for Allah is forgiving and merciful.
>
> Say, Obey Allah and the Apostle; but if ye turn your backs Allah loves not unbelievers.

These are all the passages in the Koran known to the writer which speak of God's love. The word seems to be employed rather in the sense of " approval " than of " love." Such as Allah's love is, it is enjoyed only by those who have faith, patience, reliance upon God, or who exhibit a certain type of life. The Koran furnishes in its utterances about God no parallel to " God so loved the world." Allah's love is limited to those of whom he can approve.

The Koran has much to say of God's relation to nature. Some of Mohammed's ideas on this subject were clearly borrowed from the Old Testament as is the statement in Sura 6[73]:

> He it is who has created the heavens and the earth in truth; and on the day when he says " BE," then it is.[1]

Of a like nature are the following:

> We did create the heavens and the earth and what is between the two in six days, and no weariness touched us. (50[37])

The last statement in the verse just quoted is intended to contradict the statement of Gen. 2[2] that God rested on the seventh day — a statement that seemed to Mohammed to imply that God possesses infirmity.

Another passage that has been thought to contradict Sura 50[37] is Sura 41[8]:

> Do ye really not believe him who created the earth in two days?

It is not fair, however, to charge Mohammed with inconsistency on this point (though in many other respects there are contradictions in the Koran), for he may have been thinking of that part of the story of creation which related to the seas and the dry land on the second and third days according to the account in Genesis.

In Sura 16[3-16] Mohammed refers to the creation of the heavens and earth, of men, of cattle, horses and mules, of the rain, grain, olives, palms, grapes, and other fruits, of night and day, the sun, moon, and stars, of fishes and of mountains. He argues that as Allah has made these things for man, men should give him their allegiance.

Allah sustains the heavens without columns (13[2]). In

---

[1] " BE and it is " also occurs in Sura 2[111].

Sura 6^{95-99} Allah is said to carry on all the processes of nature such as the sprouting of grain and the date-stone, the sending down of rain, and the growth of fruits. His activity is constant and unwearied. We learn from Sura 113^2 that Mohammed, like the prophet Amos, thought of God as so exclusively responsible for all that goes on on the earth, that evil as well as good is his creation.

On the whole Mohammed's conception of the relation of God to nature is borrowed from the Old Testament. It is that of the Hebrew prophets and lawgivers modified a little here and there to suit Mohammed's peculiar ideas.

If we turn to Mohammed's conception of the relation of Allah to men we find that his conception is but an expansion of the early Hebrew idea of Jehovah unrelieved by later Jewish and Christian modifications of the conception of God. Pre-exilic Hebrew prophets believed that Jehovah was responsible for both good and evil. Amos says (ch. 3^6): " Shall evil befall a city, and Jehovah hath not done it? " In Isaiah 45^7 we read: " I form the light and create darkness; I make peace and create evil; I am Jehovah that doeth all these things." The Hebrew prophets took this point of view because Satan did not emerge in Hebrew thought to relieve Jehovah of the responsibility for evil until after the Babylonian exile.[2] This phase of prophetic thought Mohammed transplanted to a later age and gave it far-reaching theological consequences. Thus he says (Sura 6^{125}):

> Whomsoever God wishes to guide, He expands his breast to Islam; but whomsoever He wishes to lead astray, He makes his breast tight and straight, as though he would mount up into heaven; thus does Allah set his horror on those who do not believe.

It appears from this passage that Allah predestines men to unbelief. Men are accordingly not responsible; in the last

[2] Satan is mentioned but three times in the Old Testament. In Job 1 and 2 written perhaps during the Exile, Satan is still an angel, though becoming sceptical. In Zech. 3^1 and 1 Chron. 21^1, both post-exilic passages, we have the only Old Testament references to a Satan at all like that of later times.

analysis Allah is such an arbitrary ruler that all responsibility even for the unbelief of infidels rests upon him. This doctrine is reiterated in Sura 39[24]:

That is the guidance of Allah! He guides therewith whom he will. But he whom Allah leads astray there is no guide for him.

Monotheism carried to this extreme becomes uncontrolled, absolute, all-absorbing will. That will overbears all other wills in the universe. Man is reduced to a cipher. Human agency and human freedom are nullified. Right is no longer right because it is right, but because Allah wills it to be right. It is for this reason that monotheism has in Islam stifled human effort and progress. It has become a deadening doctrine of fate. Man must believe and pray, but these do not insure salvation or any benefit except Allah wills it. Why should human effort strive by sanitary means to prevent disease, when death or life depends in no way on such measures but upon the will of Allah? One reason why Moslem countries are so stagnant and backward in all that goes to make up a high civilization is owing to the deadening effects of monotheism thus interpreted.

It is doubtless true that the Mohammedan doctrine of the sovereignty of God can almost be paralleled in Christian theology by the conceptions of St. Augustine and John Calvin. Nevertheless even in the most extreme forms of the Augustinian and Calvinistic systems there were always present in Christianity other elements which prevented the conception of the divine sovereignty from paralyzing the healthy activities of life as the Mohammedan doctrine has done. Moreover the Augustinian and Calvinistic emphasis upon the sovereignty of God was never accepted by the whole of Christendom as the Mohammedan doctrine has necessarily been accepted by Islam.

There are passages in the Koran which seem at first sight to allow some freedom to the human will and to recognize a corresponding degree of human responsibility, but such passages are delusive. Usually in their context one finds in some form an expression of the doctrine of the all-controlling will of Allah. Thus in Sura 34[32] occurs this:

> We will put fetters on the necks of those who are unbelievers. Shall they be rewarded except for that which they have done?

In vs. 36 of the same Sura there is also the following:

> For them (*i.e.*, those who do right) is a double reward for what they have done, and they in upper rooms shall be secure.

Between these two verses, however, there is the assertion (vs. 35):

> Verily my lord extends provision to whom he pleases or doles it out, but most men do not know, —

an assertion that is repeated again in vs. 38. Man has then, according to the Koran, no real freedom. God ostensibly rewards the good for their belief in Allah and his prophet, for their faithfulness in performing the proper religious ceremonies, and for their good deeds, such as almsgiving. In reality this is all a delusion, for they have no real merit. They are all done because Allah has decreed that they should be done by these people. Similarly God appears to punish unbelief, the neglect of the required religious ceremonies, and the violation of certain moral requirements. In truth the men who receive punishment for these things are not responsible for what they do, Allah having decreed from the beginning that they should do these things. Under his decree they could not do otherwise. This doctrine is the early prophetic conception of monotheism, divorced from its Hebrew setting, and carried to a pernicious extreme.

In the Old Testament Jehovah is often called " holy." To the Hebrew mind holiness was one of his most characteristic attributes. While in early times holiness designated terrible qualities of divinity that could not brook ceremonial impurity — a kind of divine wrath that manifested itself against all those who did not observe the proper forms of politeness in approaching Jehovah — on the lips of the prophets it came to denote moral qualities. Jehovah was pure; Jehovah was just. This thought echoes through all the later Jewish literature, and, as we shall see, became a potent thought in Christianity. This attribute of deity Mohammed failed almost, if not altogether, to perceive. The word " holy " is applied to Allah but once in the Koran. Sura 59[22] reads:

> He is Allah, beside whom there is no god; he knows the unseen and the visible; he is merciful and compassionate. He is Allah, beside whom there is no god; he is the king, the holy one, the peace-giver, the faithful, the protector, the mighty, the repairer, the great.

The Arabic word *qudûs*, " holy," here applied to Allah, may mean either ceremonial or moral purity. It is an interesting fact that Mohammedan commentators on the Koran take it here to denote ceremonial purity. Allah is characterized by those absences from ceremonial defilement which he demands of his followers. While it is possible that, when Mohammed applied the word to Allah, he meant more than this, the context in which it stands does not require more. All the other attributes referred to in the verse have to do with Allah's external dignity and work. It is probable, therefore, that in the mind of Mohammed Allah's holiness meant no more than it does on the pages of his commentators. But even if one grants that the Prophet did intend here to say that Allah is morally pure, the text would be one lone utterance in the whole Koran. Taking Mohammed's teaching as a whole no emphasis is laid on the holiness of God. Indeed holiness and justice, in the sense in which most Christians think of them as existing in the divine nature, are necessarily absent from a deity such as we have seen that Mohammed conceived

Allah to be. A God, who predestines men to unbelief and sin, and then punishes them for doing what they could not help doing and what he had ordained that they should do, lacks the elements of that exalted morality which constitutes holiness.

Indeed Mohammed appears to have thought of God as possessing about the same morality as an Arab. In Sura 3[47] he says:

> They were crafty and Allah was crafty, and Allah is the best of the crafty ones.

The same words occur again in Sura 8[30], though the context there favors the rendering:

> They plotted and Allah plotted, and Allah is the best layer of plots.

Strange as the idea here expressed is to a Christian, it is not without parallel in the Old Testament, for in Psalm 18[25, 26] we read:

> With the merciful thou wilt show thyself merciful;
> With the perfect man thou wilt show thyself perfect;
> With the pure thou wilt show thyself pure;
> And with the perverse thou wilt show thyself froward.

It is accordingly evident that in his conception that Allah was more crafty than men and would surpass them in trickery, Mohammed was still on the plane of thought of the Psalmist.

This conception of the craftiness of Allah naturally leads one to think of Mohammed's anthropomorphism in his conception of Allah. Mohammed really conceived of God as a gigantic man. While it is not easy to adduce particular texts from the Koran to prove this statement, degrees of anthropomorphism are implied in many statements. It is frequently said that Allah " sees," " knows," " wills," " decrees," etc. In all these cases the Arabic is personal. It says " the seeing one," " the knowing one," etc. It seems to have been impossible for Mohammed to conceive personality except in terms of extreme anthropomorphism. The Wahabites, who have endeavored to revive the pure Mohammedanism of the Koran, are frequently accused of thinking of Allah as a great man, and there is much justice in the charge. If the Koran does not think and speak of Allah's hands, eyes and ears, later Mohammedan writers did. Indeed, when the moral qualities of Allah were thought to be simply those of a powerful, unscrupulous despot — or at least a despot whose reasons could not be understood and so did not commend themselves to man's sense of justice — it was inevitable that in other respects he should be anthropomorphically conceived.

It is of course true that if men think of God as anything more than an unknowable Absolute, they necessarily think of him in some degree in human terms. Anthropomorphism is, accordingly, always a question of degree. It must nevertheless be confessed that in Islam the degree of anthropomorphism manifested in the conception of God has on the whole been, and still is, very great. Much more might be said of the Mohammedan conception of God, but in the characteristics named above we have the essential elements of the Mohammedan idea. All else that might be said would be by way of elaboration and tracing details.

Moslems think of Deity, then, as an anthropomorphic Being, whose aloneness and apartness from all other creatures cannot be too strongly stated. He controls all nature and rules the world so absolutely that nothing happens except by his decree. Even the unbelief and sins of men are due to his will. God is so exalted that freedom of the human will is practically denied. God is controlled by no ethical standards; good is good because he wills it; evil is evil for the same reason. While the Koran once applies to him the term " holy," it is clear that his holiness does not consist of moral perfections. He is not a loving being. Such love as he manifests is simply approval.

This conception of God can, as has been pointed out, be paralleled at almost every point by conceptions of Jehovah entertained by one or more Old Testament writers. It should, however, be noted that none of these conceptions, except the oneness and aloneness of God, ever commanded general assent among Hebrews. The others were not entertained in Judaism to the exclusion of opposite views to the same degree as they were by Mohammed and in Islam. Jewish thought has never pushed the divine will to such a logical extreme as to destroy human freedom; to the Jew Jehovah's holiness has always, since the days of the great prophets, been essentially an ethical quality. To them also Jehovah's love has meant more than approval; it possessed the passionate yearning of a father or a husband. While Mohammed's conception of God was derived from Judaism, it was so changed by the elimination of some characteristics and the exaggeration of others as to become in many respects quite different.

It should be noted also that Mohammed's anthropomorphism led him to deny to God fatherhood, and made it repugnant to him to think of God in the way that Hosea, Jeremiah, and Ezekiel thought of Jehovah as loving like a husband. To Mohammed this would imply sexual relations on the part of Allah,[3] and the thought was repugnant to him. Thus Islam lost from its idea of God the tenderest conceptions, and those most fruitful in the religious life. It must not be supposed that the conception of God outlined above has always satisfied Mohammedans or has gone unchallenged in Islam. One of the earliest manifestations of dissatisfaction produced the sect of Qadarites, who insisted that man possesses *qadar*, or power over his own actions, or, as we should say, free will. Men are everywhere conscious of the power of self-determination, and in Islam as elsewhere this consciousness asserted itself. In Islam it brought men into conflict with the doctrine

---

[3] This is at least the opinion of the commentator Zamakhshari in his comment on Sura 112[3]: " He begets not."

that everything happens by decree of the will of Allah. As early as the year 80 after the flight from Mecca a man lost his life for championing this doctrine.

Later, at Bagdad, the Qadarites were succeeded by the Mutazellites or Seceders. They flourished especially in the reign of the Caliph Mamun, 813–833 A. D., and applied to the fundamental conceptions of Islam the Aristotelian dialectic as it was understood by Persians and Arabs at the Caliph's court. According to one of these Mutazellite teachers, " we could not say that God had knowledge. For it must be of something in Himself or outside of Himself. If the first, then there was a union of knower and known, and that is impossible; or a duality in the divine nature, and that is equally impossible. . . . If the second, then his knowledge depended on the existence of something other than himself, and that did away with his absoluteness."[4]

Another Mutazellite taught " that God could do nothing to a creature, either in this world or the next, that was not for the creature's good and in accord with strict justice. It was not only that God *would* not do it; he had not the power to do anything evil."[5]

In such ways as these the orthodox doctrines of Islam vanished before the alchemy of thought, much to the scandal and alarm of the faithful. Even the Caliph became a heretic! Orthodoxy was, however, in the end made triumphant by such men as Al-Ashari (874–933 A. D.) and Al-Ghazali (1059–1109 A. D.), who, by the use of dialectic, repelled the attacks of dialectic, and made the older unreasoned views triumphant, so that they rule in the greater part of Islam today.

To a people whose conception of God is in some ways so true, but in many ways so unsatisfactory, the Christian missionary has to bring a conception of God that has, through the agency of Jesus Christ, grown from the same Hebrew root,

[4] See D. B. Macdonald, *Muslim Theology, Jurisprudence, and Constitutional Theory*, New York, 1903, p. 143.
[5] See Macdonald, *Ibid.*, p. 140f.

but which has flowered into a form beautiful, and adequate to human needs.

In spite of such schoolmen as Duns Scotus, who taught that good is good because God wills it, and that evil is evil for the same reason, the Christian conception of God has never lost the great truth grasped by the prophets of Israel, that God is essentially just — that he is controlled by innate laws of right and wrong. He is bound by the same ethical life as men.

> " Nothing can be good in Him
> That evil is in me."

Hosea and Jeremiah had taught that Jehovah loved Israel as a tender father loves and as a fond husband loves. Jeremiah had even gone beyond this and declared that God cared for the whole world. These great truths, somewhat obscured in later centuries by Jewish legalism, were revived and extended by Jesus Christ. He gave new vividness to the conception of the Fatherhood of God. Jesus' own love, his tireless service to the down-trodden and suffering, gave new depth and a new catholicity to love. After he lived men dared to believe that God was like him. The nearness of God, his human interest, his tireless and unchanging love, were realized as never before. Nothing of the old conception of God's holiness was lost. Instead, the lofty teaching of Jesus gave to this a new moral content in the thought of Christians. God the Father, Holy, Loving, Just, Tender, Near, as well as Creator and Ruler, became the Christian conception of God.

At the end of the first century the great religious genius who wrote the Fourth Gospel declared that in Jesus God's Word became flesh. The term " Word " had had a long history both in Jewish and in Greek thought. It had come to stand for something like God's power of self-expression or self-revelation. By applying it to Jesus its meaning was transfigured. The Word was no longer a philosophical abstraction; it glowed with life; it palpitated with love.

This writer, too, records for us a saying of Jesus overlooked by earlier evangelists, " God so loved the world that he gave his only begotten Son." The Christian God is a God whose love goes out to all the world and is of such a degree that he voluntarily suffers for all the world. The religious value and depth of this conception of God as compared with the kind of love which the Koran portrays God as possessing is like noonday compared with the first glimmerings of dawn.

The Johannine writings also give us our best definitions of the divine nature. God is spirit; God is light; and God is love. In these writings light and darkness have a moral significance. God is thus declared to be metaphysically spirit; morally, perfect; religiously, the loving Personality that attracts the hearts of men. Such conceptions satisfy men. To demand higher conceptions would require faculties that as yet our race does not possess.

The earthly life of Jesus was brief; his ministry much more brief. He promised to his disciples that the Spirit of God would come to be their Comforter and Guide. The fulfillment of that promise the Apostles experienced. At first they had baptized " in the name of the Lord Jesus," but before the close of the first century they began to baptize " in the name of the Father, the Son, and the Holy Spirit." Thus there came into Christian consciousness the Trinitarian conception of God. Two or three centuries later the Councils of the Church attempted to define this doctrine in creeds. The problem before them was to maintain the unity of God, and still believe that he had come into human life in Jesus Christ; to hold to his transcendence, and yet not to lose his presence from the world; to retain faith in the richness of the divine nature as it is revealed in nature, in the person of Christ, and in human experience, and yet avoid tritheism. The result of these efforts was the creeds of Nicea and Chalcedon.

These creeds may be held in various ways. They may be considered as definitions to be grasped by the mind. They may be regarded as finalities. They may be considered as dogmas to be accepted whether one understands them or not. The wise missionary, especially a missionary to Islam, will assume to them a different attitude. He will bring them into connection with the historic process that brought them into human consciousness; he will try to relate them to such religious experiences as those from which they sprang; he will dwell less on metaphysical details, and more on the spiritual significance for life which the doctrine symbolizes. If the Trinitarian conception of God is taught simply as a revealed metaphysics, it may easily degenerate, as Mohammed thought that it had done, into tritheism. If it does not do this, it may become to the mind a mere mathematical paradox, baffling to the intellect, and uninspiring to the heart. Thus conceived it appeals with little force to any one, least of all to Moslems.

We would suggest a better way. Let the doctrine not be dissociated from the Person of Jesus of Nazareth as he lived in Palestine. Let it always palpitate with the pulses of that love for men that spoke so eloquently in him. Let it not be regarded as a final expression of all that can be known of God, but as a symbol of elements in the constitution of the nature of God that are of vital importance to religion, to human experience, and to human hopes.

It has been pointed out above how a Mutazellite (his name was Ma'mar Ibn Abbad), in thinking about God as Islam conceives him, was compelled to deny that God had knowledge, or that he could will. He might equally have denied that God could love, for love, too, depends on an object to love. When a skilled thinker turns his mind upon the Mohammedan conception of God, he is compelled, as was Ma'mar Ibn Abbad, to reduce him to an indefinable something. In contrast with this, as has been pointed out by several writers,[6] the doctrine of the Trinity, standing as it does for the

---

[6] So John Caird, *Fundamental Ideas of Christianity*, Glasgow, 1899, Lecture III; George A. Gordon, *Ultimate Conceptions of the Faith*, Boston, 1903, pp. 370ff.; and George A. Barton, *The Heart of the Christian Message*, 2d ed., New York, 1912, p. 202.

conception that there are distinctions of personality in the nature of God, guarantees the eternity both of his knowledge and his love. It symbolizes to the human mind the fact that God represents in himself both subject and object, both lover and loved. From eternity the Father could love the Son and the Son the Father with a love, not selfish, but suffused with divine altruism. The greater the number of personalities in the Godhead, the greater the possibilities of unselfish love. Nevertheless the Christian conception demands such union of will and purpose on the part of Father, Son, and Spirit, that in a real sense they are one God.

The Trinitarian conception stands, therefore, for faith that the nature of God is eternally social. If it is not true, God could not be nobly loving until he had created some object to love. In that case his love is not eternal; it is an acquired attribute. What is acquired may be lost. If his love is not eternal, the firm basis is cut from under the grounds of religious appeal.

Similarly the act of knowing presupposes a subject and an object, a knower and the thing known. If God represents in himself both subject and object, his knowledge, like his love, is eternal. Thought compels one to see that, far back in the eons of time before other beings were created, a God such as Islam conceives was a lone Monad in an uninhabited universe — the most pitiable of all existences.[7] God as the Christian conceives him was, on the other hand, then as now and for-ever, the All-wise, the All-knowing, the All-loving, Spirit, Light, and Love.

God as conceived by Islam offers no social hope or social goal to the world. Once a lone Monad, now an inscrutable Despot, predestining men to Paradise or to Hell according to mere whim, — faith in him is not calculated either to warm and inspire the heart of the individual or to guarantee to man the realization of a social ideal, or even inspire in him the de-

[7] Compare Gordon, op. cit., p. 371.

sire for it.   The Christian conception of God, on the other hand, not only inspires in man social aspirations and calls forth in him social qualities, but guarantees the final attainment of the social goal.   If the nature of God was social from all eternity and will be social to all eternity, the " stars in their courses " are fighting on the side of the social ideal. The fundamental structure of the universe must, in that case, be social, not anti-social.   In the end God will not suffer force, selfishness, plunder, murder, lying, and deceit to triumph.   He will rather give the eternal victory to honor, unselfishness, altruism, and love.

The Christian conception of God affords the ground for a richer and more inspiring faith, as well as for a happier and more fruitful religious life, than the conception of God afforded by any other religion in the world.   It gives to Christian missionaries to all lands a message of glad tidings to their hearers, no matter what religious truth those hearers already possess.   It supplies the missionary to Islam with riches that his hearers sorely need, since the Mohammedan conception of God, while springing from the same root as the Christian, has been so blighted and distorted in its development as to produce in personal experience and social evolution a Sahara in comparison with the harvest-laden plains produced by Christian faith at its best.

CHAPTER X

COMMON GROUNDS WITH CHRISTIANITY

Much in Islam that gives it a mighty hold upon its followers was either borrowed from Christianity or has many things in common with Christianity. These common features are sources of strength in the religion of the prophet, since in many, if not most of these, Islam's power is recognized. The following are some of these common features and doctrines:

1. *A Book.* The Mohammedans were early given a book in which was written, with the unquestioned authority of the Prophet, the sacred tenets and commands of their religion. Mohammed referred to the Jews and the Christians as the people of a book, and to this fact he attributed a large measure of their strength. He manifestly planned early in his ministry to give his own followers a book to which they could turn and by means of which they should be cemented together.

One can easily overestimate the value to Islam of the Koran, accepted by all as the Divine revelation of Allah to Mohammed and given to them and to the world as the only safe and perfect rule, not only of faith but of their daily practices, equally applicable and authoritative in the common affairs of life as in the larger realm of faith.

2. *Belief in One God.* However much ground there is for discussion of the question as to whether the *Allah* of Mohammed is identical with the Jehovah of Christianity, the fact remains that Mohammed taught that, over the world of matter and men, one Supreme Being held undivided and unquestioned sway. We need not consider the different sources from which it is claimed by different writers the word *Allah* was derived. This matters little to our discussion. The creed

151

of Islam, " There is no God but Allah," proclaims the unity of the Godhead.

> " One God the Arabian prophet preached to man;
>   One God the Orient still
>   Adores through many a realm of mighty span —
>   A God of power and will.
>   A power that at his pleasure doth create
>   To save or to destroy,
>   And to eternal pain predestinate
>   As to eternal joy."
>
> — *Lord Houghton.*

Sura 112 is entitled the " Declaration of God's Unity " and reads: " God is one God: he begetteth not, neither is he begotten: and there is not anyone like unto him."

The Koran declares that polytheism and atheism are contrary to reason and that dualism is self-destructive.

Much of the emphasis put by Mohammed upon the unity of God was undoubtedly an attempt upon his part to counteract the polytheistic tendencies of the pagan tribes in Arabia and the many forms of idolatry that confronted him. He misinterpreted some things observed among the Jews as polytheistic and probably had reason to regard some of the practices of the Christians in Arabia as the worship of idols.

Moslem tradition has attributed ninety-nine names to Allah, although the number is arbitrary and the list differs in different books. These names or attributes, in whole or in part, are constantly repeated by devout Moslems. They include terms like the Merciful, the Compassionate, the Holy One, the Peace Maker, the Faithful, the Protector, the Almighty, the Creator, the Forgiver, the All-knowing, the Just, the Great, the Exalted, the Judge, the Truth, the Slayer, the Eternal, the Avenger, the Enricher, the Guide, the Giver. These are among some of the more striking attributes of Allah. There is no expression for *Love* in the list, although

Compassionate and Merciful are used. The Moslems reject love as an attribute of Deity.

Whatever may be said, the Allah of Islam is a mighty, ever-present Deity, whose existence is assumed by every follower of the Prophet as the center and source of his faith.

3. *The Practice of Prayer.* None of the great non-Christian religions put greater emphasis upon prayer than do the Moslems; in fact, none give prayer so central a place in creed and practice. To Mohammed and his followers prayer is called " the pillar of religion," the " key of Paradise."

One cannot live or travel in Moslem countries without being profoundly impressed with the place prayer holds in the life of the Mussulman. The fact of prayer is everywhere manifest, upon board ship, by the roadside, upon the housetop, as well as in established places of prayer. No Mohammedan seems to be ashamed that he prays or is disturbed if watched by a curious crowd of infidels. To him it seems to be a vital part of his religion and one of the most scrupulously observed of all his religious acts.

However much Moslem prayer may have lost its original spirit of devotion and become a mere means of accumulating favor with the Eternal, yet everywhere the true follower of the Prophet believes in prayer as a most important religious act and one that, in some mysterious manner, will prove in the future to be of lasting value to his disembodied spirit. The Moslem is a man of formal, stated, persistent prayer.

4. *Public Worship.* Islam was not organized when Mohammed fled from Mecca. After a hurried journey of eight days, he and his followers arrived at Coba, a suburb of Medina, where he was warmly greeted by his many disciples. For four days he remained here with Abu Bekr under the hospitable roof of friends. Here was laid the foundation of the first house of prayer. From Coba, Mohammed set out for Medina, some two miles distant, on a Friday morning, followed by a great multitude. On the road he halted and with some 100

followers performed the first Moslem public service. After
the prayer, an address or sermon was given, and at the close he
bade his followers to observe his teachings and example.
Friday has since been observed by the Mohammedans of the
world as especially set apart for the celebration of public
worship. At this spot there stands today a mosque called
Musjid al Juma, the Friday Mosque.

In Medina his first solicitude was to secure a site upon which
to erect a house of public prayer and worship. It is evident
that public worship was early designed by Mohammed as
holding a leading place in the practices of himself and his
followers. Islam is known to be a religion of public prayer and
stated services, in which, beside united prayer in concert, the
address or sermon holds an important place.

In Islam, since there is no regular order of priesthood or
clergy, the sermon does not hold so conspicuous a place as
among Christians. More emphasis is placed upon united
prayer, preferably in a mosque or a place set apart for that
purpose, but not necessarily so. One of the most impressive
sights in the religious world is that of the great mosque and
outer area at Agra, India, filled with tens of thousands of
Moslem worshipers engaged in united prayer.

Wherever Mohammedans are found, they are already familiar with the assembling of themselves together for purposes of
common and united worship and for receiving religious instruction or exhortation from one whom they recognize as
capable of instructing or inspiring. In this they more resemble
the practices common among Christians than do the followers
of any other religion.

5. *Belief in Immortality.* Mohammedanism is preeminently
a religion of the future life. Many if not most of the practices
of the Mohammedans have a strong bearing not so much upon
the life which now is as upon the life which is to come. That
future life is not one that is to terminate in time, and the
Mohammedan eternity is long. A common illustration of

A Bedouin at Prayer in the Desert with His Faithful Friend

eternity is that of a solid ball of granite the size of the earth suspended in space. Once in a thousand years a fly lights upon this ball and takes but one step and then flies away into space. The entire granite ball would be completely worn away by the attrition of that one step of a single fly every 1000 years before eternity would have fairly begun.

Whatever may be the vagaries of conception of the future life, to the Mussulman it is a reality, and much of his thought is how to prepare to enter upon and enjoy it. The Moslem gives more thought to the future life and makes more effort and sacrifice in preparation for it than do the Hindus or Buddhists or Shintoists or the fetish worshipers, and perhaps more than many Christians, especially in these modern days.

6. *A Special Religious Day.* Reference has already been made to the setting apart of Friday as a day for special public service and prayer. While the mosques are open for prayer upon all days, it is expected that at mid-day on Fridays the services will take a more public form, and Moslems are enjoined to attend. Mohammed usually conducted the Friday public services in Medina and expected all of the faithful to attend. This day, however, was never consecrated as a holy day corresponding to the Jewish sabbath or the Christian Sunday. After the services the people returned to their regular and customary life.

Friday is now observed by Moslems in practically the way in which it was inaugurated by Mohammed, although Moslems generally bemoan the fact that the attendance upon public worship, except upon special occasions, is not more general.

7. *Acceptance of the Christian Scriptures.* This subject can be but referred to here; to elucidate it would require chapters. The Koran is replete with references to and quotations from the Christian Scriptures, showing that Mohammed either had access to manuscripts of parts at least of the Bible,

or that among his followers there were men who knew much of these by heart.

Probably the first reference chronologically to the New Testament is in Sura LXXXVII, " Verily this is in the former pages, the pages of Abraham and Moses." Another, Sura LIII, " Hath he not been told of that which is in the pages of Moses and of Abraham who acted faithfully."

Sura XXXII, " And verily we gave Moses the book: wherefore be not in doubt as to the reception thereof, and we made it a direction to the Israelites."

Another, " And verily we were gracious to Moses and Aaron and saved them and their people from great tribulation; and we brought them assistance, and they were conquerors; and we gave them the perspicuous book, and directed them into the right way."

Again, " He hath ordained unto you the religion which he commanded unto Noah, and which we have revealed unto thee, and which we commanded unto Abraham, Moses and Jesus."

Again, " We gave unto Moses guidance, and we caused the children of Israel to inherit the book, — a guide and an admonition unto people of understanding hearts."

Again, " And verily we have written in the Psalms after the law, that my servants, the righteous, shall inherit the earth."

Again, " And verily we gave Moses the book and caused prophets to arise after him, and we gave to Jesus, the son of Mary, evident signs and strengthened him with the Holy Spirit."

Again, " We believe in God and in what hath been revealed unto us, and in what hath been revealed unto Abraham, and Ishmael, and Isaac, and the Tribes; and in what hath been given unto Moses, and unto Jesus, and in what hath been given unto the prophets from their Lord. We make no distinction between any of them, and unto him we are resigned."

Again, " And we gave unto Jesus, the son of Mary, evident signs (or plain revelation) and we strengthened him by the Holy Spirit."

These are but a few of the quotations from the Koran that might be given, showing Mohammed's approval of the Scriptures of the Old and New Testaments. To separate out and analyze each one of these passages (See *The Koran*, by Sir W. Muir) would be a most interesting task and could not fail to establish the fact that in the Scriptures of the Old and New Testaments there is a great and common field of belief for both the Moslem and the Christian. The importance of this fact can hardly be over-emphasized when we lay plans to bring to the attention of Mohammedans the claims of Christianity as set forth in the Scriptures of the Old and New Testaments.

8. *Regard for Jesus Christ.* When the early condition of the Church in Arabia and Syria is taken into consideration, it is a marvel that Mohammed retained such a high regard for Jesus Christ. His chief difficulty seems to have been with the doctrines of divine sonship and the trinity. And yet, in spite of this, the Koran at times breaks out into expressions of admiration if not of adoration for the " Son of Mary." Frequently Mohammed's exalted views of the Christ are obscured by his impatience with the doctrines of the trinity, as when he exclaims, in Sura V, " And when God shall say, O Jesus, son of Mary, hast thou said unto men, Take me and my mother as two Gods, besides God." Instead of the simple majesty of the Gospel as reconciling man to God, the dogma of the trinity was at that time ostentatiously forced upon everyone, and to this was added in a gross form the worship of Mary. To the mind of Mohammed she seemed to be regarded as Goddess, closely allied to the third person in the trinity, if not the consort of Deity. This fact undoubtedly led Mohammed always to refer to Jesus as the son of Mary.

In Sura III, Mohammed speaks of Jesus as the word of

God, while denying his divinity. He ventures to find proof of his own prophetic mission through Jesus who prophesied his coming. In Sura LXI he says, " And when Jesus the son of Mary said, O children of Israel, verily I am an apostle of God unto you, confirming what was before me of the law and bringing good tidings of an apostle who shall come after me: his name is Ahmad." The story of Mary the mother of Jesus was taken largely from the apocryphal Gospels but mingled with error. Sura XIX is entitled " Marian or Mary," in which much is said of her exalted character. In Sura III it is announced that before the birth of Christ the angel said to her, " And he shall speak to men in the cradle." Sura XIX gives an incident of his speaking to Mary's people from the cradle and saying, " Verily I am God's servant: he hath brought me the Book and made me a prophet." Many of the apocryphal miracles are related of Jesus, thus recording Mohammed's conception of his prophetic if not his divine character. In Sura IV we read, " O people of the book, be not extravagant in your religion, and do not say concerning God other than the truth. Truly Messiah, Jesus, son of Mary, is the apostle of God and his Word which he cast into Mary, and a spirit from him. Therefore believe ye in God and his apostle and say not three. . . . To him belongs whatever is in the heavens and whatever is in the earth."

The crucifixion of Christ was denied by Mohammedans from the earliest times. Some have thought that Mohammed regarded death upon the cross derogatory to the dignity and character of Christ. The fact that Mohammed found the Jews of his day exulting in having put Christ to death, may have led him to take the opposite ground that he was not killed. The Koran repeatedly asserts that Christ died like other men and that he himself foretold his own death, as in Sura XIX, which seems to declare also his resurrection, " Peace upon me the day I was born and the day I shall die, and the day I shall be raised up alive." Tradition adds much to the belief of Moslems in the Christ and his relation to Mohammedanism and the world. The Koran and Moslem tradition abound with statements about and references to the Christ, so that the name and certain characteristics are not unfamiliar to all Mohammedans. While it is true that the representations are inadequate, often distorted and frequently ridiculous, nevertheless they are sufficient to form a common basis for discussion with Christians. Mohammedanism has a Jesus, the son of Mary, whom it is possible to introduce to them as the Christ, the Son of God.

9. *Need of Salvation.* While the Moslem's conception of salvation differs widely from the Christian's, yet the fact remains that among Mohammedans there is a general desire to be saved from some possible pending destruction. This does not seem to be so much a sense of need of salvation from sin as from the consequences of sin. The great sin of the world is the failure to become Moslem. All such " shall be overcome and thrown together into hell." Sura III sets out at length the state of the unbelieving and the rewards of the faithful. To the former salvation means accepting Mohammed as the prophet of God, to the latter rewards depend upon a scrupulous observance of the laws and usages of Islam.

The first step towards salvation is the repetition of the creed, marking withdrawal from infidelity and entrance into the ranks of the true believers. This is an indispensable step in order to escape the wrath which is sure to come upon all who persist in their denial of the unity of God and the validity of his prophet. But even this step is not sufficient to insure complete salvation, even though Mohammedans are un-questioned advocates of the doctrine of the perseverance of the saints. No matter how much a Moslem may neglect to perform the ritual of his religion, or how black may seem to be his sins, he will escape the eternity of hell to which all unbe-lievers are destined, although his approach to heaven may be by a long and circuitous route.

The devout Moslem needs constantly to repeat his creed, observe the five periods of prayer, preceded by the proper ceremonial purification, keep the month of fasting, give alms and make the pilgrimage to Mecca. These are all necessary to his complete salvation. To these may be added more prayer, greater works of charity, and, if the opportunity offers, martyrdom, through which the journey to the highest heaven becomes greatly shortened.

10. *Fraternity.* Brotherhood among Moslems is one of its characteristic features and has been from the first. It is not the brotherhood of the Christian so much as the sense of unity in a body moved by a common impulse aggressively to achieve a certain end, or to defend a common cause. This spirit was developed in the days of Mohammed in wars waged to secure a foothold in and about Medina and in the battles fought for booty. The experiences through which Mohammed and his followers passed tended to weld them together into a more or less united body, not because there existed a sense of obligation to defend or protect all co-religionists, but because success as a theocracy in the face of strong and bitter opponents demanded unity.

The followers of Mohammed, through their entire history, have been so beset with political, racial and religious enemies, that they have hardly been free from the necessity of holding together to maintain their existence. These outward conditions have unquestionably led to the solidification of Islam, giving the impression to others, even though at times this impression was not borne out by the fact, that a sense of fraternity even greater than that which actuates the followers of other religions, marks the life of the Moslem.

The abolition of caste in India wherever the Mohammedan faith spread is evidence of the sense of brotherhood permeating the entire body. This fraternity does not extend to those outside the faith. Islam recognizes no race, no color, no rank and no caste; whoever is a true follower of the prophet is a brother of every other follower and as such can claim his protection and hospitality. Many circumstances beyond those here mentioned have tended to create and perpetuate this unity. The uniform ritual, manifesting itself in common forms of worship, the services in the mosques on Friday, when great masses of worshippers under the common leader together perform their ritual of prayer, tend to create a sense of oneness not capable of production by rules and regulations. The annual pilgrimages add their measure of unification and create a sense of brotherhood.

11. *Emphasis upon Faith.* Islam is to the Mohammedan a supernatural religion. Its revelation came down in a miraculous manner from God, its prophet maintained relations with the unseen and the demands of his faith are incapable of explanation, and what is more, the Mohammedan seeks no explanation. He recognizes that Mohammed was a messenger from God and thereafter all that proceeds from him is to the Moslem but natural. Miracles, divine intervention, the efficacy of religious ceremonies, the reality of the unseen world, the commanding supremacy of Allah, all follow as naturally as the day follows the rising of the sun. There is no attempt at explanation because there is no call for it. The Moslem does not pretend to know how prayer and alms and fasting and pilgrimages can add to the happiness of his eternal existence, but he believes it does, and so he goes on praying and giving and fasting.

The sin of doubt is an unforgivable sin. Against it Mohammed exhorts and warns. Christianity puts no more emphasis upon this important feature than does Islam. These two religions surpass all others in the stress placed upon faith. Both ask to be taken upon authority. It is only in recent years that Christianity has looked with complacency upon the attempt to apply reason to faith and religion, while Islam is yet far behind. Christianity is able to meet the test of reason, but Islam can hardly be expected to do so.

The Moslem believes, because it is his religion, and he is certain that it all came from God. In this he rests his hopes of the world in which he lives as well as the world to come. It is useless to attempt to secure from a Mohammedan a reason for his acts or for his faith. To him religion is above reason and faith more than knowledge. When faith and reason and knowledge come into conflict, the Moslem clings to faith and lets the others go. The supreme test of his religion is faith.

12. *Centralized Religious Functions.* When Mohammed began his career he was familiar with the Jewish and Christian feasts centering at Jerusalem. He was astute enough to see the value of such a custom to the unity and enthusiasm of a company of co-religionists, speaking different languages and living under different tribal or racial conditions. It is also probably true that, antedating the advent of Mohammed, there was a well established custom among the tribes about Mecca of coming to that central city periodically for certain religious ceremonies connected with the Kaaba. Hence the adoption of a centralized worship, accompanied by pilgrimages, not only affiliated the new religion with that which it was attempting to supersede in Mecca, but it offered to both Christians and Jews who accepted him a substitute for Jerusalem.

However this may be, the fact remains that, through centralizing Moslem worship in Mecca, which closely connected Islam with the person of Mohammed, there was introduced and perpetuated a fixed custom that has wonderfully unified the Mohammedans of the world and given them a sense of solidarity procurable in no other way. Most religions have recognized the necessity of occasional pilgrimages to central shrines of special religious significance for the reflex influence upon the pilgrim and the far-reaching effect upon the religious life of the tribe, or nation, or body of worshippers. Christians at the present time are no less devotees of the pilgrimage accompanied by the assembling of masses of Christians in one place in the interests of their faith. Annual, triennial, quadrennial, or some other stated conventions, councils and conferences are in constant practice by the Christian bodies of America and Europe. In these latter days we are holding somewhat similar interdenominational and international assemblies, like great Missionary Conferences, Sunday School Conventions, etc., etc., terminating in mass assemblies, and all in the name and in the interest of religion.

It was for something of the same purpose that pilgrimages to Mecca and Medina were inaugurated and have been continued to the present time as an important part of the practice of devout Moslems. In places remote from these sacred shrines, secondary pilgrimages have come into practice, as in India, where frequently Moslems and Hindus make use of the same shrines for religious purposes.

13. *The Place of Sacrifice.* This point is considered here quite apart from some of the Moslem customs of sacrificing a lamb, or some other animal, at weddings or upon other occasions. We are here speaking of that element in the Moslem belief that exalts personal sacrifice in the name of religion and in the interests of the believer who makes the sacrifice. This fact is capable of extensive illustration from the teachings of the Koran and tradition and from the practices of Mohammedans. We can mention but a few of these.

The first demand upon the Moslem is that he give time and daily attention to prayer. He is to engage in prayer at the stated periods, wherever he may be. He is to shrink from no publicity and be frightened by no ridicule. But, more than this, he is to rise before day and engage in his devotions which he last participated in two hours after sunset. At noon, two hours before sunset, and at sundown, besides the two other seasons of prayer already mentioned, the true Moslem must devote himself to prayer, after the necessary acts of purification, in themselves no simple task. The rules for prayer make severe demands upon the natural indolence of the Oriental; they are rigid and persistent.

The giving of alms is universally required from all believers. This custom performs a double purpose in the economics of Islam; it provides the pious fund for the support of the religious establishment, while it secures merit to the one who makes the gift. Mohammed was drastic in his demands that alms should be given to the poor and to the religious organizations. Belief in the efficacy of alms-giving is evidenced today in all Moslem countries by the large number of professional beggars who throng the entrances to the cities frequented by Mohammedans. These are accustomed to throw to each, as they pass, a small coin. Although this is not done because of any special care for, or sympathy with, the recipient, the act prompted by religion leads to the frequent giving of money to others as well as extending wide hospitality to strangers.

The fasts of Islam are often taxing in the extreme. The fast of Ramazan demands severe self-denial and personal sacrifice. It is fortunate that most Moslems live within 30 degrees of the equator, so that there is not so marked a difference throughout the year between the length of the days and nights. Still, however much night may be turned into day, the month of Ramazan to every Mohammedan is a period of real trial and hardship, but to those who are compelled to work, it is doubly severe. While exceptions are permissible, there is no simple recurring custom in any religion that is more painfully exacting as a personal test and that requires a greater sacrifice of personal ease and preference.

The pilgrimage to Mecca may be called one of the crowning sacrifices demanded by Islam of its devotees. Every free Moslem who is of age, male or female, with means sufficient to meet the expenses of the journey, is expected to make the pilgrimage once in his lifetime. It is permissible to hire a substitute, if for any reason the journey cannot be made in person. To those who live in Arabia, or Egypt, or Syria, the task is not so burdensome or perilous; but when the pilgrim starts from Russia, Persia, Morocco, India, China and the interior of Africa, months are required for the journey, which is usually taken upon foot or with slow-moving caravans. Quite apart from the actual money expense of the trip, a large percentage of those who start out for the holy city of Islam never return. The hardships of the road, disease, exposure, and often pestilence cause many to perish in this act of devotion and sacrifice. There is no accurate census of the numbers who annually make the journey to Mecca, but it is known to mount up into the tens of thousands. It is not difficult to make an estimate of what this one command of Islam costs all followers of the Prophet.

The Jihad should be mentioned in this connection as including the supreme sacrifice demanded in case of necessity. This is not periodic, and millions of Moslems may never be called upon to offer themselves as soldiers in a holy war; but when the demand is made every able-bodied true Mohammedan male of proper age must be ready to give himself, not to his country, but to his religion, even to facing death. It is incumbent upon every Moslem to take up arms for his faith whenever the call shall come, and he should be grateful for the privilege of martyrdom as a test of his devotion.

Mohammed laid out before his followers no flowery paths of ease. His call was to a sturdy and exacting religion, demanding the sacrifice of self to a marked degree, in order to attain unto the paradise of the faithful.

While the thirteen points named above do not include all of the parallels or partial parallels in which Christianity and Islam stress common acts or virtues, they are sufficient to show that there is much common ground where Christian and Moslem may meet and in which a wide field may be discovered for mutual discussion. These afford points of contact where the two religions approach each other and suggest the door of entrance to a clearer and more fraternal understanding. There is much of a similar nature not touched upon here, affording fields for investigation that promise rewarding returns to him who would reach the Moslem heart with the message of the Crucified Christ.

CHAPTER XI

INADEQUACY OF ISLAM

To some this discussion will seem unnecessary, yet there are many who question the need of attempting to Christianize Mohammedans, since "they are already believers in one God and accept Jesus Christ as a prophet of God." It is not our purpose to consider the insufficiency of Islam as a religion from the standpoint of belief or creed. It is one thing to profess a creed; it is quite a different thing to embody that creed in the life of the individual and in the mass of believers.

The value and worth of any religion is revealed by its effect upon life. Expressions of belief, be they ever so beautiful and perfect, are meaningless and without value if they fail to make beautiful and more perfect the lives of those whose belief they seem to voice. This is the test Christ puts upon creed and religion as applied to His own followers, and the standard of performance has never been improved upon. The value of a religion cannot be measured by its influence upon the life of the individual believer only, for every adequate religion must take into consideration communities of men and women, living in relation to each other. Any religion therefore that does not exalt human relationships and make more Godlike human society in all of its diverse and complicated organizations cannot be adequate for the world.

In applying this test, distinction must be made between defects in the religion that inculcates or permits practices detrimental to human welfare, and the defects in individual adherents who ignorantly fail to apply the teachings of their faith, or who misinterpret those teachings. It would be as manifestly unjust to charge the Inquisition to Christianity as to make Islam responsible for all of the acts of the Bahaists.

167

It is, however, fair and just to demand that any religion, professing to be adequate to meet the needs of men, shall so reveal in its adherents a power for good in both individuals and in society that the only fair conclusion would be, that, if this religion should become general it would benefit mankind. Any religion that meets this test must pass as a good religion; but if it aspires to become a universal religion, it must show that it is capable of meeting the needs of humanity in all relationships more completely than any other religion can do. Islam claims to be not only a good religion but the best religion for the world, hence the necessity of showing that it is best suited to the conditions and needs of all men and in all of their varied relationships. Christianity is compelled to meet the same tests as must every other religion.

We are here inquiring whether or not Islam is a religion calculated to meet the needs of the world, and, for our reply, we record the answers that come to us from the fruits it has produced in its adherents. The twelve centuries of Mohammedanism can be regarded as a sufficiently long time in which to demonstrate not only the strength of Islam but also its tendency in producing exalted character and a safe and worthy social order. After careful study of the life and character of Mohammed himself and the history of the development of the religion to which he gave his name, we are inevitably led to the conclusion that Islam is wholly inadequate to meet the needs of the race. It has been weighed in the balance of the centuries and has been found wanting. We will enumerate some of the reasons for our conclusions as here stated.

1. *The Character of the Founder.* No religion can lay claim to perfection in whose founder so much imperfection exists. The life of Mohammed as written and taught by Mohammedans makes the fact of his defects in character patent to the world. It would be an alleviating feature if these moral lapses were condemned, or even concealed. Instead of this, everything said or done by the prophet became permissible for

his followers and often mandatory. A study of the Koran and the accepted traditions but reveal the true character of Mohammed as sensual, cruel, ambitious, inconsistent, and untruthful, putting the Moslem state above religion and making plunder and violence the weapons of faith.

In a religion that puts its founder at the very center of its teaching and practice, the significance of his defective character is greatly enhanced. The tendency to exalt if not to deify Mohammed among some modern Moslem sects, and his universal exaltation as the supreme head of the faith, reveal the fact that, at its very source, Islam is corrupted, and so, from the beginning, its influence has been, in many of its leading features, and must continue to be evil rather than good.

2. *Its Conception of God.* Mohammedans hold an exalted conception of Allah as a deity of unlimited power and knowledge, who sits upon the throne of the world and rules according to his unquestioned and almighty will. In his presence man is but a slave, helpless and hopeless except for infinite mercy. Not only is Allah a kind of absentee god, presiding over a universe for whose creation he had no responsibility, but he is also a strict keeper of accounts, balancing debits and credits with all of his subjects. The god of the Moslems is feared but cannot be loved, since he in turn never loves. In this he partakes of much of the character of the gods of the heathen who use their power not chiefly to help men, but to afflict and punish. Hence the Moslem worships because he fears to do otherwise, or that he may have placed to his credit in the eternal records that which will be due him for the acts of worship regularly performed. Allah, in his majesty, exacts tribute and homage and unquestioned obedience from all his subjects, visiting dire vengeance upon those who fail to submit to his supreme will.

A god of this character compels to formalism in all acts of devotion and worship, since the worshipper approaches his god not from any sense of affection, or personal pleasure, or desire, but because stated acts of homage must be performed and approved expressions of allegiance must be uttered to avert the visitation of divine wrath. The Moslem's god opens no fountains of affection, calls out no manifestations of love and strengthens no tender passions in the heart. The inevitable result is the creation and development of a severity and cruelty of disposition that partakes of something of the nature of the Allah worshipped and that looks with contempt upon those who exalt love as evidence of the divine in man and as a characteristic of deity.

3. *Conception of Sin.* Sin to the Mohammedan is not the doing of that which is wrong, but of that which is forbidden. The greatest sin of all is to refuse to accept Islam, and all other sins arise from a failure to accomplish the full ritual of the true Mussulman. The requirements of Islam are so many and so exacting that it is impossible for one to fulfil them all and so there is no hope of achieving the perfect in life. That this may not be too overwhelmingly discouraging, a variety of compensating acts are made possible, whereby sins may be cancelled. These indulgences are varied and are put within the reach and power of every follower of Mohammed so that none need perish. The means of escape from the consequences of sin are through stated prayer, repetition of the names of Allah and the creed, almsgiving, pilgrimages, fasts, etc. Repentance for the sin is not required, neither is confession necessary, nor even a desire or purpose not to repeat the offense. The only requirement is to perform that which will accrue to the eternal merit of him who wishes to escape from the penalty of unperformed duties or overt acts against his faith. The only restraint, therefore, upon the acts of the Moslem is that inspired by his inability to escape the penalty by doing works that will keep his eternal credits sufficiently large.

4. *Prayer a Form Only.* Although prayer holds a large and central place in the Mohammedan system, it is almost as

mechanical as the prayers of the Buddhists of Tibet, who use the mechanism of the prayer wheel to save personal exertion. The fact that prayer can be acceptably offered only in the Arabic language removes from this function all elements of intelligent participation, unless the worshipper knows that language. Since only a small proportion of Mohammedans are familiar with the Arabic, to the great majority the act is as meaningless as the prayer wheel and possibly more so, since the Buddhist knows the prayer that is written upon the paper in the wheel. There is then no possibility of intelligent prayer, except to the few. There is little place in Islam for the voicing of real petitions or of spontaneous adoration, even in an unknown tongue. The Arabic prayers comprise quotations from the Koran and expressions of adoration and devotion often of a lofty and exalted character. By multitudinous repetition these become to most if not all Moslems but high-sounding phrases, either in a known or an unknown language, awaking little or no spirit of devotion in his own breast and establishing no conscious relations with God. The Mohammedan does not pray that he may draw near to his god, or that he may spread before him his sins and secure from him needed blessings. The Moslem prays at stated intervals because his religion commands it and that the credits due those who obey this command may be his. Prayer to the Moslems is quite a different act from the prayer of the Christian. It is a ceremony from which the spirit has departed for the most of the Moslem world, an act whose value to the one who prays consists only in the doing and that has no power to bring the worshipper into spiritual relations with his god.

5. *Attitude towards Women.* Islam not only does not provide for the spiritual and physical protection of women, but it discriminates against them. The place they hold in the home, in society and in religion is far below that claimed and held by men. The teaching of the Koran and the traditions as well as the practices of that religion, even to the present

time, have tended to degrade womanhood. This has resulted in the suppression and even extinction of the finer sensibilities and qualities of Moslem women, while it has deprived the Moslem world of their uplifting and refining influence. There are good grounds for the conclusion that the blunted moral sensibilities and many of the cruel practices of Mohammedans in all their history may be in a measure due to this fact.

No one can read with care that Sura in the Koran entitled " The Cow " and then trace throughout Moslem history the place accorded the wife and mother, without being driven to the inevitable conclusion that a religion that thus treats the motherhood of the race can never be recognized as adequate for the race's need.

6. *Toleration of Slavery.* Because of the almost universal modern sentiment against human servitude, Mohammedans have not been bold to proclaim their belief in and practice of slavery. It is well known, however, that the practice is common in regions where it can be safely practiced. In recent years the leading slave dealers in Africa have been and yet are Mohammedans, and in Moslem countries like Turkey there has been little attempt to conceal the fact of its practice. It is in the harem that modern Moslem slavery is most common, especially in countries least frequented by Europeans, where its existence is difficult to trace. Even today in Turkey Christian girls are bought and sold as chattels, and he who is able to present the Sultan with a slave girl of rare beauty is sure of royal favor. Slavery is in large measure but a part of the ill-treatment of women and is a consistent outcome of the Moslem conception of a woman's place in society as well as the normal state of a religion that openly practices inhuman treatment of peoples powerless to defend themselves.

7. *Discouragement to Intellectual Growth.* Islam has made but scant contribution to the advance of knowledge or science or art or invention, especially within the last five centuries.

This may be partly due to the fact that Moslems are confined mainly to the tropics and live in regions of minimum rainfall, but their lack of intellectual advance cannot all be attributed to that fact. The fundamental tenets of their faith discourage if they do not actually put the ban upon independent thought. God has revealed all wisdom and all knowledge to men through the Koran. Whatever is there is clear to all and needs not to be learned from other sources. Whatever is not there is immaterial or contrary to the will of God and need not and ought not to be studied.

Moslem faith is not a matter of understanding but of acceptance, and when once accepted there is no place for reason; obedience is the only fitting attitude and whoever would question becomes at once an unbeliever and a heretic.

The attitude of Moslems everywhere towards education is the inevitable outcome of their religion. It is a serious question as to whether Mohammedanism can survive the impact of modern science, philosophy and history. It is evident that many of the leaders, conscious of this peril, are seeking to stem the rising tide by exalting the old and warning against the new, while others are endeavoring to discover a way by which a Moslem may become a modern scholar and remain true to his faith. Wherever modern education has advanced among Moslems it has been against the inertia and even open opposition of the leaders of that religion. Islam is the religion of ignorance.

8. *Unchangeable Character.* Islam was decidedly a new and radical departure from the religion of Arabia which it supplanted, as it has been since for other peoples like the Tartars and the wild races of Africa. Most unfortunately for its permanent success and worth, Mohammed crystalized it into an unchanging form where for centuries it has remained immobile. No provision was made for adapting it to peoples of other countries and of succeeding ages and to meet new conditions. Not only was the revelation closed with the

death of Mohammed, but there remained no authority to alter religious practices or to make a modern interpretation of utterances and directions given for the people of the desert. Islam became a dead religion not only without the liberty of growth but without the power to grow. This characteristic is so marked that Lord Cromer, after his long experience with Islam in Egypt, where it has advanced as much as in any other country in the world, declares that Islam has no power of growth or change and should it commence to do so it would begin to be something else. The effect is the same upon the individual, upon society and upon the national life of all who embrace Islam; the final character is fixed and progress ceases. One needs but to study the history of the Moslem peoples to be convinced of the validity of this statement. Owing to this fact alone, if to no other, Mohammedanism cannot be a satisfactory religion for any people.

9. *The Koran Final Authority in Civil as well as Religious Matters.* This is but a part of the unchangeable character of Islam and accounts in large part for it. Not only is the Koran and accompanying tradition the last word in religion, but it is also the last word in civil law and national control. This grew out of the dual office assumed by Mohammed, who was at the same time Prince and Pope. The religious state he established was to have and did have but one code of law, and that was the divinely revealed Koran. So long as the Islamic state embraced only Arabia, as it did at the time of Mohammed's death, the laws were adequate and fairly satisfactory. It was when other countries and people were brought under Moslem rule that new difficulties in the application of this law to civil matters began to appear. The Caliph of Islam, the Sultan of the Ottoman Empire, recognizing this difficulty, created a new officer, the Sheik-ul-Islam, whose business it was to interpret the Koran with reference to its application to specific cases. The officer had no ecclesiastical authority to change what was revealed but only to interpret it.

In Mohammedan countries the court of appeal in the settlement of civil cases is to the Koran, from whose decision there is no appeal. The anomaly of this condition is shown by the fact that the Turkish Parliament at Constantinople, before taking final action upon measures under consideration, often referred them to the Sheik-ul-Islam that he might report upon whether or not the proposed act accorded with the teachings of the Koran. Whenever it was shown that the measure was contrary to revelation, it was either dropped or modified.

The mere statement of these facts is sufficient to reveal the inadequacy of Islam as a national religion as well as the unsuperable difficulties it faces in attempting to adopt modern forms of government.

10. *Union of Church and State.* It has already been stated that Islam by its very nature is a state religion. Mohammed was the head of the ecclesiastical or religious order and the ruler of the country and people who had accepted Islam. The genius of Mohammedanism is to exert national force through a Moslem state. The church was the state and the state was the church. Strictly interpreted, all the citizens of the state must be Moslem; but Mohammed, seeing the difficulty of accomplishing this, made provision for non-Moslems to continue to reside under a Mohammedan government subject to certain regulations made to cover their case. The church gave the laws to the state and the state protected and perpetuated the church.

As Moslem countries have come under the control of non-Moslem governments it has been necessary to make many concessions to Mohammedans lest their fanaticism be aroused into violent resistance. It is difficult for a Mohammedan to think of Islam in terms of religion alone. To him it is a system that should control the state and give him a code of laws to govern all his relationships. As in all other cases where religion has sought to control the state, whatever spiritual forces that religion possessed at the outset have been dissipated in the endeavor to maintain and exercise temporal power. In all countries where Islam has exercised national control, religion has been dominated by the necessities of politics.

11. *Destitute of Spiritual Power*. Mohammedanism never claimed that it is a spiritual religion, that it brings God to men or lifts men to God. Emphasis has always been placed upon the system or organization by which men were able to make themselves right with God, and upon the political order that provided a government for all who came under the sway of the Caliph. It has always ingloriously failed to provide a way by which the sins of men were forgiven, much less a way through which the desire to sin was removed. Islam told men what they could do and what they must not do, but it never has attempted to reach to the fountains of human action for their cleansing. It has dealt only with that which was external, ignoring the fact that a bitter fountain cannot send forth sweet water.

The redemptive side of the nature of God does not appear in Islam. To the Mohammedan, God is not seeking to save men from their life of sin and create in them a new and a better life, but he only desires to bring all men under one form of religion, which is Islam, and over whom he will rule as supreme Lord and Master. God does not seek to save men, but men seek God for the advantage that is to accrue to them.

In spite of this fatal defect, Mohammedans have now and then appeared who seemed to have a deep insight into spiritual realities, but this has been not by the aid of their religion but in spite of it. The large number of mystical sects that have sprung up within Islam and contrary to its teachings and practices are but evidence of its own spiritual barrenness.

As one studies the inner life of the Mohammedan trained and reared in accordance with the Orthodox faith, the absence of spiritual ideals and impulses, and usually of desires, is conspicuously manifest. The Moslem lives in a secular and material world whose supreme pleasures are sensual and whose paradise has little trace of exalted ideals and spiritual conceptions. It is of the earth, earthy, and in itself has no power to rise above the conditions of its origin and the records of its centuries of materialistic legalisms.

This absence of spiritual power has produced in Islam a mighty force for the destruction of spiritual impulses and religious ideals in the individual as well as in society. While it fails to save, it has become a dominant force for evil.

CHAPTER XII

MOSLEM DISSATISFACTION

Experienced missionaries among Moslems who have carefully observed their attitude toward the beliefs and practices of their own religion, have given the following as some of the principles and practices of Islam that are failing to satisfy their own followers. This list might be prolonged almost indefinitely. Space forbids much more than the cataloging of the various points mentioned, although each one alone is worthy a chapter. It should be particularly noted that these are points raised by Mohammedans against the adequacy of their own religion. The attitude of criticism is becoming more common and outspoken, and especially among the more intelligent.

(1) The present idealization of Mohammed compared with his character as revealed in the Koran and in authorized tradition is one phase that invites criticism. The life of the prophet reveals elements of character against which the devout Moslem revolts, and which others regard inadequate as the basis of a true religious order for the salvation of men and the redemption of society. There is an increasing dissatisfaction with the character and life of the founder of their faith, on the one hand, and, on the other, with the present tendency in some sects to assign to him attributes of divinity or at least characteristics that belong to a supernatural person.

(2) Another subject of criticism is the puerilities and contradictions in the Koran. The multiplication of mystical sects has driven to a more careful and critical study of the Koran. The result is that many are repelled by it. It does not measure up to the book that, according to their conception, ought to be the foundation of a great and universal religion.

Its trivialities and inconsequential utterances on personal and minor affairs are repelling many and leading them to seek for something more satisfying.

(3) A third basis of dissatisfaction is the detailed commands, prohibitions and legalistic and casuistical provisions of the Koran and especially of their many traditions. Legalism has paralyzed the natural religious forces inherent in the people and made them only the observers of times and seasons and ceremonies from which the true spirit of religion has disappeared. They recognize that already Islam has become largely a service of the lips and obedience to unalterable religious exactions, in which there is little place for the exercise of the spirit of personal devotion and where none is required.

(4) They also revolt against the practices and abuses of individual leaders who are more and more usurping authority. Religious orders are recognized to be contrary to the teachings of the prophet who rejected an ecclesiastical hierarchy and proclaimed the eternal priesthood of the individual believer. Instead of a reform movement to bring again into play the religious forces of the people, they see authority concentrating in the hands of the few and without the real religious good of the masses at heart.

(5) Dissatisfaction also arises on account of the many elements that have entered from without. Contamination through contact has appeared most prominently in the last generation in the rise of the new modern movements among Moslems, many of which base their activities upon doctrines and principles not only not found in the teachings and traditions of Islam but in direct antagonism to them.

(6) The pride and self-satisfaction which Moslem piety has engendered is recognized by the truly devout followers of Islam as contrary to the teachings of their prophet and against their religion.

(7) The evil practices experienced upon the pilgrimages to Mecca and Medina are another stumbling-block. The

severest condemnation of these practices as un-Moslem and even anti-Moslem in their character, are becoming more and more frequent in periodical literature and in tracts by leading Mohammedans.

(8) The intelligent find the requirements of compulsory fasting vexatious and the ceremonial of daily prayers irksome. It is inevitable that these forms and ceremonies become insufferably irksome when they express no spirit of devotion or longing of the soul through these acts to enter into closer relations with God.

(9) The retrogressive tendency in political and social relations also estranges many. The loss of Moslem prestige as a political force among the nations is a severe blow to all who have entertained the belief that it was to increase in power to the complete conquest of the world. They have seen one by one the Mohammedan nations lose their prestige and become subject to non-Moslem powers. At the same time in the social realm there are indications of the same retrograde tendency.

(10) The lack of personal and religious freedom in religious and social matters is another cause of dissatisfaction. A desire for freedom but expresses the natural longing to escape from laws which seem to contravene reason and rules that forbid individual initiative. The fixed laws controlling the relations of the sexes are resented by an increasing number.

(11) There is an increasing revulsion against slavery. Slavery is not a practical question in countries under Christian rulers, but the better class among Mohammedans rebel against the recognition of slavery as a divine institution.

(12) Many also revolt against polygamy and concubinage. It is natural that the student of the laws of society as well as of religion should recognize the self-destructive character of this law and custom of Islam.

(13) The legalistic character of forgiveness in which the debits and credits of the life are balanced by a stern judge and

the verdict pronounced without love for the sinner, fails to satisfy. It does not meet the longing of the soul of the devout Moslem.

(14) The practical difficulties of fatalism also estranges some. It is recognized that this belief has from the days of Mohammed, stood across the pathway of progress in intellectual, social and religious matters. In a hundred ways it has destroyed the power of initiative and made the believer a mere puppet in the hands of a supreme power against whose foreknowledge and divine decrees no human agency can prevail.

(15) Compulsion in matters of religion is also resented. The Moslem world is not united in its acceptance of the doctrine and practice that the Moslem faith may be forced upon unwilling subjects. Even today in Turkey many Moslems revolt against the forcible conversion of Armenians and Greeks to Mohammedanism.

Thoughtful and devout Mohammedans are studying and thinking and even writing against these things. They evince a restlessness of spirit and a deep-seated longing for genuine and far-reaching reforms. A Mohammedan student recently stated before the students, Moslem and Christian, in one of the Christian colleges in Turkey, that unless a leader is raised up to reform Mohammedanism and lead it to victory, it is already doomed. Many are experiencing the same difficulty in that and other countries. They exhibit a changed and changing attitude of the followers of the prophet towards their religion that seems to fail to meet in this twentieth century the requirements of thinking men and of society.

Many public statements have been made by Mohammedans expressing keen dissatisfaction with Islam as a religion and as a government. We must always remember that Islam is a theocracy and that dissatisfaction with its political leaders is also dissatisfaction with one of its chief religious functions. When a protest is made against the acts of the Sultan of Turkey we cannot forget that he is, even after more than three years of Turkey's participation in the war, the only Caliph of Islam to be found anywhere. The proclamation of the Shereef of Mecca announcing himself as King of the Hejaz and deposing the Sultan of Turkey as Caliph of Islam has gone forth. Whoever inveighs against the Caliph of Islam arrays himself against one of the central and most sacred doctrines of that religion. It is significant that in the attitudes quoted, criticism is not constructive. Existing things are severely condemned but no better way is shown. One must search long and carefully among the utterances of Islam to find a case of hopeful, constructive criticism of Mohammedanism as a force in national affairs and as a religion. There is manifest a widespread sense of inadequacy and impotence with no evidence of a spirit of hopeful courage and religious daring. As the Moslem student declared, they all seem to feel that only by miraculous intervention can Islam be saved. Some examples of this spirit of depression may be given.

In 1899, a company of delegates from the Moslem world assembled in Mecca and gave fourteen days to discussing the causes for the decay of Islam. Fifty-seven reasons were given, including fatalism, the opposition of science, the rejection of religious liberty, neglect of education and inactivity due to the hopelessness of the cause itself. A leading Moslem editor in India wrote in 1914: " We see that neither wealth nor ' education ' nor political power can enable the Muslims to achieve their national salvation. Where then lies the remedy? Before seeking the remedy we must ascertain the disease. But the Muslims are not diseased, they have reached a worse stage. A diseased man has still life in him."

We find the same note of despair in the recent volume of essays by an educated Indian Moslem, S. Khuda Bukhsh, M.A. He speaks of the " hideous deformity " of Moslem society and of " the vice and immorality, the selfishness, self-

ENTRANCE TO A MOHAMMEDAN MOSQUE IN CHINA

seeking, and hypocrisy which are corrupting it through and through." Those who live among Moslems and read Moslem newspapers and books are more and more surprised that Islam itself is so little conscious of its strength and so sensitive to its weakness and decay, and that everywhere Moslems are bemoaning a day of opportunity that is lost. The Moslem pulpit and the Moslem press in the great centers of Islam unite in a wail of despair. " O ye servants of God," said a Cairo preacher recently, " the time has come for Moslems to look after their affairs and to regard their religion and conduct as a sick man looks toward his remedy and the man who is drowning toward dry land." In the *Review of Religions* for September, 1915, the head of the Ahmadiyah movement writes:

" Today the Mussulmans are to be found in every corner of the earth and Islam claims its followers among all ranks of people. And though much of the former glory and power have been lost, there are still left a few ruling states which yet profess the faith. But withal it is apparent that the hearts of Mussulmans at large are fast sinking at the thought of the future of Islam. There are thousands, nay, millions of Muslims, who, at the sight of the power of Europe and its daily rising tide, have already come to the conclusion that for Islam to continue in its career of saviour of nations, nay, even to maintain its position, is now a thing outside the range of possibility. Nay, many a foolish one has gone so far as to predict that within a hundred years Islam will be obliterated from the face of the earth. As a matter of fact, the way in which at the present time Islam is being assailed from all sides, and every religion is treating Islam as the one common object of its onslaught, is sufficient to shake the heart of every shallow observer. And this is why the educated section of the community, who are acquainted with the condition of the times, are in a state of utter despair, and consider it but a bootless toil to take any measure or to make any endeavor for the regeneration of Islam. Such is the condition of the generality of Muslims of the present age, when in spite of there being myriads of them, they have reached the state of such utter despair.

" . . . What is the condition of Islam today? Country after country is passing out of the hands of the Mussulmans. Nay, rather, they have already lost them all and one by one all the kingdoms have been snatched away from them. It is true, kingdoms and nations do, in the nature of

things, come to an end, and no one familiar with history finds any reason
for surprise in their ruin. For just as the individual is subject to death,
so also the life of kingdoms and nations cannot help being affected by the
passage of time. The nation, that today holds the rule, does tomorrow
lead a life of dishonour and dependency. Thus it is a sign of ignorance to
grieve over the fall of any nation. But the case becomes peculiarly significant when we find a number of kingdoms belonging to different peoples
and situated in different parts of the world, but all professing one common
faith, following one another in ruin in such quick succession. It is possible
that the different dependencies of one empire may descend the steps of
decline at one and the same time, because it often happens that there is a
similarity in the condition of the different parts of one empire. But when
kingdoms situated so wide apart as Algeria, Morocco, Tripoli, Egypt,
India, Persia, Afghanistan, Turkestan, the Philippines, the Sudan, Abyssinia, established at diverse times and flourishing under the auspices of
different nations, all come to an end almost simultaneously and the rule is
everywhere transferred from Muslim to non-Muslim hands, the events
prove that the fall has a special significance and is not the result of occurrences that happen every day.

" In short, the natural condition of the Mussulmans is so weak that a
materialist is forced to exclaim that the end of Islam is now at hand, and
that within a few days there will be, for Islam, not a place to hide its head.
The sight of such a predicament is sure to pain every sympathetic heart,
and I know not if there is any Muslim who can view the plight without
experiencing a pang."

Mohammed Sarfaran Khan of Naini Tal, India, in his
address to the Moslem Religious Congress said:

" With the growth of European civilization and the cultivation of
English manners among our educated classes, the question of our religious
requirements and how best they can be met is becoming more and more
prominent day by day, and it is worth while discussing the question,
especially as we have fortunately among us a few eminent persons who are
fully alive to the growing needs of modern civilization and have also keen
sympathy for the spiritual welfare of their community. . . . The majority of the well-to-do Mussulmans will be seen possessed of European
civilization and manners; our ways, our dress, and even our food will be
changed, and last, though not least, our thoughts will also be completely
changed. You cannot certainly check the growth of civilization, even if
it should seem to parade against your fixed notions of religion. . . . The

rudimentary principles of Islam, such as to believe in the unity of God, to acquiesce faithfully in the teachings of the prophet, to admit the necessity for prayer, fastings, etc., and conforming to them practically, must be held sacred and adhered to till the last. The changes to be introduced will then be of the following nature. These changes, or at least some of them, though not formally sanctioned by the spiritual authorities, have virtually been imperceptibly adopted by many of the enlightened Mussulmans, and are not only the outcome of their practical and honest everyday life, but are also the dictates of their conscience."

James Munroe of Bengal quotes a Mohammedan writer upon this subject as follows:

" What is now called religion is simply a lifeless form. A man mumbles certain sounds, and makes flexions of the body, and he has done all that this religion requires of him to do. He is now at liberty to go and cheat his employer, render false accounts, and speak a multiplicity of lies. . . . The Ulema have always been against a diffusion of knowledge; they wish to keep the Book of God, and all religious books, in a foreign and unknown tongue. They desire to keep the people in ignorance and superstition, so that their influence and power may continue unabated. . . . It is futile to hope for the regeneration of our community by means of a revival of Arabic literature. . . . Historical works in the Arabic language are a bare narration of occurrences, and were written at a time when there was no idea of the sequence of events in the history of human affairs, so that we must have recourse to English for the acquisition of the knowledge of history as well as science, or we must place this knowledge before our young men in the garb of their spoken language. . . . The translation of the Koran will be regularly read, and our people will not have the mummery which is now called religion, but will have true religion as their constant reference and real guide."

Mr. Mohammed Aziz Maqdoum, pleading for a Mohammedan University, wrote in the *Muslim Review* (1910):

" The truth is that western education as imported at present demolishes the old building of one's beliefs, but does not arrange for the construction of another and more beautiful. The mind is unhinged; it knows not where to go to find repose, till at last Jeremy Bentham and Herbert Spencer dawn to it as embodiments of sound logic, wisdom and common sense. The consequence is not very pleasant to look upon. The Hindu rails against the rulers, the Muslim turns traitor to the traditions of unflinching loyalty to Islam. Islam is a dead letter in educated circles. Where the Koran was read daily in the morning formerly, there, now, the *Pioneer* (an English daily newspaper published in Allahabad) has taken its place."

There is profound dissatisfaction with the political position of Islam as represented by the Ottoman Empire as ruled over by the boasted Caliph and claiming to be the keeper of the sacred relics and cities of Mohammed.

The defeat of Turkey in the Balkan War came as a great surprise to Moslems in India. A Moslem, writing of it in the *Hindustani Review*, says:

" The defeat of Turkey in the Balkans came as a great surprise to the whole world, like the defeat of Russia by Japan a few years ago. But it was more than a surprise to the Mohammedan world; it was a crushing blow, a staggering revelation. And because Turkey was regarded as the sole surviving power of Islam, its only hope of glory, this revelation of its weakness was accompanied with all the bitterness of a present disappointment and the uncertainty of a gloomy future. It was such a grievous shock that it unnerved the whole Mohammedan world." [1]

The effect of the world-war upon Mohammedan opinion concerning Turkey may be indicated by the following quotations of Mohammedans in various parts of the world. We first give some quotations from Indian Moslems before Turkey entered the war.

The Hon. Mr. K. G. Ahmed Maracar, of Madras, issued a circular letter to the Moslems, in which he says:

" I would request that all of us should hold meetings of Anjuman and other Moslem bodies, to send telegrams to the Consulate-General of Turkey, at Bombay, to intimate to the Sultan of Turkey that in view of the King-Emperor having observed strict neutrality during the time of the late Turco-Italian war, and in view of the very kind treatment we have been receiving at the hands of the British Government, the Sultan of Turkey should now join the British cause, in case His Majesty is unable to maintain strict neutrality."

[1] Quoted from Dr. Zwemer's " *Mohammed or Christ.*"

Another leading Mussulman merchant writes in the course of a letter:

" We, the Mohammedans of India, as a whole, appeal to the Sultan of Turkey on no account or persuasion to give heed to the detrimental counsels of turbulent Germany. We know, and the whole world sees, that Germany is aiming at trampling on the sovereignty of all Europe, Turkey included, and aiming at the dictatorship, as Napoleon did."

The leading Moslem papers, like the *Hablul Matin*, *Al-Hilal*, *Zemindar*, *Sultan*, *Mussulman*, *Comrade*, and *Observer*, have warned Turkey not to expect any sort of help from Indian Mussulmans if she sides with Germany. The *Observer* further remarked:

" So great is the debt that the Moslems of India owe to England and her culture that they cannot for the moment think of transferring their affections to Turkey, which, though allied to them by the bond of a common creed, has certainly no claim upon their sympathy, if it chooses to enter the fight and take up cudgels against the sovereign of this country."

The Near East for January 22, 1915, contained the following:

" An interesting pamphlet on the entrance of Turkey into the war has been published in Bombay by Mr. Cassamally Jairazbhoy, Vice-President of the Moslem League, and is now being distributed, both in English and the vernacular, throughout India. It is entitled ' The Suicide of Turkey.' The author's object, says the *Morning Post*, is twofold. He wishes to help any of his coreligionists who find themselves doubtful as to how they should act in that which he describes as ' this great crisis in the history of Islam.' He also desires to give adherents of other religions ' an exposition of a common point of view among Mohammedans that may once again assure them, should they need assurance, of the loyalty of Islam to the British Raj and to the cause of justice and freedom for which the sword of England has been drawn.' He shows that Turkey is being used by Germany as a tool to serve her aims, and asks what liberty of religion could Islam expect if Germany were to defeat the Allies. ' Islam,' he says, ' realises only too well that Turkey has slain itself, and Islam looks forward to the not far distant time when the Mohammedans who still groan beneath the tyrannical influence of Stamboul will be free men beneath a just and progressive Government, even as the Mohammedans of India and of

Egypt. We therefore clearly recognise that it is to the interests of Islam as a whole, and of one section of it in particular, that Turkish misrule should for ever be ended.' "

The attitude of the Moslems of Sierra Leone to the war is sufficiently set forth by this extract:

" An important mass meeting of Moslems of Sierra Leone, presided over by Alfa Mohammed Al-ghali, Sheik-ul-Islam, was addressed by the Secretary for Mohammedan Education, the convener, on December 8, says the *African Mail*. The object of the meeting was to explain the position of affairs consequent on the unwarranted action of Turkey in having joined hands with Germany, and to prevent the spread among Moslems of an erroneous idea that the cause in which Turkey has embarked is a religious one.

After a comprehensive address by the secretary, some of the principal alfas spoke, all strongly condemning the action of Turkey as unjustified and opposed to the interests of Islam. Alfa Al-ghali, the chairman, in summing up, expressed sorrow for, and astonishment at, what had happened in Turkey, and, among other things, cited from the Koran and the Hadis, or Traditions of the Prophet, passages and sayings indicating the circumstances under which a Moslem State may take up arms against another State, none of which, he said, applied in the present case. He was therefore greatly surprised and sorry that Turkey should have allowed herself to be so misled from the path of rectitude.

A resolution was then unanimously passed strongly condemning the action of Turkey as unjustified by the Koran and the Hadis and endorsing the opinion of his Highness the Aga Khan, as expressed in his message to Moslems, and the Secretary for Mohammedan Education was requested to reduce the resolution into writing for transmission to the British Government by the Governor." [2]

The following resolutions, sent to the British Secretary of State for the Colonies from the Moslem population of Trinidad and Tobago, sufficiently attest their attitude toward the British government on the one hand and the Sultan of Turkey on the other:

" (1) That this meeting of the leading Moslems residing in the Colony of Trinidad and Tobago have read with intense regret the declaration of

[2] *The Near East*, January 15, 1915.

war by Great Britain against Turkey, and as loyal British subjects resident in this colony desire to offer to his Most Gracious Majesty the King and Emperor our sincere devotion and loyalty, and to state publicly that no Moslems here are in sympathy with the Sultan of Turkey.

(2) That the resolution so unanimously carried be immediately forwarded to his Excellency Sir George Le Hunte, Governor of Trinidad and Tobago, expressing our sincere and loyal cooperation to the British Crown as British subjects.

(3) We Moslems, on behalf of other Moslems residing in his Most Gracious Majesty the King and Emperor's Colony, beg to assure the Government that we are loyal and faithful subjects of the British Crown, and that we are always ready to shed our blood for the honour and prestige of the British Flag, under which we are enjoying free liberty, peace, and contentment." — *Abdul Aziz.*

The following is a translation in part of a letter addressed by the Moslems of Cyprus to the Colonial Secretary:

" The Right Hon. Lewis Harcourt,
    Secretary of State for the Colonies.

SIR,— We, the undersigned, have the honour to request that our following statements may be taken into favourable consideration by his Majesty's Government.

We learn with very deep regret that the Greeks of the island have taken advantage of the proclamation of the annexation of Cyprus to renew their demands for the cession of the island to Greece.

We rejoice in the annexation of this island to the British Empire, being thereby assured that we shall continue to enjoy the blessings of an enlightened administration. . . .

We must humbly and earnestly pray, therefore, that an assurance may be given to the Moslems of Cyprus that they will be permanently united with the British Empire — an assurance which, in view of their tried loyalty to the Empire since 1878, we feel cannot well be refused. — We have the honour to be, Sir, your most obedient and humble servants."

(Signed by seven high religious and civil officials.)

The *El-Moqattam*, a Moslem paper published in Cairo, had a significant signed article in its issue of February 16, 1915, upon " Moslem Independence." We make here a few quotations that show the tenor of the entire article:

"Moslem as I am, I might likewise bemoan the lot of Islam. But my faith does not prevent my reason from ruling my emotions. . . . Moslem independence has, thanks to Enver and Talaat, become a mere shadow of a past reality! The fact is that Moslem independence was in no age nearer to annihilation than it is at this time, nor have the Ottoman Mohammedans ever suffered more crushing humiliation than they are now suffering because of Enver, Talaat and Jamal. Lands lost, provinces wrenched away, honor at stake — catastrophes unparalleled in the days of Abdul Hamid! The consequence is that our enemies have become more covetous of our property and more bold to do us harm. How then could we express sympathy at this time for Enver and his friends?

. . . How can Enver, Talaat and Jamal rightly be called the defenders of Moslem independence while they throw themselves, and us with them, into the arms of the Germans, who treat us as a man treats his goods and chattels. Nor do I understand how they can claim to be the real defenders of Mohammedan independence while the Germans are the absolute rulers of Turkey. These 'defenders' are driving our children and brothers and cousins into the jaws of death, not to restore something that has been lost, but to enlarge the boundaries of the German Empire and hoist its flag over every fortress and citadel! Yes, how can they claim to be the defenders of this independence while, ever since they came into power, they have punished every one who has had the welfare of Islam at heart? How can they, while they are fighting against the Quran and the language of the Quran? Yea, what right have those braggarts to boast of the government of Enver and Talaat and Jamal as being the real defence of Moslem freedom while the Ottoman Empire has, owing to them, fallen to the lowest depths of misery?

. . . It is desired by some to have an independent Moslem state, free of all European control. Indeed, this is both legitimate and patriotic. But this requires first to purge the nation of all fanaticism and superstition, and to allow reason full control over passions. Moreover, active and energetic men are wanted who would work wisely and sincerely and with true moral courage to realize these golden dreams."

"Shawky Bey, the Khedive's poet laureate, has (says the *Egyptian Gazette*) composed a fine poem on 'the Kaiser's tremendous dream,' of which the following are some stanzas literally translated:

'What is the judgment, Lord, what is Thy view, of the Kaiser's tremendously expansive dream?

' Wilhelm has delivered a speech showing that of the great Kingdom he will appropriate the larger part and leave only the smaller for Thee. Which Sword, O Lord, is sharper — Thine or his?

' Should his dream become true the Moslems' calamity would be great. We are neither Germans that we might get a share, nor Romans.

' O God, forget not Thy flock at a time when Thy flock appears to be the humble party. The crime of ignorance always falls upon its perpetrators. We are the victims of a reckless band of men.'

The closing lines, of course, refer to Enver Pasha and the military adventurers then ruling Turkey."

One of the most influential Moslem daily papers, published in Cairo, Egypt, boldly declares:

" The interfering on the part of Turkey in the present conflict was an uncalled-for foolishness, and by her action Turkey has forfeited her right to the Caliphate. Nor is Turkey's claim to the Caliphate justifiable. Why should the Turk, that old Mongolian descendant of Othman, usurp the Caliphate from the hands of the true descendants and successors of Mohammed? Besides, Turkey's policy for several decades has been detrimental to Islam, and in many cases the Constantinople Government has shown a hostile spirit to Mohammedans themselves, not to say anything of her ill-treatment of Christians."

The leading Sheiks and dignitaries of Morocco published a pamphlet called the *Moslems' Verdict*, which has been widely circulated through North Africa. Among other significant things this pamphlet says:

" The deplorable state in which the Ottoman Empire finds herself today is really due to the unsound policy of the Young Turks, who have brought the empire to the verge of ruin. The internal unrest and poverty was enhanced by the Young Turks' casting in their lot with the Germans and staking the heritage of those glorious ancestors who built up the Turkish Empire. This indeed is a great crime. But how could Turkey avoid losing her honor and independence when Anwar Pasha is nothing but an instrument in the hands of the Emperor William, blindly obeying his commands, while the entire Turkish army is under the control of German officers? Even the religious institutions are now in the hands of the Germans!

This particular crime, committed by the Young Turks in broad daylight, has aroused indignant protest throughout the Moslem world. Moslems have unanimously condemned this shameful conduct, and have raised their voices in India, Persia, Arabia, Egypt, Tunis, Algiers, Morocco, Central Africa, and other Mohammedan countries, censuring those wretched persons who are precipitating their country into an abyss of sure destruction. Even Moslems in Turkey have striven to oppose them, for there are those in Turkey who are genuine Moslems, of noble sentiments, and who have the real welfare of Islam at heart, notwithstanding the consternation and terror to which they have been subjected by Anwar Pasha and his confederates. Those true Moslems disapprove of this war which was kindled by Germany and declare openly their friendliness to France, England and Russia. The Moslems in the French colonies in Africa have also availed themselves of this opportunity to express their sincere love and loyalty to France. *Muftis*, judges, *sheikhs*, and *'Ulema*, well acquainted with the Mohammedan law and the precepts of true Islam, not to mention the chiefs, dignitaries and even petty farmers, have expressed what their hearts feel towards France. We may refer to the declarations coming from the great chiefs of the Sufi sects, and published as an appendix to H. M. the Sultan of Morocco's declaration and that of the Bey of Tunis. Such statements are indeed compatible with the Law; and if we add to them the numerous epistles coming from different quarters of the entire world, it would be clearly seen that by casting in Turkey's lot with that of Germany the Young Turks have committed an unpardonable sin against Islam and have excommunicated themselves from the brotherhood."

In the summer of 1916, the Grand Shereef of Mecca, who is the Chief Magistrate of that sacred city of Islam, after having announced two months before, his independence of Ottoman rule, addressed a proclamation " To All Our Moslem Brothers." This proclamation, which is given in full in the Appendix, should be read in connection with the utterances from Moslems of the rest of the world which are collected here. It is one of the significant evidences of the disintegrating effects of the war upon Islam.

While the Moslem world is thus disintegrating, there are those who recognize its significance. They see that the success of Islam depends upon the existence of a victorious Caliph.

Soon after the outbreak of the European War, Enver

Pasha issued a signed statement in a Moslem paper, *Esh-Sha'ab*, in which the following passage occurred:

" The life of the holy Caliphate and of the entire Moslem world depends on the sacrifice which our valiant army will offer."

The following statement was made after the call for a holy war had been issued and when it was apparent that the Sultan of Turkey was no longer recognized by the Moslems of the world as the successor of the Prophet.

" Both Sunnis and Shiahs are agreed that the religious efficacy of the rites and duties prescribed by the Law (the Shari'at), in fact the very existence of Islam, depend on the existence of the Vice-gerent and representative of the Prophet (The Caliph) who, as such, is the spiritual head (Imam) of the faith and the faithful." This is the utterance of Right Honorable Ameer Ali, who thoroughly understands Islam from within, printed in the *Contemporary Review* in April 1915.

In view of the evidence from Islam itself that we have passed in review, the following statement of Prof. C. Snouck Hurgronje of Leyden is of interest:

" The Mohammedans have become inferiors in this world, politically and socially; so much so that the idea of a world-dominion founded on their religion could not keep anything of its attraction for any but the ignorant. The others are almost ashamed of the presumption expressed by the teaching of the *jihad*, and try hard to prove that the law itself restricts its application to cirumstances which do not occur any more."

That the Mohammedans are beginning to realize the possibilities of a united Christendom is revealed by an article published in a Calcutta, India, Moslem vernacular paper, *Muhammadi:*

" Where is the spirit that existed in our forefathers when they withstood so boldly the crusades of the Christians? Then Muslims were united and with great self-sacrifice and for the glory of Islam fought and conquered, 'stamping the Christians beneath their feet.' But now the Christians are attempting to rise. They are everywhere sinking their sectarian differences with the one aim to destroy our faith. They are not marching on us today with unsheathed sword to shed streams of blood, but with peaceable methods, which are a thousand times more deadly. First of all they are urging the need for Christian Unity. Conferences have often been held at which it has been confessed that missions have utterly failed to arrest the progress of Islam. Now the Christians maintain that only a united Christian Church can overcome Islam.

Surely when Christians are planning such a huge campaign it is an evil day for Islam. Will you not bestir yourselves? If you spend one rupee where Christians spend a thousand, then the victory of Islam is sure and not a Christian will be able to remain in Asia.

The fact is, Christians are becoming more united, while in Islam, alas! we are all divided. We spend our time watering the poisonous trees of domestic and social quarrels when we should be starting missions everywhere to check the inroads of the Christian faith. . . ."

Other papers in different countries have sounded similar warnings to the Moslems to unite and resist the threatened overthrow of Islam.

A Zanzibar Arabic paper voices a similar cry of despair:

" The Christian Powers of the West have made a determined attack upon the East with cavalry and infantry and ironclads and their political organizations. The pillars of the East are tottering, its thrones are being destroyed, its power is being shattered, and its supremacy is being obliterated. The Moslem world is divided against itself, and every one is busied with his own private interests. Brother no longer listens to the cry of brother. . . . The missionaries are strengthening themselves in their attack upon the Moslem faith, not being satisfied with gaining possession of the Moslem kingdoms and their states. What has befallen the Moslem world from their poisonous breath is due to the divisions of the Moslem world, their mutual hatred, and the divisions in their kingdoms. In this way they have lost the whole world: and their sickness is incurable."

In addition to dissatisfaction growing out of the war and the unity of Christendom there is also dissatisfaction arising from internal poverty, as the following indicates.

An enlightened Moslem of India reports of his experiences

in Mecca, according to statements printed in a Calcutta paper and quoted by Dr. Zwemer in his *Mohammed or Christ:*

" Today the mullahs of Mecca mount a pulpit and air their erudition; that is, their knowledge of the traditions, as they interpret them according to their respective schools, and end with a few wandering, lifeless sentences in condemnation of all heretics, in contempt of this life, and in praise of the world to come. A philosopher would consider their sermons ridiculous. . . . The wonder is that the faithful can be found to obey the behests of these tradition-ridden miracle-mongers, who do nothing to lessen the breach between the sects, but leave the more enlightened laymen to lead the way to reunion. My Meccan experiences prove this, that the faith of the priest is stagnant from the want of the breath of reason. In its decadence Islam is priest-begotten and priest-ridden."

These quotations from recent utterances are but a fraction of what might be given, but perhaps they will suffice to fix an impression of a widespread dissatisfaction within Mohammedanism itself and a recognition of its inherent weakness as a world power and as a living faith.

CHAPTER XIII

ATTEMPTS AT REFORM FROM WITHIN

Mohammedanism is not a unified religion. Mohammed is said to have predicted that his followers would be broken up into sects. This has been true from the beginning and resulted in the two great divisions, the Shiahs and the Sunnis, who, while antagonistic to each other in many respects, still hold to and venerate in common the principal tenets of Islam, including the holy places honored alike by each.

While these divisions of long standing are of supreme interest to the student of Islam, for the purposes of our present study we are more concerned with some of the modern cleavages that have crept in among the true believers. These show a state of spiritual or religious unrest, seeking satisfaction through some addition or innovation not taught by Mohammed and frequently not permitted under Moslem rules. We can refer to but a few of these attempts at reform among Moslems, and that in the briefest manner. We shall confine our studies to modern movements, since we are considering our subject with the practical end in view. These modern movements among Mohammedans can be of interest to us here only as they reveal a state of mind or conditions showing a tendency that would suggest a method of successful approach with the Gospel message.

The Ahmadiye Movement in Northern India. This sect sprang from the village of Quadin, in Northern India, some 50 miles from Lahore, about 1880. It seems that one Mirza Ghulam Ahmad claimed that he was the long anticipated Mahdi of Islam, also the Christian Messiah and the Avatara of the Hindus. The founder died in 1908, when a sharp division entered into the sect through a dispute over who should be the successor of Ahmad.   With this division we are not particularly concerned.

The original sect was supremely concerned with religion, although political questions succeeded in penetrating somewhat their inner circle.   One of the characteristic teachings of Ahmad was that Christ did not die upon the cross but that he was rescued alive and miraculously healed; that he journeyed to Cashmere, where he served long as a preacher to the lost sheep of the house of Israel.   He there died a natural death and was buried at Strinagar.   It is somewhat difficult to reconcile this belief with Ahmad's vigorous anti-Christian prejudices.

Owing to controversy this sect now has two Khalifa, who through rivalry double their zeal for conquest.   Both publish periodicals and carry on educational enterprises, and a society among them for the advancement of Islam claims to be supporting 12 missionaries in different parts of India, Ceylon, Mauritius and London.   They also entertain the idea of extending their missionary endeavors into Java, Japan, China, the Philippines and beyond.

In East Bengal, the Punjab, the Deccan and Malabar they are gaining converts.   The missionary spirit is strong with them.   It is impossible to give the number of followers of these sects.   Ahmad claimed a little before his death that they numbered 500,000, but this is probably much too large.

The principal peculiar Ahmadiya doctrines are that revelation did not end with the death of Mohammed; that Mohammed is the intercessor for the faithful upon the day of judgment, that Ahmad was the promised Messiah, the second manifestation of the prophet of Arabia, the sinless one.

Bahaism.   " Bahaism," says Dr. S. G. Wilson, " is a definite revolt from Islam within its own fold.   It has won its way in Persia to a position of a separate religion."   Mirza Ali Mohammed of Shiras, in 1844, when only twenty-four years of age, laid claim to being the promised Messiah.   He took the name of " Bab," the gate or the door. His followers were called Babis. The Bab was executed in Tabriz in 1850, only six years after he had entered upon his public ministry. Many of his disciples were slain. As in the case of the Ahmadiya of India, upon the death of the Bab many Messiahs sprang up, introducing confusion and controversy. One of the aspirants to leadership was Baha Ullah, who succeeded in attracting most of the Babis to himself. These then became known as Bahais and their religion as Bahaism. Baha claimed for himself the credit of being the Lord of a new dispensation and the founder of a new religion.

Baha was at Bagdad from 1852 to 1867. For a time he was in Adrianople, European Turkey, under Government surveillance, from whence he was sent to Acre in Syria. Here he soon was given larger liberty, where he built a palace, received pilgrims, sent out tablets and composed his Books of Revelation. These books were published in Bombay, India. In May, 1892, he died at Acre.

Two successors arose, being the sons of different tribes, but Abbas drew the greater number and under the name of Abdul Baha he set out to make the faith a world religion. After 1908 he resided in Egypt and has since made several journeys to Europe and North America.

As to their peculiar tenets, the Bahais claim that from time to time a new religion is needed; that the old religions, all of them, were true in their day, but that from them the spirit has departed and hence the need of something new to take their place.

In this crisis, when all the existing religions have come to nought, Bahaism comes as the Divine revelation, a new dispensation or covenant. Abdul Baha claimed that he is building upon the foundation laid by Jesus Christ but which has been forgotten.

Baha Ullah claimed to be the Incarnation of God the Father, the Father of Christ, " Creator of whomsoever is in the world," "The Ruler." The Persian Bahais accept this teaching. The Revelation of Baha is collected in the books and Epistles and Tablets which it is claimed contain knowledge that was sealed by the prophets of bygone cycles. It claims itself to be superior to all former religions, as its books are superior to all existing religious writings. Bahaism also claims to be the universal religion which is offered to the entire world.

This subject is too extensive to admit of discussion here, except to say that the order has become split into many rival and mutually incriminating sects, a sad commentary upon the words of Baha, that they are to consort with all religions with spirituality and fragrance. No language is sufficiently rich in vituperatives to express the bitter hatred revealed by them in speaking of those from whom they theologically differ. They have also indulged in gross exaggerations regarding their adherents.

Dr. Wilson, after careful investigation, puts the Bahai believers of the world as follows:

Persia	100,000 to 200,000
Turkish Empire and Egypt	5,000
India	1,000
Russia and the Caucasus	5,000
North America	4,000
Europe	200
Others	100

This makes a total, outside of Persia, of only 15,000. Owing to their proselyting zeal and delight in reporting fabulous numbers of imaginary followers, the number is often believed to be greater.

Dr. Speer speaks of them as follows:[1]

"It is doubtless this mystical, allegorical character of Bahaism which attracts a certain type of mind in America, in the main probably, the same type which follows after spiritualism, esoteric Buddhism, Swamis

[1] Quoted in Wilson, *Bahaism and its Claims*, p. 264.

from India, theosophy, and other movements which play around the edges of the occult and magical, and help to dull the edge of present realities with the things which are neither present nor real. . . . Indeed it is probably this soft compliance with anything and the absence of the robustness of definite truth and solid principle which makes Bahaism attractive to many moral softlings in the West. . . . It will run a brief course and amount to little in America. . . . The novelty will soon be over and the people who did not have sufficient discernment to discover the truth that will satisfy them in Christianity, will not find it in Baha Ullah or Abbas Effendi." — R. E. Speer, *Miss. and Mod. Hist.*, Vol. I, pp. 143, 162–168.

The Mahdist Movements [2]

The Mahdists indicated a socialistic rather than a religious propaganda, although its basal ideas were religious. These movements have arisen from amidst the decay of Islam and seem to be but an attempt to resuscitate and to secure justice for a disheartened people. They have come forward out of a period of degeneracy, corruption and weakness, and have attempted to open a way of escape. Thus have arisen the Mahdis of India and the Sudan, and yet they were not able to save Islam from its weakness and give it the prosperity enjoyed by the Christians whose success they envied.

The Mahdi of the Sudan is one of the latest and the best known through the death of General Gordon. Mohammed Ahmad of Dongoli proclaimed himself Mahdi in 1878. He had received strict religious instruction, being able to repeat the Koran by heart when twelve years of age. In his preaching he impressed upon the people the wrongs they suffered and assured them that he was the Chosen of God to lead to their emancipation. The conditions of unrest were favorable and the people gathered about him in great numbers. The forces of the Egyptians were subdued, as province after province was overrun. Each victory, especially that over Hicks Pasha, convinced his followers that he was indeed the promised guide and leader to victory.

[2] *Mahdi* is usually understood to mean ' the guided one.' It is a term in Islam something like *Messiah* in Judaism. Mahdis began to appear in the first century of Islam.

Religious laws were enacted. Rules were laid down for the government of his followers, touching many of the details of their daily living. Every kind of corruption characterized him and his court, religion, except as a cloak, being laid aside. At the last, only the merest resemblance to Mohammedanism remained, while the pride of power in numbers increased. The people under his leadership suffered untold horrors from wars, pestilence and famine, until in the battle of Omdurman the Mahdi was slain and his followers scattered.

General Gordon's lamented death at Khartum led to the destruction of this devastating movement and the bringing of the Sudan under the control of a Christian power.

The Mahdist movements are what must be expected from Islam so long as fanatical races are left to themselves to be guided and swayed by emotional religious leaders. They always end in disaster and they inevitably must bring only sorrow and suffering in their train. They demonstrate the failure of Islam to satisfy its followers in matters belonging not so much to the spiritual as to the social, economic and even civic and national side of life. Herein too there lies a suggestion for the Christian missionary who would appeal to the entire man with a Gospel of redemption.

Sufiism

Sufiism[3] gave to the rigid monotheism of Islam a monistic conception of the universe. This has affected millions of the followers of Mohammed. The creed, " There is no God but God," has come to mean to such, that outside of Allah there is no being and that the universe is but a mode of existence for deity. It is primarily a philosophy that has so become involved with the religion of Islam that it has produced many transformations.

Like Bahaism it achieved its first development in Persia,

[3] Sufiism takes its name from *Sufi*, " wool," because in the early days its devotees wore rough woolen garments.

where it permeated the literature and dominated the thought. Many Persians were pantheistic in their philosophy, and so the more readily welcomed an interpretation of their religion that harmonized.

Belief in the unity of God was easily carried over to mean final unity or absorption in him. In his Spiritual Guide Mullah Jalal ud-Din said, "O my Master, you have completed my doctrine by teaching me that you are God and that all things are God." This removes the possibility of idolatry since all worship to whatever directed is rendered to the One Supreme God.

The teaching, doctrines and the rites of Islam are given allegorical and mystical interpretation. Spiritual communion is clothed with all the imagery of amorous passion, and sensual delights are made into symbols of divine realities. Thus Sufis regarded themselves as free from the rites of the law as well as from its restrictions upon their actions and conduct. Shams-i-Din says,

> "The man of God is beyond infidelity and religion,
> To the man of God infidelity and religion are alike."

Salvation to the Moslem means to escape from the just punishment due to his violation of law, but according to Sufiism, it is to be freed from self, to be in union with God. Some go so far as to say that it means such a complete absorption of the individual in God that he can say " I am God."

The steps by which this goal may be obtained are contemplation, meditation, adoration, etc., in accordance with certain rites or ritual called the *Zikr*. Professor Margoliouth refers to this as a " compound of various hysterical and hypnotizing processes." These are of two kinds, silent and vocal, and are sometimes accompanied by a great variety of bodily motions or vocal gymnastics. Musical instruments are also used. There are many different orders and a wide variety of practices in the use of the zikr. Some of the fakirs or der-

vishes seem to enter into a state of trance in which they see
visions, have ecstatic experiences, or become unconscious.
Startling feats are sometimes performed by them when in
this ecstatic or frenzied state.

Prof. D. B. Macdonald urges that the zikr be studied by
the Christian missionaries with a view to discovering if possible some underlying principle or truth to aid in propagating
Christianity among Moslems and especially among the followers of Sufiism. Dr. Wilson, however, seems to be convinced
that the zikr is a religious rite of little or no value to the Christian, and that Sufiism, in the extent to which it has gone, offers
but a doubtful door of approach to Islam.

Out of Sufiism have come several orders of dervishes[4] with
a variety of tenets and customs, some of them claiming their
founder to be Abu Bekr or Ali. It is certain, however, that
by the 2d century after the death of Mohammed an order,
perhaps the first, of dervishes was established, but in the face
of great opposition from the orthodox. Some Sufis were
punished as heretics. They were persistent in claiming that
they were loyal to the faith, the Koran and tradition. Some
claimed — as Iman Al Gazzali — that Sufi mysticism stood out
in opposition to scholasticism.

These orders have spread throughout Islam, each order
with its separate founder and with distinct rules and practices.
When a Sufi dynasty was established in Persia in 1501, the
Ottoman Empire made an attempt to suppress the dervish
orders in Turkey as opposed to Sunniism. This attempt was
repeated in 1656 and again in 1826, but none of these attempts permanently succeeded. There has been great growth
in the number of the orders of dervishes and in their influence in recent years. Sufiism is today exerting a preponderat-
ing influence in Moslem civilization and is rapidly spreading
in Turkey and Syria. There are said to be 200 lodges in

---

[4] " Dervish " is derived from a Persian word which means " seeking doors," because the
early dervishes were mendicants.

Constantinople, and among the members are counted the reigning Sultan and his predecessor. Professor Macdonald claims that the religion of the bulk of the Moslem population of Egypt is Sufiism. This is said also to be true of the Dutch East Indies, North Africa and the Sudan.

Sufiism owes its origin to Hindu, Greek and Persian philosophy, and demonstrates that a foreign element modifying its doctrines, worship and life can enter into the system of Islam. This also demonstrates that Mohammedanism does not satisfy the mystical and the spiritual craving of the soul in its desire to draw near to God and to find a way of approach to Him. It proves that the Moslem possesses a longing of the heart that only a spiritual deity through spiritual worship can satisfy.

Mysticism

Rev. Herbert E. E. Hayes, of Egypt, writes in the *Moslem World* for April, 1914, on the subject of Mysticism as follows:

" Mysticism, it is hoped, will provide the missionary with a point of contact whereby he may read the Moslem heart. And today a study of Mysticism is being advocated, because it is thought that it will solve many of the problems that stand in the way of approach. There is no doubt that much is to be found that is common in the mystical thought of all ages and creeds. And it is known that Christian, like Islamic mysticism, owes a good deal to the mystical and philosophical thought of paganism. There is a good deal of difference, however, in the development of the two schools of thought. Christianity has purified the mysticism of the West from errors that still exist in that of the East. A characteristic of Mysticism, in all its phases, is that it tends to Pantheism. This tendency in Christian thought has been controlled and held in check; but Sufiism is essentially pantheistic, although the Islamic conception of the Infinite is deistical. The Christian mystic is satisfied when he attains to union with God, which he describes under the symbolism of marriage. The result of this union is a life of intense activity on behalf of un-enlightened men. The Sufi mystic yearns for absorption in the Infinite, when his own personality is destroyed by being merged in the Divine. Thus, unlike the Christian, he becomes an impracticable visionary. Real mysticism involves an acceptance of the two great aspects of God — the transcendental and the immanental. The Sufi's error is that he neglects the first aspect for the second; his quest for Reality tends to become purely a subjective process. In his system there seems to be no possibility of approach in order to bring him into touch with the claims of Christ; for, in his contemplation, he rises above the need for any intermediary (and in so far as this is true, as will be seen, he cannot be a true Moslem); he reaches a certain stage in the mystic way when prophet and book alike are unnecessary. One of the Sufi poets says, " Love is the object of my worship. What need have I of Islam? " And an authoritative writer on the subject declares, " The Pantheism, Idealism, and Quietism, which are the body of the Sufiistic doctrine, are rather the outcome of his own spiritual tendencies than the result of the teaching of Islam."

These mystical movements among Moslems are but a demonstration of the fact that the strict legalism of Islam fails to satisfy the craving of the heart. The cases here cited and the large number of dervish orders thriving wherever Moslems dwell in any considerable numbers represent the craving of the hearts of the followers of the Prophet for a mystical union with God not provided by the strict formalism of their orthodox religion. These movements have led into all manner of excesses and many of them have widely departed from the teaching and practices of Mohammed and his immediate followers, and yet who can deny that they have been the means of holding many in outward adherence to a faith which otherwise might have been discarded. Many of the followers in these various sects or orders have exhibited a sincere purpose and endeavor to come into closer and more personal relations with God.

PART III
RELATIONS TO CHRISTIANITY

CHAPTER XIV

EARLY ATTEMPTS TO CHRISTIANIZE

So far as history reveals, during the first centuries of Mohammedanism there was no attempt upon the part of the Christian Church to persuade Mohammedans of the truth of Christianity. We have no record of an endeavor to Christianize the Moslems or of any discussions to that end. Perhaps one reason for this is that Christianity was so upon the defensive that its entire energy was expended in preventing its own forces from being overwhelmed by the onward rush of Mohammedans as they moved outward in their attempt to conquer their immediate neighbors, if not the entire world. Christianity therefore was in armed conflict with Islam, largely in defense, but occasionally in aggressive warfare, not to win Moslems to Christianity but to subject the Moslems to Christian rule. One of the most outstanding and conspicuous examples of this was the various Crusades.

Thus Christianity and Mohammedanism were arrayed in deadly conflict for the possession of a country. There was no question raised as to the merits and demerits of the two religions embroiled, but the question was simply that of physical supremacy. The Christians temporarily won in the Crusades and held control of Palestine for some years, but were afterwards defeated and Mohammedanism again came into control.

One would hardly refer to the Crusades as an attempt at Christianizing the Mohammedans, although it was manifestly an attempt to subjugate Mohammedans to the rule of Christian countries. That this was not entirely a clash of arms is apparent from the reliance of the Crusades upon divine intervention, many of them depending wholly upon miraculous aid in their attempt to subjugate the forces of Islam.

We find a similar conflict in Spain when the Saracens won and held the country for so long a period, and were later attacked by the Christian forces and ultimately expelled. Here again we find Mohammedanism and Christianity arrayed in open battle, the Christians being the aggressors, in the reaction against the Saracen occupation of Spain, and representing an aggressive movement upon the part of the Christians in their attempt, not to win Moslems to the Christian faith, but to subject Moslems to Christian rule.

These were in no sense attempts to Christianize the Mohammedans, since, so far as we know, there was no underlying sentiment or purpose, in any of these attacks upon Mohammedans, to make them Christian. The only result which we could expect from such attacks was to harden the hearts of Mohammedans against Christianity and to make them hate the Christian and all that for which the Christian stood. Thus Christianity came to be regarded as in cruel conflict with Mohammedanism and as the political enemy of Mohammedans, wherever they existed, and the principle became thoroughly established in the minds and in the hearts of Mohammedans, that there was then and was ever to be a continuous physical conflict between the forces of Islam and the forces of Christianity.

In speaking of the result of the first crusade, Sir Mark Sykes, in his " The Caliph's Last Heritage," says:

" With the conquest of Jerusalem began the strangest interlude in the history of our modern map of Turkey in Asia. Islam was rolled back, the whole of the Mediterranean littoral became Christian once more. Egypt alone survived unconquered. The Cross was carried as far East as the Syrian desert in the South, as far as Edessa in the North, while the whole of the Western end of the Asia Minor Peninsula was freed from Moslem dominion."

The crusaders held the coast, but did not establish themselves in the strategic centers of the country they had won. Had they united with the Greeks, the Suljuks could have been driven into Persia, and Christendom would have regained all it had lost, and probably for all time. Religious feuds separated and weakened, making united action impossible.

Christianity and Mohammedanism have come into conflict more than any other two existing religions. Buddhism sprang out of Hinduism, but very soon emigrated to other countries, leaving Hinduism in command of the field. Buddhism also came into contact with Confucianism, but as Confucianism is not a religion, the two were able to blend harmoniously. But Christianity and Mohammedanism from the very beginning were in armed conflict. With the Christian king of Abyssinia alone did Mohammed have friendly relations. The Christian tribes among the Arabs were early made to feel the power of the Mohammedan arms and were quickly and readily subdued.

The entire history of the Ottoman Empire is in a peculiar manner and to an unusual degree the history of the conflict of Islam with Christianity. The extension of Ottoman power in Europe, by which Greece, Hungary, Bulgaria, Roumania, Servia and other countries were overcome, is but the story of the conflict of Christianity and Islam, each striving for secular mastery.

These various conflicts of arms and rivalry of government which have existed from the beginning between Moslems and Christians have necessarily engendered in the minds of the followers of both religions a traditional hatred of each other. It is impossible for the Moslems not to regard the followers of Jesus Christ as openly and intensely hostile. It is impossible for them to understand, therefore, any approach of Christianity to Mohammedanism except that of a martial approach with a view to temporal control.

The use of martial hymns by the church is always understood by the Moslem as referring to carnal warfare and to material conquest. " Onward, Christian Soldiers," to the Mohammedan auditor signifies a crusade and he is confident that it means a crusade against Moslems. This is true of all martial terms by which the church has endeavored in all periods of its history to express spiritual struggle and victory. Even the old hymns of the Crusaders have lost for the Christian their former significance, but not for the Moslem.

Some have constantly referred to the relationship between these two great bodies of religionists as a controversy. Viewed from the standpoint of history, there has always been controversy between these two classes, but, viewed from a purely missionary standpoint, any preconception of controversy should be set aside and the approach to the Moslem be put wholly upon the basis of the life and teachings of Jesus Christ. The animosity and hatred, thus engendered through centuries of conflict, it will require much time to allay, and a longer time completely to obliterate.

It is but natural, therefore, that wherever the Christian missionary comes in contact with the Mohammedan, or a Christian nation with a Mohammedan state, there shall be revealed at the outset a temper and spirit of hostility and resistance, which exist nowhere else, but which is the only natural attitude that could possibly be maintained by the Mohammedan world, after its twelve centuries of experience. This historic and natural attitude of mind must not be forgotten as plans are made for approaching the Mohammedan with the Gospel message.

Born from the heart of a few devout leaders, who stand out in their age and generation as men of vision, who saw in the Mohammedans, not a people to be brought under physical subjugation, but a people to be won by the love and saving power of Jesus Christ, but few new movements have been inaugurated. We will mention two or three of these as an illustration and demonstration that the spirit of Christ was still alive in the Christian Church and that there were prophets in those days who, through the universal prejudice and hatred, saw the heart of the Mohammedan for whose redemption the Lord Jesus Christ gave up his life, and who boldly preached redemption for the Mohammedan as for the pagan.

Perhaps the first Christian disciple to present to Mohammedans the Gospel of Christ in its loving simplicity was Francis of Assisi, who was born in 1182 and became the founder of the great order of the Franciscans. He forsook his home and became an itinerant preacher of great power, adding multitudes to his followers who devoted themselves to consecrated poverty. With self-sacrifice and burning ardor and spiritual industry he made extended missionary journeys to Illyria, Spain, and to the East, in order to preach to Mohammedans. He obtained, it is said, audience with the Sultan and preached to him the gospel of self-abnegation and surrender. He spent some time in the Holy Land, where he gained many disciples by his earnestness, devotion, and his eloquent presentation of his message. Conspicuous for his loving spirit and gentle manner, he made a powerful impression upon Mohammedans. Little remained as external evidence of the effect of his labors among Moslems, yet the fact stands out in noonday clearness of a Christian of that age attempting to carry to Moslems in a loving spirit the gospel of friendship and brotherhood.

The second we will mention is Raymond Lull, who was born in 1235 on the island of Majorca, off the coast of Spain. He became a distinguished University lecturer in theology and philosophy in Paris, where his pupils characterized him as the " Enlightened Teacher." He was instrumental in persuading the University of Paris to found Chairs for teaching the Greek, Arabic and Tartar languages, while he himself combatted the Moslem philosophy, which was becoming the philosophy of the Church. At the Church Council held in Vienne in 1311, he was influential in securing a decree establishing professorships of Hebrew, Greek, Arabic and Chaldee in various Universities. This philosopher and theologian, poet and profound scholar burned with a consuming zeal to preach a Gospel of reason and love to the Saracens of North Africa.

Before following the immediate career of this man, let us turn for a moment to the situation in Europe at that time, against which dark background the life and zeal and vision of Raymond Lull stand out with startling brilliancy.

The world at that time was one of medieval legend and classic learning. The 13th century was noted for eventful epochs in European history. The power of the great empire was waning and separate states were springing up in Italy and Germany. Civil liberty was bringing forth fruit in the enlargement of ideals and the founding of universities. About the time of the birth of Raymond Lull, Ferdinand of Castile was winning back Spanish territory to Christian rule from the hand of the Saracens. The Ottoman Turks were coming into power in Western Asia. The Crusades had just come to an end, and the Crusaders, returning to Europe, had carried back a new spirit of education and a new consciousness of the great world, — although then geographically limited to a comparatively narrow area. Political change and social expectation marked the spirit of Europe.

At the same time the Mongol hordes under Genghis Khan were spreading over the countries of the East. The Caliphate of Bagdad had fallen, and the Turks were disputing with the Mongols the control of Persia and the highlands of Eastern Turkey.

A lofty faith and a dwarfing superstition characterized the spirit of the age. The Church revealed a cruel temper toward infidels, Jews and heretics, while those who erred from the faith were severely persecuted. The Mohammedan world was also in a state of turmoil and unrest. They had been alarmed by the strength of the first Crusade, and reassured by the weakness of those which followed. The defeat of their forces in Spain had convinced them that there was yet in Christianity a militant power that needed to be considered. Islam was only then receiving its second great check, the first having been administered in the 8th century by Charles Martel, and the second by the European forces in aggressive battle to drive Mohammedans out of Spain.

It was at a period like this that Raymond Lull, at the age of fifty-six, set out in 1291 from Genoa to Tunisia, where, with varying degrees of success and opposition, after imprisonment and expulsion, favorable hearing and the exhibit of fanatical hatred, he preached the Gospel of redemption through Jesus Christ. He withdrew for a period, and finally returned to his work in 1314, in his old age. Physically shrinking from the task, but with his love burning and his zeal alive, he went, longing for and expecting a martyr's crown; in which he was not disappointed. He was finally stoned to death on the seashore at Bugia, 300 miles west from Tunis, on June 30, 1315. His body was taken back to the home of his childhood and lies in the Church of St. Francis at Palma on the Island of Majorca, the place of his birth.

Raymond Lull may be set down as the second apostle to the Mohammedans. He taught and led the way to preach the gospel of love and redemption to a fanatical and hostile people, at a time when the whole Church was filled with an intense hatred and with a spirit of heartless cruelty toward all infidels, among whom the Mohammedans were classed as chief. Naturally timid, he faced certain martyrdom at the age of eighty years, in order that he might seal his oral message with his life blood. He left, beside the example of his consecrated life, as a priceless heritage to the church of all ages, his deathless declaration, — " He who loves not, lives not; he who lives by the Life, cannot die."

There seemed to be no one in the whole Christian world to take up the work of love after his martyrdom. For centuries no special effort was made to penetrate the formidable and even cruel wall of separation that divided Moslem from Christian. While Raymond Lull's life was honored in the Church, there were none to rise up and follow in his footsteps. It seemed for centuries as if his and St. Francis' life had been thrown away. It is only in recent years that we have begun to study their lives and especially that of Raymond Lull and to catch from him the inspiration which the Church so much needs, to be ready to make sacrifice for the redemption of the Mohammedans.

Henry Martyn, another apostle to the Mohammedans, was born in England in 1781. He may be called the first successor to Raymond Lull and the first modern missionary to the Mohammedans. He received high academic honors in England and was ordained in 1803, and went to India in 1806 as chaplain of the East India Company. Before going to India he studied Sanscrit, Persian and Arabic.

Within two years after his arrival in India, he translated the New Testament into Hindustani, one of the leading Mohammedan languages of India. He did other translation work, but took up especially the study of Persian with the purpose of reaching the Mohammedans of that country. In 1811 he sailed from Calcutta to Bombay, with the Persian Gulf in view. He was compelled to withdraw from India on account of broken health, while at the same time his heart was burning to give the Mohammedans of Arabia and Persia the Bible in their own tongue. He composed tracts in Arabic, talked with the Arab sailors, studied the Koran. He visited Muscat and Arabia, and solemnly decided that if his life was spared he would, in Arabia, translate the Bible into Arabic and into Persian.

He regarded the translation of the Bible into the languages spoken by Mohammedans as his supreme commission. He went to Persia, since the climate there was more favorable for his failing health than in Arabia, and there actively entered into the discussion of the merits of Christianity as over against

Islam whenever opportunity offered. His health, however, that had been completely broken, failed so rapidly that he started to return home by the way of Constantinople, making the entire journey across Asia Minor and Eastern Turkey on horseback, until on October 16, 1812, he laid down his life, at the city of Tocat, some four days' journey from the southern shore of the Black Sea, in the heart of Anatolia.

Few lives have accomplished what Henry Martyn accomplished before the age of thirty-two. He was a missionary of the Church Missionary Society, and was followed by others who had caught something of his zeal to give the Gospel to the Moslems of India, Persia, Arabia, Afghanistan, Turkey, Egypt and Africa.

The next outstanding apostle to the Moslems is Keith Falconer, the third son of the Earl of Kintour. Born in Edinburgh, July 5, 1856, reared by a God-fearing mother, and with unquestioning faith in Christ, by a series of events he came to be interested in the Mohammedan world and its conversion. In 1874 he became an undergraduate in Cambridge University, a student of Trinity College. His special interest in his studies was in mathematics, not especially calculated to inspire one with zeal for missionary work. He, however, gained distinction in the study of Greek, Church History, Divinity, and the Hebrew language. He put special emphasis on the study of Hebrew from the first, until it was reported he was able to compose with accuracy and elegance in that language. After his graduation he settled down in residence at Cambridge, and took up the study of Syriac and Arabic.

In 1875 Keith Falconer came into contact with Dwight L. Moody, who was then on a visit to England, in an evangelistic campaign. He was one of the leaders of the move to get Mr. Moody to Oxford, and it was in one of the meetings at that time that he made his first attempt to speak in public. This was followed by other and more aggressive Christian work, not only in Cambridge but in other parts of England. He followed the work of General Gordon with the closest interest, as he went for the relief of Khartum, and when the news came of the treachery of the Moslems and of the death of Gordon in the midst of a bloody massacre, he received a mighty impulse to give his life for Christianizing the Moslems.

After a visit to Leipzig, he went to Egypt, making his home at Assiut, some 200 miles above Cairo on the River Nile, for a more thorough, systematic study of the Arabic language. Here he came into personal contact with the Scotch missionary, Dr. Hogg. He returned again to England, and after further studies and special evangelistic work there, he turned his attention toward Aden, a peninsula projecting itself into the Gulf of Aden, at the northern extremity of the Indian Ocean, a stronghold of Arabia. Here he proposed to devote himself to presenting the Gospel of Jesus Christ, through the Arabic language, to the Arabs of Arabia. His careful preparation in the languages, to which he had devoted many years, gave him an unusual hold upon the people with whom he came in contact.

His zeal burned warm and his faith was strong as he took up his work in Aden in 1885. Roman Catholics had already begun work there forty-five years before this, and the Church Missionary Society was considering the question of an Arabic mission. Keith Falconer put the hospital to the front as one of the most valuable means of approach to the Moslems. He himself knew something about drugs and had some little familiarity with practical details of surgery.

Hitherto he had been wholly unattached to any missionary society. Feeling that such an attachment would help him, he applied to and received appointment from the Committee of the Free Church of Scotland, with which his father had long been connected. He returned to Scotland and appealed for the equipment of a medical work, and there before a meeting of the General Assembly he made an impassioned appeal for taking up missionary work among the Mohammedans, pointing out that they are not heathen but that they have a strong belief in the Lord of heaven and earth. His appeal had a mighty effect. He returned again to his beloved work in Arabia, where, in just six months after he had left England full of hope and joyous anticipation, he died and was buried amid the scenes of his labors.

CHAPTER XV

MODERN EVANGELISTIC EFFORTS

The attitude of the Roman Catholic Church toward Islam is different from that represented by Raymond Lull or Keith Falconer, and it is necessary in this study that we give it brief attention. We will not attempt to go into the scholastic divisions which the Roman Catholics make of their methods of operation, as they divide their work into three special divisions: the ruling power (Imperium), sanctifying power (Ministerium) and doctrinal power (Magisterium).

Under the first, Imperium, they assume that Christians are the true heirs of Abraham, to the exclusion of Moslems and Jews. That was the principle underlying the Crusades, and has been uttered by various Papal bulls. It was on this principle that the Crusades were organized and the forces of Christianity massed to resist the advance of Mohammedanism and even to drive Mohammedanism back from regions already possessed. It was this spirit which has kept hope alive and faith firm in Christian sects under the rule of Mohammedans. According to their belief the movement of emancipation will go on until the Church shall be wholly free from Moslem control.

Under Ministerium, the sanctifying power of the Church, according to Catholic belief, is manifested toward Islam in three different ways: (1) By giving the Universal Church the spiritual forces necessary to overcome the spirit of Islam. This was used at the time of the Crusades in giving plenary indulgence to those who made pilgrimages to the holy sepulchre and who fought for its emancipation. Later, this plenary indulgence was extended to all the stations of the cross. (2) It was used in keeping up the supernatural life of the sacraments in the churches subjected to Moslem rule; by the maintenance, unification and development of the hierarchy. This is the preservatory function of the Church. (3) By the recognition of the spiritual and temporal power of the Pope, an authority which Islam ignores. This condemns the Islamic state, regarding Mohammedan princes and rulers as simply holding temporary power, later to be displaced. It was not until the 15th century that the dogmatic definition of Islam was formulated by the Pope. But on this we need not dwell.

In practice, the Catholic Church has sought almost exclusively the conversion of Moslem rulers as the only means for gaining mass movements toward Christianity. Their legates were instructed to aim at the conversion of certain leaders, as the Khan of Persia, the Ottoman Sultans of Turkey, the Moguls of India. They were not expected to attempt the conversion of the masses, but to wait in a state of expectancy for mass movements after the leaders had entered the church. Cases of individual proselytism have been few and isolated. Even at the present time the leaders in the Roman Church have refused to organize special apostolic missions, on the ground that the autonomy of the Christian churches under Moslem rule is too precarious to assume the risk, and that it was of prime importance that the Church be maintained, even in its present condition, intact, rather than to have it become the aggressor and thus arouse the animosity of the Mohammedans, which might be sufficient even to destroy what now is. Although there have been faithful servants of the Church who have endeavored directly to bring to bear the forces of Christianity upon Islam, little has been accomplished.

The " White Fathers," one of the latest of the Catholic orders, was founded under the name of the African Missionary Society. Their object seemed to be the spiritual welfare of the infidels living in Moslem territory which, through the conquest of Algiers, has since become French territory. It is assumed by the Catholics as an imperative duty to work for the conversion of their Moslem neighbors in colonies under their mother country, and effort was made by their leaders to reach the Moslems in the Sahara, where a military religious order was attempted, and for forty years the "armed brothers" have existed; but the original object seems to have been lost sight of, through unforeseen obstacles, and instead of making a direct approach for the conversion of the Mohammedans, they seem to be working for the leading negro races who have not yet been reached by the Moslem propaganda. Their best missions are in the region of the Great Lakes, where Islam has made strong inroads. They also have missions in Jerusalem.

In their methods, they make use of the mystical power of the Church, through prayer and sanctification and intercession, followed by oral presentation of the Gospel. They invite to union with the Church, and employ the printed page, distributed and presented by missionaries and by converts. These are the three stages of evangelization employed by the Catholics, and the first two are supposed to be preparative for the third. Special emphasis is placed upon the preparation of the missionary himself in conforming his whole life to the discipline of his duties, in order that he may become a living stone in the edifice of the Church which it is hoped to construct out of the Moslem material lying at the hand of the missionary.

This fundamental principle is one which the Protestant missionaries of all time may well imitate: first, that the disciple himself become an example of the evangelical life, showing forth the Gospel in his life by being himself a living Gospel, so that, being seen of men, they may catch the meaning of the true Christian life, may get the interpretation of the Gospel, and may come to know Jesus Christ himself.

The attempt of the Protestant Christian world to reach the Mohammedans with missionary endeavor has been scattered and has manifested varying degrees of energy and devotion. It is only in the latter half of the last century that there seemed to be any real effort to reach Moslems with the direct message of Christianity. The Church Missionary Society of England, to which reference has already been made, was probably one of the first to send out missionaries to Persia and India, Arabia and Syria, with a view to carrying the direct message of the Gospel to the Mohammedans. One of the reasons why this was not done earlier was the hatred and spirit of antagonism existing between Mohammedans and Christians; and another was, that the Christian world had not been fully convinced that the Mohammedans were not partly Christian, in that they worshipped the one true God. Even today there are many people in England if not in the United States who raise the question as to whether we should send missionaries to Moslems.

The United Free Church of Scotland began to work in Aden, and the Danish Church has only recently sent out missionaries to that same field. Missionaries from these three European Societies have gone to Bagdad, and occupy stations on the East coast of Arabia.

The American Board began work in the Turkish empire nearly a century ago, and at the beginning had the Mohammedans chiefly in view. A large work was accomplished among the Moslems, until a spirit of persecution and opposition arose through the government, making it impossible for Mohammedans to accept Christianity.

In Egypt, the United Presbyterians have a large and extensive work established, and are now reaching Mohammedans in considerable numbers. In North Africa, beginning even before the middle of the last century, the Church Missionary Society sent missionaries to work among the Moslems, meeting with very little success. This work has been taken up in more recent years by the American Methodist Mission. Throughout the continent of Africa, less that one-twentieth

of the entire missionary body are seeking to reach the Mohammedans, and some Boards that set out to do missionary work
for Moslems have swung back to the native pagan populations.

Sumatra and Java present typical fields of work for Moslems
in Malaysia. The Baptist missionaries reached Sumatra in
1820. The American Board sent missionaries fourteen years
later, who were put to death. The Rhenish Missionary
Society entered the field in 1861 and other Societies from the
Netherlands are at work in the islands. There are probably
the largest returns in Java of converts from Mohammedans
of any Mohammedan field. There are six Dutch Missionary
Societies laboring in the islands, where, out of some 29,000,000
of population, more than 24,000,000 are Mohammedans.

The first effort made by the Protestant missions to reach
the Moslems of India was made by Henry Martyn, who has
already been mentioned. Missionaries of English, American,
European and Australian Protestant churches have at different times undertaken definite work for Moslems as well as
Hindus. This work has chiefly been devoted to the preparation of versions of Scripture in the languages spoken by
Mohammedans. The Missionary Societies most active in this
line are the Church Missionary Society, the Society for the
Propagation of the Gospel, the London Missionary Society,
Churches of Scotland Mission, American Presbyterian Mission, United Presbyterian Mission, American Methodist
Episcopal Mission, and the English and Australian Baptist
Missions. There have been a large number of conversions
from Mohammedanism to Christianity during these years,
but there has been little attempt to segregate and classify the
work for Mohammedans as over against work for Hindus.

The largest results and most effective work for the evangelization of Moslems in India has been through schools, where
spiritual lessons have been regularly taught, and those who
have sought baptism have given, as their reason for changing

their faith, reading the Bible or some religious tract, or the instruction received at the hand of some Christian teacher. The work in India has already been so aggressive that it has aroused the Moslems to a defense of their position.

As Moslems lay much store by " The Book " it was essential that the Christian Book shall be presented to them in their vernacular. This is in direct contrast to their own custom and tradition that the Koran cannot be translated into any other tongue.

It was a strategic move therefore to put into the hands of Moslem peoples, whom the Christian missionaries were attempting to reach, copies of the Christian Bible in whole or in part, in their spoken tongue. These versions, now in use and capable of production in any needed quantity, are as follows: the entire Bible in Arabic, Persian, Urdu, Osmanli Turkish, Azarbajani, Pashto, Kiswahili, Chinese, Ki-Ganda, Kashmiri, Gujarati and Punjabi. Translations of parts of the Bible or New Testament are in Uzbeg, Bashkir, Jagatai, Kalmuk, Karass, Bilochi, Malay, Javanese, Hansa, Kurdish, Bengali, Berber, Kabyle and Albanian. These, with the sacred scriptures in other languages understood and read by Mohammedans in various parts of the world, have made the Bible, in whole or in part, available for reaching by far the greater portion of the Moslem world. The most available of all the versions above enumerated is the Arabic, since it is so widely read by Moslems and also because Arabic is the sacred language of Islam.

In addition to these versions of the Christian Scriptures, there has been prepared an extensive Christian literature in many of the Moslem languages. This is primarily in the Arabic, Persian, Urdu and Turkish languages. Chinese Christian literature is available for all who speak and read the Chinese language. Dr. Tisdale tells us that, even now, nearly every Mohammedan who can read can obtain in his own tongue at least a portion of the Christian Scriptures or some other instructive Christian literature.

The preparation of an up-to-date general Christian literature for Moslems has not yet been seriously undertaken. The establishment of the Nile Mission Press in Cairo, Egypt, is for the purpose of meeting, in part at least, this crying need. Hitherto too much emphasis has been put upon controversy and too little upon constructive instruction in the fundamental facts and principles of Christianity. This preparation of an adequate Christian literature for Moslems can be achieved only by the united effort of different communions conscious of the fact that the Moslems do not need to understand sectarian differences; they do need to know the beauty and love of the glorified Christ. Translations from other languages can never meet the need. An adequate Christian literature for Moslems must be written for them, and not translated from books prepared for other peoples.

By no means has the Mohammedan world been covered by the modern missionary endeavor; in fact, it has hardly been touched. There are great centers of population in which no effort whatever is put forth to reach the followers of Mohammed. Although in these cities many missionaries may reside, no concerted effort to reach the Moslem peoples of the city has been made. There are more than thirty of these great cities containing many Moslems and a population of 100,000 or more, in nearly every one of which today are a few Christian missionaries, yet at none of these important centers are the efforts to reach the Moslems in any measure commensurate with the opportunities. Every one of the cities is calling for more missionaries and for an increased force.

One needs to take but a cursory glance at the parts of the world occupied by Moslems and compare their large populations with the small number of missionaries and Christian workers among them to get an impression of the fact that the conversion of the Mohammedan world has not yet been seriously undertaken. One of the reasons why so little effort has been concentrated upon the conversion of Mohammedans is the greater facility for approach and the more sympathetic response from other non-Christian races, peoples and religions.

Some of the reasons why, up to the present time, missionary work directly for and among Mohammedans has been looked upon as almost a failure may be enumerated. It should be noted, however, that it has not been by any means a failure, though the statistical returns have not been at all commensurate with the effort put forth or with similar efforts that have been made in Buddhist, Hindu or Confucian countries, or even among the pagan races of Africa. The following fundamental obstacles to the Christian approach needed first to be overcome. (1) The prejudice that exists among Mohammedans against Christianity. All Christian workers among Moslems must make tremendous effort in every direction to overcome the deep-seated and long-standing prejudice of most Moslems, wherever found, against Christianity. Various reasons have been given for this already, but we will recapitulate a few of these. The first is the fact that the Mohammedan contact with Christian nations has been the contact of war, in which Christians have shown little or none of the spirit of Christ. and it was natural for the Mohammedan to interpret what he saw in the acts of the Christian nations as a direct representation of what Christianity actually is. We need not refer back to the conflict beginning even in the days of Mohammed and extending all down through the centuries, but to the more recent contacts of Mohammedans in Turkey, for instance, with the Armenian, Greek and Syrian races, which have from the beginning been more or less in conflict with the Mohammedan government, — and it must be confessed that in multitudes of instances they have not revealed the true spirit of Christ in dealing with their Mohammedan neighbors. Turkey has repeatedly complained of her treatment at the hands of Russia, a so-called Christian country, and it must be confessed that Russia's dealings with Turkey have not all been along Christian lines. The same may be said of the Christian nations of Europe, who have exploited Turkey and have used, in this exploitation, their great military strength and power. The result has been that the Mohammedans of the Turkish empire, and undoubtedly, through them, the Mohammedans of other countries, have been greatly influenced; they have looked upon Christianity as a hostile religion, believing that a nation that has become Christian will necessarily be opposed to any Mohammedan country, this fact being emphasized by the gradual elimination of Mohammedan nations and peoples as independent governments, and the setting up over them of Christian rule. It is natural that the Mohammedans of North Africa, Arabia, Egypt, the entire Turkish Empire, and Persia, should regard Christianity as a religion of oppression that sets itself up as the enemy of Mohammedanism and the subjugator of Mohammedan countries. The Mohammedans of India recognize British rule, which assumed control over them without their consent or approval, but to which they are bound to submit. They have not always been friendly to the British Government, although they have probably been as much so as the Hindus. The conflict in India between Christianity and Mohammedanism is not so marked as in the other countries above named.

Quite in addition to this is the personal contact of a multitude of Mohammedans with Christians, and here again we go back to the contact with members of the Oriental Churches, which have kept up the form of Christianity and of Christian worship but have lost, often entirely, generally largely, the spirit of Christ himself. They have seen men professing to be Christian, even Christian leaders in the work of the church, whose word could not be trusted in matters of business, and they have seen Christian leaders excessively use intoxicating drinks. They have seen members of marauding bands who were representatives of Christian peoples. This has gone on to such an extent that among many Mohammedans the idea is firmly fixed, that the Mohammedan is honest, upright, truthful, while the Christians are the reverse.

Among the wild tribes of Africa who have recently come into Mohammedanism this prejudice is not so deeply fixed as in the Turkish empire and in other sections where for generations Mohammedans and Christians have lived side by side, and where the Mohammedans have seen the examples of un-Christian living on the part of their so-called Christian neighbors. A Mohammedan who had read the New Testament with great earnestness once told the writer, in the presence of a large number of Armenians, that, after reading the teachings of Christ and the apostles, he had come to the conclusion that there was not a single Christian in his town, that every one of them lived contrary to the teachings of Christ.

It is only in comparatively recent years that missionaries have taken up their residence among these Mohammedans and have begun to make an impression upon these prejudices that have become almost a part of the Moslem creed. There is yet, however, much to be done before the way will open for an unprejudiced approach to the Mohammedan with the direct Christian message. This prejudice has constituted a barrier that seemed at times unsurmountable and has led many to say that Christianity can never make progress among Mohammedans.

(2) The methods of approach have not always been intelligent. Missionaries who have been sent to the Mohammedans have gone unprepared for their task, with little—often with no knowledge whatever of the Koran or of Mohammedan or Eastern tradition, and without capacity to look at religious questions from a Mohammedan point of view. Not infrequently these missionaries have fallen below the intel-

lectual and educational standards which we now see are essential for a strong and confident approach to intelligent Mohammedans. This has handicapped the missionary, who has thus been forced to deal blindly with the great fundamental questions of the Mohammedan religion and to trust to chance for his ability to present the Christian message in any way calculated to command the hearing and the respect of those whom he attempted to reach.

One sometimes marvels, in the face of these facts, that so deep and wide an impression has already been made upon the Mohammedans during the last century, and that so many, especially in Java and in India, have been led to accept Christianity, and that so much success has been witnessed in the breaking down of prejudice and opening the door of approach to the Moslem mind and heart.

(3) The absence of a satisfactory literature has been a handicap to all missionary endeavor. It is only in comparatively recent years that the Bible, especially the New Testament, has been in any large measure translated into the languages spoken by the Mohammedans, so that the missionary did not have even the Bible at hand through which he could approach the Mohammedan and put into his hands the Book which was the foundation and guide of Christianity.

There has been almost an entire absence of other religious literature that was calculated to command the attention of the Mohammedan and secure for it a thoughtful reading. This subject has been touched upon already, so need not be here widely discussed, but it is an important topic and must account for much of the failure of the missionary effort hitherto to make a deep impression upon Mohammedan followers.

(4) We of the western world have failed to recognize that Mohammedanism is an Oriental religion, that as such it has survived the centuries. Because of this failure, we have approached the Mohammedan with what is really an Oriental

religion, but which has been so thoroughly Westernized that the modern or Western features have been put to the front and so changed that, quite apart from Mohammedan prejudice, the presentation of Christianity has awakened opposition because of its appearing to the Moslem as Occidental.

This too reveals the importance of a careful preparation upon the part of all those who would influence Mohammedan thinking and especially Mohammedan belief, to get themselves into the Eastern atmosphere and to come to the Mohammedans with a religion that is adapted to them, presenting those phases of Christianity which were received from the East and which, if stripped of their Western garb, are just as suited to the East as to the West.

(5) The missionaries to the Mohammedan have put too much emphasis upon a formal creed and too little upon the great fundamental principles of Christianity. They seemed to forget that the heart of Christianity is in the life, and that it is manifested primarily not by statements of belief but by a changed life that is hid with Christ in God. Some of the missionaries to Mohammedans have seemed to feel it to be their duty as Christian teachers to put forth, early in their contact with the Mohammedans, some formal statement of doctrine or belief and demand assent to that statement. Such creeds have invariably repelled the Mohammedan and impressed upon his mind a conviction that Christianity is as formal as Mohammedanism, and that one is initiated into it by the acceptance and utterance of a creedal statement, and that thereafter nothing remains but to conform to the demands of Christianity so far as details of worship are concerned. Presentation of a creed at the outset has blinded the eyes of the Moslems to the spiritual nature of our religion and has made it very much more difficult thereafter for them to grasp this fact.

(6) The isolated, fragmentary and unconnected character of the attempts to reach the Mohammedan world have but

displayed the weakness of the approach. The different Societies have entered upon the conquest of Mohammedanism without connection with each other, without plan of campaign, with no unity in policy and with an absence of plan for the training of missionaries for their great and almost impossible task. It is inevitable that a great campaign entered upon in such a way must lose much that might have been won by unity of plan and purpose and by the closest kind of cooperation.

(7) There has also been a failure on the part of the Christian church to grasp the immensity of the task and to plan for it accordingly. While the efforts were fragmentary and isolated on the field, they but exhibited the attitude of the Church at home,—an attitude of isolation and of uncorrelated plans. The Church has failed to comprehend the fact that the 230,000,000 of Mohammedans, presenting a more formidable opposition to the Christian approach than any two hundred and thirty millions of any other religion or race, cannot be won incidentally or fragmentarily. They have failed to grasp the fact that there is a general spirit of unity running through the Mohammedan world in matters of belief, and an opposition more significant and powerful than that which exists among any other race or any other people, with the possible exception of the Jews. Such unity in faith, in practice, and in protest, cannot be won except by a corresponding unity in the Church of Christ.

CHAPTER XVI

CHANGED ATTITUDE TOWARDS CHRISTIANITY

A missionary, writing in the *Punjab Missionary News*, speaks of the great change that has taken place in the last fifty years in the attitude of the Mohammedans of India toward Christianity. A few years ago it was common for a Mohammedan on hearing the name of Christ to show his disgust by spitting. Sometimes he went so far as to attempt to drown the sound of Christ's name and to cleanse his ears from the pollution of hearing it by a loud repetition of the creed of Islam. It was not uncommon for the Bible to be snatched from a missionary's hand, thrown on the ground and trampled on. All this within the experience of missionaries now in the field.

This hatred and contempt does not seem to exist at the present time, but there is a certain fear of the mystical power emanating from the name of Christ and from the Bible itself. Many Mohammedan boys come to mission schools with strict injunctions not to touch the Bible for fear of some occult influence.

The same missionary reports that, at the present time, they meet Mullahs as well as other Moslems who possess Bibles and who read them. Mohammedan men of all classes are seeking to secure copies of the Bible. In the higher educational institutions where regular Bible readings are given, and where the students are not requested to buy a Bible, more and more these students come and ask where they can get copies, and after procuring them, they bring them with them to the class. Occasionally a Bible is left lying about, and examination shows that the Mohammedan owner has been studying it carefully and making notes in the margin, while now and then a student will say, " We come to college to learn the

233

Bible. We learn the Koran at school but not the Bible, and the Bible is as much our book as it is yours. We want to know it."

The three steps in the changing attitude of Mohammedans toward Christianity as reported are: (1) that of contempt and hatred; (2) of fear and a certain degree of reverence; and (3) a desire to study and learn the contents and claims of Christianity.

As to the sale of Bibles among Moslems in recent years, we glean from the report of the British and Foreign Bible Society regarding its work in the Singapore agency for 1914:

" At the close of 1912 there had been an increase of nearly a hundred per cent. in Bible sales over the previous year. Java, with its population of 33,000,000, does not contain more than 3,000,000 who can read, but the outlook is splendid. Everywhere new schools are springing up."

" The value of the sales in Java is greatly increased and ninety-eight per cent. of the sales are to Mohammedans; but only those who have worked as Christian missionaries in Moslem lands can fully realize what that means. But even better is the knowledge that many of these Mohammedan people who buy a portion of the Bible subsequently return to our colporteurs and purchase a Testament or other parts of the Bible. ' A little leaven, leaveneth the whole lump,' and we are certain that these silent messengers are working into the lives and homes of Java's millions, and are already bearing fruit unto Life Eternal. . . .

" One hears from time to time criticisms of our work, more especially as regards the work amongst Mohammedans. Such critics generally say that the Malays and Javanese do not want our books, and only buy them for their pretty covers. To deal with these criticisms, and also to give information to those who have the welfare of the Moslems at heart, I will deal with both these matters. All our Malay and Javanese books are bound in thin covers of common grey paper, useless for any other purpose, and worth only a fraction of the price charged for the books. In reply to the former, I would quote the following figures of our sales for the past three years of Malay and Javanese books, almost all of which were bought by Moslems:

	1911	1912	1913
Malay Arabic sales	10,709	13,500	17,230
Malay Roman	10,011	11,223	15,930
Javanese	14,155	26,499	40,947

" If the Mohammedans do not want our books, how is it that they purchase them in increasing quantities every year? I am more inclined to believe that a man who has bought one book and read it, goes and tells his friends what a treasure he has found, with the result that they buy for themselves, while he buys several other portions next time he sees a colporteur."[1]

Dr. George F. Herrick, for fifty years in Turkey and in close personal contact with Mohammedans throughout the entire period, in an article in the *Moslem World* for October, 1914, states that we need to go back only about fifty years, in all parts of the Moslem world, to find an attitude toward Christians of conscious superiority coupled with contemptuous indifference or with pronounced repugnance. Today, Dr. Herrick reports — and he speaks primarily for the situation in the Turkish empire—that among intelligent Moslems the contemptuous indifference has everywhere disappeared; that the repugnance has, in recent years, deepened into more bitter hatred among many; that this has been caused especially in the Near East through the conviction of intelligent Moslems, that among the Christian nations of Europe injustice and disregard of solemn treaties has been exhibited toward the weakening Moslem states. At the same time he reports that, among the thinking Mohammedans the question is seriously being raised as to whether in Christianity itself, as over against that which has been exhibited to them by the so-called Christian nations, there is that which is able to uplift and elevate a people? This is a question raised by the great number of Moslems who are solicitous for the moral and spiritual elevation of their people. With these, the assumption of the superiority of Islam over Christianity has been destroyed.

Dr. Herrick expresses his conviction that never before has the Moslem world been so open to the influence of the Christian as it is today. The only question therefore for us to

[1] *Moslem World,* January, 1915, p. 86.

consider is how to meet the opportunity. In answering this, he puts first the spirit of conciliation, sympathy and fraternity. Anything that reveals that side of Christianity is welcomed by the Turks as a demonstration of Christianity working in the hearts of those who live a friendly, sympathetic life among them and who show that spirit in their beneficence.

Dr. Herrick also says:

" It is my conviction also that there are many things in Islam which the Christian can approve and accept. We can accept their theology as far as it goes, supplementing it with the doctrine of the fatherhood of God, and of sin as guilt, sin not simply ignored by divine pity, but demanding an almighty and atoning Savior. We can approve, and might well adopt, the Moslem's reverential attitude and spirit in worship. The name of their religion, ' Islam,' surrender, and ' Moslem,' one self-surrendered to God, appeals strongly to the thoughtful Christian. We can pray the prayer of the first sura with our Moslem brethren. It would hardly be a loss to Christianity, it might be a gain, if our call to prayer, like theirs, were by the trained human voice from a high position, instead of by a bell.

Conciliation, however, does not imply nor demand compromise. When your Moslem friend says, ' Why, we are agreed. All that remains is for you to accept our faith with yours,' we have to call a halt. Christianity and Islam are not at all identical. When we touch the life, the moral and spiritual life, they are not even similar.

The Moslem's apprehension of the moral attributes of God differs widely from that of the Christian. Paternal love has no place in his view of God. According to Islam, mercy and justice have no relation one to the other. Sin is not guilt, but weakness, and is forgiven through pity to the formally penitent. Religion and the life are strangers, one to the other. ' Yes, he is a liar, but very religious. To be sure, he is a murderer, but he prays five times a day. He is a thief, but he says, " bismillah," in God's name, when he goes on his robber's errand.' "

Direct evangelistic work for Moslems is carried on in Egypt perhaps more aggressively and successfully than in any other part of the Levant. Public preaching services for Moslems are held in Cairo at four centers every week, and the meetings are largely attended. Tent meetings have been held in some of the villages. At all meetings a considerable quantity of Christian literature is distributed as well as among the thousands of pilgrims starting on their journey to Mecca. These services are simple and unostentatious. A table is there for holding the Bible, a chair for a pulpit, with singing in Arabic, a prayer and then an address. It is only occasionally that someone tries to draw the crowd away or enters into controversy with the preacher. Usually good order has been maintained, with an attendance running from 50 to 125 and with real interest manifested. The Scriptures in the vernacular are sold at the close of the meeting.

Dr. Zwemer sums up, in his *Mohammed or Christ*, the modern movement in the Near East in the following words:

" There is not the least doubt that tens of thousands of Moslems in Turkey and Persia, and even in Arabia, are intellectually convinced of the truth of Christianity as opposed to Islam. The philosophical disintegration of Islam, which began in Persia by the rise of Moslem sects, is now being hastened by means of newspaper discussions. There is a general unrest. There are frantic attempts to save the ship by throwing overboard much of the old cargo. The attack on orthodox Mohammedanism was never so keen or strong on the part of any missionary as has been the attack from those inside Islam. If you will read the report of the Mecca Conference, when forty Moslems met together in secret conclave to point out the causes of decay in their religion and listed them — fifty and more defects in this religion of their Prophet — and published the list as a document to scatter over the Moslem world, you will no longer accuse any missionary of dealing harshly with this issue of falsehoods buttressed by some great truths which we call Islam. If Islam reformed is Islam no longer, then what will take the place of the old traditions? When the shriek of the locomotive is heard at Mecca, will Arabia sleep on in its patriarchal sleep? Will the nomads beat their swords into plowshares and their spears into pruning-hooks, when modern irrigation transforms the desert into a garden? Will Mohammedanism with its ideals prevail, or Christianity? Will polygamy or monogamy? Will a free press or a press that is throttled? Will the Constitution or the Koran be the law of Western Asia?"

The Moslems are attempting to stem the tide of Christian advance by a kind of back-fire. In Lahore, India, they have organized a Mohammedan Tract and Book Depot. On May 30, 1914, they issued a catalogue of 67 books and pamphlets, all in English, besides some also in Urdu. In a brief preface to the catalogue, the following statement is made respecting the purpose of the new enterprise:

" This depot was opened after long and careful consideration. Its main object is the publication of books, the study of which would not only be a source of pleasure but also afford moral and spiritual instruction, teaching men to hate vice and love virtue; to bear a good moral character; to shun evil company; to regard the Supreme Being with due awe and reverence; to kindle a desire for piety; to fulfill the duties laid upon man by God; to promote mutual sympathy and goodwill; to put away prejudice, malice, annoyance, irreligiousness, bigotry, disobedience, etc.; and especially to become perfectly acquainted with the Tenets of Islam, in order to be able to cope successfully with its opponents; and, lastly, to have a true and complete knowledge of our illustrious predecessors and their glorious deeds."[2]

There is an Islamic Society in Edinburgh which was instituted in 1908 in the University Union, meeting on Sunday afternoons during the winter and summer terms. " The objects of the society are: (1) To promote the religious, social, moral, intellectual and commercial advancement of the Moslem world. (2) To provide and maintain means of social and literary intercourse for its members. (3) To remove misconceptions prevailing among non-Moslems regarding Islam and its believers. (4) To render legitimate assistance to the best of its ability to any Moslem requiring it. (5) To provide facilities for conducting religious ceremonies. (6) To hold debates and socials, and to read papers likely to further the interests of Islam. (7) To acquire, arrange and preserve literary and scientific works on Islamic subjects for the use of its members. (8) To collect funds in order to carry out the various objects of the Society." [3]

[2] *Moslem World*, April, 1915, p. 186.
[3] *Ibid*, p. 203.

The Mohammedans look upon Christianity as representing the advanced spirit and thought of the West. They are accustomed to consider Western civilization as Christian civilization, as over against their own, which is of the East. Many of the more progressive Mohammedans are attempting to engraft upon Mohammedan institutions the spirit and progress of the Western world. In apologizing for Mohammedan history they attempt to show that Islam has not been propagated by the sword; that slavery is not one of their religious institutions; and that the Prophet did not permit polygamy. The educated Moslems are breaking away from their old traditions and are attempting to drive all religious ideas and interpretations back to the Koran itself. Intelligent Mohammedans see the value of modern education, and while the conservatives are suspicious of everything that is modern, including all forms of education, the more advanced thinkers and the more enlightened are endeavoring to find some way of escape, by which Mohammedanism may be retained as a religion and at the same time secure for its followers all of the advantages of the advancement and education of the West. The Moslem press, in many countries, is taking up and discussing at length these new and even revolutionary ideas. Various and popular movements and leagues are being formed among the Mohammedans of India, Java, Egypt, etc., in an endeavor to promote the new spirit while retaining the old religion. Many of these movements were inaugurated since the beginning of this century. Perhaps the most advanced step in this direction has been taken among the Javanese, where for the last twenty-five years a very marked advance has been made in modern thinking and in liberality of interpretation. One of the most interesting features, and most encouraging withal, is the way in which in tracts and in newspaper articles these matters are openly discussed. There could be no better way to enlighten the minds of the reading Moslem public; and as the discussion goes on, the defenders of the new movement become more bold, and at the same time the spirit of independence and of freedom of thought is developed.

" Perhaps it is a fair estimate to say that from two to four millions of the total Moslem world population have so far adopted Western education and broken away from the old Islamic standards of orthodox tradition that they should be classified as ' New School Moslems.' These are found especially in India, Egypt, Turkey, Algiers, and Persia. Not all of them have adopted Western civilisation, but Western educational methods and ideals have compelled them to restate their own beliefs or doubts, and to modify their social and moral standards to such an extent that they have clearly separated themselves from the masses.

Although Moslem education still divides itself along Western and Eastern lines, the methods and ideals of the West are pushing their way everywhere. Colonial expansion and commercial exploitation in Africa as well as in the Mohammedan lands of Asia by the marking out of spheres of influence, the building of railways, the growing influence of the Moslem press, the competition as well as the example of the mission schools — all these tend to accelerate this movement for higher education."[4]

Moslems are seriously discussing in these days the comparative religious values of Christianity and Mohammedanism, and they are considering the two central personalities of these two religions and their respective merits — Jesus Christ and Mohammed.

" A proof of the extent of preaching in the mission schools is the fact that you cannot find two Moslem children one of whom is taught in a Moslem school and the other in a Christian school but you see them quarrelling in the street on such a question as this: Who is the greatest, the Messiah or Mohammed? and very probably both of them are the sons of one pious Moslem. The other day while I was reclining in my house I heard a quarrel in the street between a boy and a girl. A negro servant was helping the boy in his argument. The boy was crying ' Christ is not greater than Mohammed,' but the girl replied, ' Teacher told us that Christ was greater than Mohammed and all other creatures, for He saved men from their sins.' When they came to me, I made clear to the boy that his sister was in the right and he in the wrong."[5]

[4] S. M. Zwemer, " Mohammed or Christ."
[5] For further discussion of this subject, see S. M. Zwemer's " Mohammed or Christ." Chap. XIV.

Many Mohammedan tracts are being issued in Egypt and in North Africa bearing titles taken from Christianity, many of these being bitter attacks against Christianity. At the same time, the Mohammedans are free to discuss the acts of Christian nations of Europe, judging them by the Christian standards of the New Testament, thus showing that they are not only studying the New Testament and the great fundamentals of our Christian faith but are passing judgment upon so-called Christian nations whenever they violate the clear teachings of the Gospels. All this is encouraging in the highest degree, since it shows an intelligent investigation of what Christianity is and an intelligent and practical application of Christianity to the life of the nation as well as to the life of individuals. Much reliance can be put upon the Moslem press in the future for the dissemination of Christian truths and for providing the arena in which Christian and Mohammedan teachings are arrayed, one against the other.

" The Christian theologian can denounce the Koran as a fabrication and a fraud, but the Mussulman, although he may allege interpolations in the Biblical text, is prevented by his own religious belief from denying the Divine origin of the Christian Scriptures. Similarly, a Christian may call the prophet of Islam an impostor, and an evil person, but a Mussulman's religion imposes upon him respect for the personality and character of Jesus Christ as a Messenger of God."[6]

Dr. Zwemer says that the World Missionary Conference at Edinburgh was reported at length in the leading Moslem papers of Cairo, that the translations of missionary literature published in New York appear in the daily papers of Lahore, India; that the Moslem press is alert on all important matters taking place in the civilized world.

Dr. Zwemer quotes 'Ata Hussein Bey who, in a volume on political economy and the history of civilization, wrote at length of Jesus Christ and his teachings. In this article the

[6] The *Comrade* of Calcutta, India (May 30, 1914), quoted by Dr. Zwemer in his "Mohammed or Christ."

Mohammedan author quotes with fair sympathy some of the very fundamental teachings of Christ. He speaks of his interest in the poor and despised, of his mingling with them and blessing them and thus laying the foundation of the community life, of his commendation of fellowship and service and brotherhood. But he speaks most emphatically and unreservedly of the universal love which Jesus taught to his disciples and to the world, claiming that this was the fulfillment of the entire law, even commanding that men love their enemies and those that harm them. The Mohammedan author goes on to say that this is the principle of life higher than all other principles, and closes his statement as follows: " All this the well balanced mind accepts and approves of, but the question arises, is it possible for a man to love his enemies and do good to those that hate him?"

" The prophets and reformers have been and always will be men of like passions with us, with this all-important difference — that in them the Divine spark was not suffered prematurely to die away. They felt the inward message and determined to carry it out. . . . Socrates condemned as a corrupter of youth, Jesus crucified as a setter forth of strange things, Mohammed persecuted for his religious mission . . . the world, however, only sees at rare intervals the vision — the supreme beatific vision of a Socrates, a Jesus, a Mohammed. . . . Is it not religion . . . which falls on dry hearts like rain, and which whispers to self-weary moribund man, ' Thou must be born again '? ' Sons of God,' he writes, have the wisdom of this world as well as of the next; the highest goal in life is to become like to God with a pure mind, and to draw near to Him and to abide in Him"; and again, " The governing principles of all religions is the same. In the language of the apostle James (sic): ' Pure religion and undefiled before God and the Father is this, to visit the fatherless and widows in their affliction, and to keep oneself unspotted from the world.' "[7]

At the Moslem Anglo-Oriental Educational Conference held in Lucknow, India, in December, 1912, a reception was given to the delegates by Reid Christian College and Isabella

[7] Mr. G. Khuda Bukhsh (*Essays, Indian and Islamic*, quoted by Dr. Zwemer, on page 266 of his *Mohammed or Christ*).

Thoburn College. Two hundred Moslems were present. The Chairman, Major Seyyid Hassan Bilgrami, M.D., there made an address in which he praised the efforts of missionary education from the days of Carey and Marshman. He mentioned not only the educational institutions of India but some of the leading Christian Colleges of Turkey. A leading Moslem paper in Cairo, Egypt, strongly advocated the establishment of the Cairo Christian University, now in process of organization, and prophesied for it a great future, " although," said the writer, " we know that the college will be established in the name of evangelism and be guided by the missionaries."

Dr. Zwemer says that there never was so much friendliness, such willingness to discuss the question at issue, such a large attendance of Moslems at Christian hospitals and public meetings, and even preaching services as there is today. And this is true in spite of public warnings against having dealings with Christian missionaries. The American Mission in Egypt has a committee on evangelistic work, and has made the following report:

" At no time in the history of the Mission has there been such an urgent call for aggressive evangelism among all classes. The special religious awakening among educated Moslems in all parts of Egypt has brought upon us the two-fold burden: First, how to deal with convicted and converted Moslems; and second, how to meet the antagonistic opposition of Moslem societies. This awakening has brought about such a spirit of inquiry, with the result that an overwhelming number of Mohammedans are prepared to hear the Gospel and to study the Bible, that we find ourselves insufficient in number and equipment to deal successfully with the present situation."

This chapter might be increased to an indefinite length, showing that wherever Christian missionaries have been brought for a long time into contact with the forces of Islam a changed attitude on the part of the Mohammedans is becoming rapidly and increasingly apparent. Old prejudices seem to be breaking, and the Mohammedans are beginning to see that Christianity has something which they do not possess and which is necessary for moral, intellectual, social and national advance. The light is shining into the darkened Mohammedan mind; or, to change the figure, the old barriers that separated so effectively the Moslem and Christian worlds are becoming shattered and the way of approach to the Mohammedan mind and the Mohammedan heart is becoming easier because of the marked change in the way in which the Mohammedans look upon Christian truth and the openness of mind with which they are ready to consider fundamental truths against which they set their faces like steel a generation ago. What may we not expect from Turkey, disintegrating as a great national force, its people conscious of the failure of their religion to meet the requirements of their national life? What may we not expect from Arabia, with its brilliant history of the past but for several centuries subject to the oppressive forces of Ottoman Turkey, now emancipated from the cruel military autocracy and left free to control her own institutions and to fall into line with the progress of modern civilization? Arabia allied herself with the great Christian forces of the West, and we may expect that she will take her place as one of the constructive elements in the Near East. The same is true in a measure of the Moslems of India and of Egypt and of North Africa, whose attitude toward the Christian West has already met with fundamental revolutionary changes.

CHAPTER XVII

DIFFICULTIES CONFRONTED

In approaching Mohammedans with the message of the Gospel, missionaries have too frequently failed to comprehend the methods of thought and habit of mind characteristic of the Oriental. We have made the same mistake with all Orientals, endeavoring to influence and convince them by the same arguments we would use at home. The missionaries are only more recently beginning to comprehend the fact that to an Oriental an illustration is vastly more persuasive than a syllogism, and is more liable to secure his assent and win his allegiance.

Another trait of mind common if not universal in the East is inability to recognize that it is at least contrary to what we term the laws of thought to entertain at the same time two mutually contradictory or exclusive systems of philosophy or religion. When one encounters an unquestioned case of this kind, he is at first inclined to charge gross insincerity, but longer acquaintance convinces him that it is quite possible for a man of decided intelligence to accept without question the teachings of one religion and continue faithfully to practise the forms of another. The writer has conversed with a university trained Brahmin in India who freely and emphatically declared his belief in Jesus Christ as the true and only savior of men, while he continued to practise Hinduism. When asked how such things could be, he replied, " It is impossible to study the life and teachings of Christ and not be convinced of their unquestioned truth, but I continue the practice of Hinduism because that is my religion." This has been clearly expressed by Professor Macdonald in his *Religious Attitude and Life in Islam*. He says (page 7):

" The Oriental has the most astonishing keenness in viewing, grasping, analyzing a single point, and when he has finished with that point, can take up a series of others in the same way. But these points remain for him separate; he does not co-ordinate them. They may be contradictory; that does not trouble him. When he constructs systems — as he often does — it is by taking a single point, and spinning everything out of it; not by taking many points and weaving them together. Thus, he may criticise one point and be quite indifferent to the consequent necessity, for us at least, of criticising other points."

The Oriental, and especially the Moslem, seems to have no vivid sense at all of the presence of law in the physical, intellectual and moral universe. He postulates the supernatural and to him all actions and reactions spring from the immediate will of God. It does not occur to him to attempt to reconcile the phenomena that he observes or by any process of investigation to trace these phenomena to their source. To him anything, everything, is equally possible, and his mind demands no explanation of what he sees. Nothing to him is incompatible and the most contradictory facts engender in him no spirit of inquiry.

This state of mind may not be found in all individuals in precisely the same degree, and yet one who expects to lead the man of the East to change his philosophy or his religion must recognize the laws, or, should we say, the lack of laws by which the mind of that man operates. He must not expect to find in the thinking of the Oriental ability to see life steadily as a whole and to grasp firmly the principles and system of our Christian theology. It is at this point more than at any other that we declare the necessity of the Christian missionary's orientalizing himself before he may expect to achieve success in reaching the other man. Hitherto the effort has too often been to occidentalize the Oriental when he accepts Christianity. This is by no means desirable. The Westerner should recognize that Christianity is capable of being grasped and applied by the Oriental, in his Oriental method of thinking, and made a vital part of his Oriental philosophy, and of becoming a power in his Oriental life and in the society in which that life is passed. We must remember that all the great religions, including Christianity, had their rise in the East, and that the West has never produced a commanding religion and probably has little to contribute to the religions that exist. Additions to Christian thought made in the West do not make it more acceptable to the Eastern mind.

In addition to what has already been said on this subject, it may be well to bring together some of the many reasons why the conversion of Islam presents such a formidable task to the Christian Church. They are the following:

(1) The attitude of Mohammed himself to Christianity — an attitude bequeathed to his followers — constitutes a very great obstacle to missionary effort among Moslems. Judaism and Christianity were known in Arabia in the time of the Prophet. He hoped to be recognized by both and to win both. He thought at first that the Jews would recognize him as the successor of their own prophets, and that Christians would recognize him as a successor to Jesus, who, being later than Jesus, superseded him. In both these hopes Mohammed was disappointed. Judaism and Christianity rejected him. He accordingly regarded them as rivals, and took pains in the Koran to fortify Islam against them. His knowledge of Christianity was imperfect. It was gained partly from Zeid, a slave boy from a Christian family whom Mohammed freed and adopted, partly from " Coptic Mary," the slave concubine sent him by the Christian governor of Egypt, partly from Christian anchorites in Arabia, and partly from such slight contact with Christians as occurred on his two trading expeditions to Syria, one when he was twelve, and the other when he was twenty-five years old.

From these sources he gained such knowledge of Jesus that he had the highest reverence for him. He regarded him as a Prophet (see Sura 5^{50,77}), believed in his miraculous birth

(Sura 3[40 ff]), and credited the marvellous stories concerning his childhood that are told in Apocryphal Gospels (see Sura 5[110 ff]), yet he strenuously denied that Jesus was the Son of God (see Sura 2[110]; 10[69]; 23[92]). Jesus was a prophet or an apostle, but nothing more.

In the 7th century the Eastern Church practised the worship of icons — images or pictures. This Mohammed, no doubt, witnessed in Syria and he regarded it as idolatry (compare Sura 43[86] with 10[29]). He seems also to have curiously misunderstood the doctrine of the Trinity, supposing it to teach the deity of God, Christ, and the Virgin Mary. This fundamental Christian conception of God he accordingly denounced in the Koran, asserting that Jesus denied its truth, or, at least, never said anything to justify men in believing it (see Sura 5[116 ff]). He asserts emphatically that Jesus is not God nor equal to God; that those who say so lie (Sura 5[76]; 9[30 ff]). Sura 2[115], when taken in its context, charges Christians with misinterpretation of their own Scriptures and implies that this is the basis of their false doctrines, while Sura 15[90 ff] is usually understood to charge Jesus and Christians with alternating their Scriptures. Mohammed thus not only denied the central doctrines of Christianity but gave the Mohammedans in the Koran itself authority for charging that those doctrines rest upon a perversion of the meaning and text of the Bible. In addition to all this in Sura 5[56] the Prophet warned his followers against taking Christians for their patrons, declaring that those who did so were, like the Christians, unbelievers; (compare Sura 5[76,77]). The experiences of Mohammed and his misconceptions concerning Christianity led him in this way so to arm his followers against the real Christ that it is difficult to pierce their defenses.

(2) The fact that Mohammedans are widely scattered over the world. It is not one compact people, like the Hindus of India, found almost wholly within the bounds of one country, or like the Buddhists, who, although occupying two or three

different countries, are very concentrated in Ceylon, China, Japan. The Mohammedans occupy widely separate areas, while maintaining a unity as strong as, if not stronger than, that which binds the Hindus or the Buddhists together.

When we set out to consider the Mohammedan world, we have before us large sections of Russia, the Balkan peninsula, Turkey, Afghanistan, Morocco, Algeria, Tunisia, The Sudan, the Sahara and other sections of Africa, the Malay Archipelago, nearly all parts of India, widely separated sections of China, the Philippine Islands, besides other scattered areas. One has but to read over the names of the countries in which Mohammedans are found to see how difficult it is to think of them as a unity or to plan any campaign that would embrace Mohammedans in all parts of the world. While there may be some advantage in this fact, owing to their separation and therefore their inability to rally for each other's protection against the encroachment of Christianity, there are many disadvantages which must be taken into consideration by the Church in its plan for Christian conquest.

(3) These widely scattered Mohammedans do not speak the same language. There is no language that represents the spoken tongue of the Moslems of the world. Arabic has been called the Mohammedan language, since it is the sacred language of Islam, in which for centuries the Koran only existed. While there are probably more Mohammedans who speak or read the Arabic than any other language, yet one with a speaking knowledge of the Arabic would find himself greatly limited in his attempt to approach the Mohammedan world.

The 20,000,000 of Mohammedans in Russia do not all speak the same tongue; neither do all the Mohammedans of Turkey, where the Albanian, Turkish, Kurdish and Arabic languages are widely used. The same is true of the Mohammedans of India. There is no one language that reaches them all. Neither is there any one Mohammedan tongue for China; the Mohammedans of the Mandarin-speaking districts speak the Mandarin language, and in areas where other Chinese tongues are spoken, that is the language also of the Moslems.

This difficulty is not confined wholly to the Mohammedans, for we find it in India in working for the Hindus, where a variety of languages are spoken; and there are several different languages and dialects in China. But probably the Mohammedan world is more affected than any other two hundred thirty millions of followers of any one of the great religions in any part of the world. This makes it impossible to prepare any one piece of literature for all Moslems. They must be dealt with in language zones.

(4) The deep-seated prejudice, more so than in any other religion, against Christianity, amounting in some places to an outspoken and almost violent hatred. This subject has been touched upon elsewhere, hence there is no necessity for extensive statements here. It is a well recognized fact that Mohammedans look upon Christians as their hereditary enemies and Christianity as their only rival among all other religions; only Christians have attempted to change their belief; only Christians have sent missionaries among them and prepared a literature in their tongue calculated to reveal Christianity as a superior religion. If Christians were out of the way, Islam would have a free hand among all other religions.

(5) The divided character of Christendom. . . . Repeatedly Mohammedans, when approached with the Christian message, have referred to the fact that Christendom is hopelessly broken up into sects that are hostile to each other, and that it is futile for Christianity to attempt to win Mohammedanism until it can become united in itself. Many Mohammedans who bring this protest against Christianity fail to recognize the divided state of Islam, to which reference has already been made; and yet, in all of the divisions of Mohammedanism, there is one underlying current of unity. To them this

seems to be wholly lacking in Christianity, giving the impression that the Christian Church does not represent union but rather a combination of contending and hostile bodies, none of which follow the teachings of Jesus Christ, who enjoined love upon his disciples and who fundamentally believed in the doctrine of the brotherhood of all men, for which, in their judgment, Christianity stands.

On April 16th, 1916, there was printed in the *Boston Herald* a communication from a Mohammedan living in Arlington, Mass., expressing the Mohammedan point of view on the subject of the division in the Christian Church. This Mohammedan writes in part as follows:

" After reading various sermons on the Haverhill riots (which occurred two or three weeks before, caused by the efforts of a preacher to set forth in public the weakness of the Catholic Church, and which led to wide discussion in the press and in the pulpit) I was impressed with the idea that the Christian religion as practised and preached in Christendom, instead of inculcating the Golden Rule, seems to increase the religious bigotry and hatred throughout the world. The trouble with Christian churches is that they lay more stress upon their creeds and ceremonies than upon the practical daily application of the teachings of Jesus. The churches have entirely misunderstood Christianity as given to the world by its founder. Why does the Turkish Government maintain a guard of soldiers in the holy sepulchre at Jerusalem?

Most of the ceremonial in the churches is an adaptation of the old pagan ritual grafted onto Christianity at the time Rome became Christian, and the churches stand for authority and obedience to their rites rather than the conduct of the individual in right living.

. . . There must be something wrong with the ethical teachings of the Bible which makes the love of money the controlling object in life of the Jew and the Christian, for where else in the world do you find such enormous fortunes, gotten no matter how, as you find among the multimillionaires of Christendom. And this spirit of greed and covetousness is demonstrated by the great world powers of Christendom who have robbed the rest of mankind of their countries and liberties. Why is it that the Turkish Government has always given an asylum to the Jews when they were persecuted by Christian powers? Because, of all the people of Turkey, not Mohammedans, the Jew was the only one that never manufactured, sold or handled intoxicating liquor."

(6) It is probably more difficult to get the point of view of Mohammedans than that of the followers of any other non-Christian religion. There are so many conflicting elements, so much wrapped up in tradition, or in special interpretation of utterances of Mohammed, or the doctrines of the Koran, that it is almost impossible for one reared in the West to get clearly the point of view of the Oriental Mohammedan. Some have ventured the statement that they believed it was more difficult to understand the Mohammedan than it is the Hindu or the Buddhist.

(7) The aggressive character of Mohammedanism constitutes another obstacle. It is not a quiescent religion like Hinduism and Buddhism, but it is a religion which is aggressively progressive in self-extension among the non-Mohammedan nations. In this respect, the Christian Church is face to face with a new problem in missionary propaganda. While Buddhism is a missionary religion, it is not aggressively so, and in these later centuries it has practically ceased to be self-propagating except by the natural law of inheritance. The Buddhists are not endeavoring to win the world to Buddhism. On the other hand Mohammedanism in some respects seems to be more alertly missionary than Christianity itself, in that its followers go out into non-Mohammedan countries and among non-Mohammedan people, as in Africa, and carry on a propaganda among the native races that surpasses in effectiveness the endeavors of the Christian Church in those same countries. The methods used by the Mohammedans, as in these later days in the Turkish Empire, to compel Christians to give up their Christianity and to accept Islam, are such as Christianity can never adopt, but they are methods which demonstrate the tremendous earnestness and purpose of Mohammedans to force conversion. In 1914 the Mohammedans started out on a propaganda of conversion among the Armenians of Turkey, circulating documents which they forced Armenians under severest threats to sign. These

MOHAMMEDAN MOSQUE AND WORSHIPERS IN LAHORE, INDIA

documents declared that the signers "had looked into the principles of Mohammedanism and had decided that it is the only true religion."

Christianity faces in Mohammedanism an aggressive, living, militant religion, that, even yet, in some circles, believes itself destined to be the religion for the world.

(8) The Mohammedans believe, as the followers of no other religion except Christians, that their religion is the only true religion. The Hindu accepts the fact that the Christian religion is probably true for the Christian, while Hinduism is true for the Hindu; and the Buddhists have often taken that position; but the Mohammedan starts out with the conviction that his religion is true, and that all other religions are false; that Mohammed is the true Prophet of God, and that he superseded all other prophets, and that, when he propagates Mohammedanism, he is propagating that religion which must win all men, and that all who are not Mohammedans are lost both in this world and for the world to come.

The Mohammedan is a firm believer in the right of the Mohammedan to rule the world, and while he is not now witnessing the triumph of Mohammedanism, he still retains the belief that it is ultimately to triumph, and to this end he watches and waits for a great leader, yet to be raised up by Allah, who will unite Mohammedanism in a worldwide movement for complete conquest.

(9) The most important obstacle is the indifference of the Christian Churches. However great are the obstacles above mentioned, none approach in vital seriousness the one here considered. This has paralyzed the arm of the Christian forces and neutralized their efforts. It has held back recruits and dried up the springs of available resources. How different would have been the outcome had some earnest, able Christian missionary approached Mohammed at Mecca as he was beginning to feel the insufficiency and even folly of the religion of his pagan city and of the Arabian tribes! Had the

church then been strong and alert, the prophet of Arabia might have been another Saul of Tarsus, giving his life and splendid talent to the extension of the Gospel of the Son of God through Arabia, across North Africa and over Asia Minor and Persia. It was the indifference of the church of the 7th century that made possible the Mohammedanism of the 20th century.

At the time of the crusades it was the church militant with drawn sword and burning hatred for the " Infidels who held the Holy Sepulchre " that planted deep in the heart of Islam a corresponding hatred for Christianity and a lasting distrust of all who profess to be followers of the meek and lowly Jesus. Europe that claimed to believe in the fatherhood of God and the common brotherhood of all His children, taught the Mohammedan to hate all Christians and to regard all who bore that name as enemies forever.

Raymund Lull attempted to undo the evil the church had committed by taking to the Mohammedans a Gospel of loving compassion, but the church was indifferent and he was left to struggle and even to die a martyr's death in Africa alone and unsupported. For five centuries more the church was dead to the need of the Moslem world for the Gospel of Christ and unconscious of its opportunity to reveal the better way.

At the present time there are large numbers, even in the church, who raise the question of the wisdom, or even propriety of sending missionaries to Mohammedans. They contend that Moslems are already believers in one God and in Jesus Christ as a prophet and that more is unnecessary. The beautiful passages in the Koran are recited as proof that Islam is an adequate religion and therefore to attempt to Christianize Moslems is to act under the impulse of a fanatical zeal and not according to reason. Others, dwelling at length upon the traditional hospitality of Mohammedans, especially in the Near East, and praising the kindly spirit and ostentatious professions of brotherhood claimed by the few, have taken the position that Islam produces men as exalted in character and ideals as does Christianity and hence it is absurd to think of improving them by preaching to them the Christ. These have failed to comprehend the vast gulf existing between the creed and the life and that the few exalted Moslem characters which have never failed to stand out against the dark and forbidding background of normal Moslem living, are rare exceptions, that the sum total of Moslem life and history has been insufferably bad.

Over against the class just mentioned are others who take the position that the Moslem is hopeless. For twelve centuries he has successfully defied the approach of the church and unquestionably he will continue to defy it. Even Professor Hurgronje maintains that Mohammedanism will never yield to the aggression of the Christian missionaries and it is futile to expect it to do so.

This is the policy of surrender before the battle has been begun. It is yielding before a difficult task without making an honest and sincere effort to accomplish it. Never has the church made a real effort to win the Moslem world for Christ; and yet the results already are adequate to prove that the task can be accomplished. Others do not deny that the Moslems need Christ and that they can be won, but the results of the effort and the sacrifice already made are less than the same effort and sacrifice made among people of other religions. They see the peoples of pagan Africa coming over in tribes and note the mass movements in India and at once assume that a life and money given to these and similar countries will accomplish more for the Kingdom than if given to reach Mohammedans where the response is slower and far less spectacular. It is natural to seek the easier task among a more responsible people while the Mohammedan waits. During the last century of modern missions, much has been said of the importance of christianizing the great coming nations of the East. Japan and China have been much upon our lips and have run through all modern missionary literature. These powerful nations, for the sake of the entire world, must be Christian and to that end no sacrifice is too great to make. On the other hand, there is no great Mohammedan nation. The Ottoman Empire that once was, has lost its glory and Persia exercises little independent power. No modern Moslem nation of commanding proportions commands the attention of the world and mutely pleads for Christian sacrifice. It is only 230,000,000 people, most of them politically helpless, scattered over the face of the earth, speaking many languages and united by no bond but that of their religion, who are waiting to know Him who is the way, the truth and the life.

The church and its membership have not yet caught the spirit of the Christ who loved all the world, even the humblest, most helpless and most needy. They have passed by the wounded and bleeding Moslems, who for these twelve centuries have been close by the way over which the followers of Christ have passed and repassed upon the farther side. The indifference of the church at home has been and today is really the only obstacle to the conversion of the Moslem world. If the church would but rally her forces of men, money and intercession, all that has been mentioned as obstacles would disappear. After all, the key to the conquest of Islam is the church here at home.

CHAPTER XVIII

CONCESSIONS REQUIRED

The Christian missionary in approaching the Mohammedan, must be ready to make concessions respecting Christian customs and traditions. This in no way implies that there must be a concession in Christian truth, but a concession in practices and methods. We have been altogether too fixed in our forms of preaching and of conducting church worship, when approaching the Mohammedan of the East. He is also fixed in his methods and is often repelled at the outset by what he sees and hears, when the things that repel him have no particular significance to Christian worship, doctrine or life.

One of the points that should be considered is the matter of architecture. There is manifestly no inherent reason why the Christian church or chapel should be Gothic, or that it should bear any form corresponding to the architecture of the West. Can there be any reason why the church in the East should not be Eastern in its entire appearance, without and within? If that church is located within a Mohammedan field, why should it not be Saracenic, if that form of architecture is more acceptable to the worshipper or to the people? In the interior, there is no reason why the whole general appearance should not be Eastern, so that when the Mohammedan comes within its walls, — and even before he has reached the building, — nothing will confront him to repel or awaken a spirit of resistance. One can readily see that, if he comes with a spirit of approval, he will be in a better frame of mind to express approval of that which is taught within a building that harmonizes with his conception of what a place of worship should be. The Moslem places of worship are dignified, with nothing to repel the Christian except as they may be associated in his mind with Mohammedanism. The Christian must be ready to concede so much to Mohammedan prejudice, that he may be made a sympathetic listener to the presentation of Christian truth.

This matter of architecture is of such importance that we may well pause and give it special consideration. Much of our success or failure in work for Moslems may turn upon this question.

Mohammedanism has grown up in and around an architecture quite distinctly its own. It is called by different names. In one place it may be called Moorish, in another Saracenic, in another Arabian, in another Mogul, and in another Ottoman; nevertheless these are all referred to as Moslem and have grown out of the practices and beliefs of Mohammedanism.

One of the principal reasons for considering this subject here is the fact that Christian churches have so generally adopted images and pictures as a part of their architecture and ornamentation. These appear not only in the statues that surround many of the great churches of history, but in the pictures that adorn the walls and in the ornamentation of the stained glass windows. Naturally this form or ornamentation repels the Mohammedan, who has been taught to believe, with all the sincerity of his being, that the making of anything in the image of man or of animal, and especially the using of these for decorative purposes, in or about places of worship, is idolatry.

Mohammedan architecture started from a humble beginning. The first mosque erected at Medina was undoubtedly of the simplest character, plain and without ornamentation. As strength and wealth increased, more substantial religious buildings were demanded, and in the 2d century of the Hejira Christian architects were employed to design and construct mosques so that, in that period, the Moslem places of worship came to resemble to a degree the Greek churches, although much plainer.

In considering the characteristics of the Moslem architecture, we note the following points:

(1) Its simplicity, with entire absence of decoration in the form of images, or pictures, or representations of human beings or animals. They were, however, not prohibited from using Arabesque decorations, which are displayed to great advantage in some of the remnants of the Saracen architecture in Spain. Geometrical forms in great variety were used by the Arabs with marked success for ornamental purposes, and the coloring frequently employed stands out even today in conspicuous prominence. While there is wide variety in the details of Moslem architecture as between that in Turkey, for instance, and that in India, nevertheless the one feature here referred to runs through it all. There is a beauty and a fascination about it that impresses itself upon the traveler, and often, as in some of the great mosques at Constantinople or at Agra, the whole presents a grandeur that seems to speak of Allah, the one All-Mighty and All-Merciful.

(2) Another feature is the use of the arch. It is probably true that the finest specimens of arches are to be found in Mohammedan countries and are the product of Mohammedan architecture. It is stated that the Arab gave to Europe the pointed arch, the trefoil and the quatrefoil. It was only in the 12th century that the Christian church began to use the pointed arch, but among the Mohammedans it was known as far back as 780 A.D. In the Moslem ruins of Spain, the horse-shoe arch repeatedly appears, as well as in the buildings of Morocco and Algiers. Even today this style of arch is little used in Christian lands, although so conspicuously and successfully employed by Moslems. India has many illustrations of mighty archways, as at Secundra, near Agra at the tomb of Akbar, the greatest of the Mogul Emperors.

(3) The third point is the use of the minaret. This is a

clear illustration of the way in which religious architecture grows out of the tenets and practices of the worshipper. Mohammed established the custom of calling to prayer rather than using a bell or any other instrument. In order that the summons might reach all the would-be worshippers, it was necessary for the one who issued the call to have an exalted position above the houses of the people. This led to the building of a tower, either as a part of the place of worship, or close by, from the top of which the call could be issued.

These minarets are today characteristic of the mosque or Mohammedan place of worship, and while their detailed style of architecture differs in many points, nevertheless the fact remains that the tower always characterizes a Mohammedan place of worship. In some of the larger and more conspicuous mosques more than one minaret appears, as, for instance, in some in Constantinople, in Egypt, and in India, where as many as five minarets are found connected with a single mosque. There seems to be some rivalry in securing the highest minarets, but we do not understand that the height has any particular significance except to reveal the pride of the worshippers and their ability to excel others.

(4) We will mention one other point, which is not strictly confined to religion, that is, the respect shown by the Mohammedans to their dead through the erection of costly, even magnificent, tombs over their bodies or in their memory. Some of the most impressive pieces of architecture in the world today were erected by Moslems in the memory and as the tomb of someone who is departed. St. Salim's tomb at Fatehpur Sikri, in the vicinity of Agra, India, is a good illustration. The Taj Mahal at Agra is probably the most beautiful, elaborate and expensive tomb anywhere in the world, visited by tens of thousands of tourists each year from the ends of the earth. Probably no building is more frequently

drawn and photographed and described than this master-piece of Mohammedan commemorative architecture.

Christians, in endeavoring to approach Mohammedans and bring to their attention the claims of the Gospel of Jesus Christ have undoubtedly been too neglectful of the Mohammedan preference for a simple and a particular style of architecture. Take, for instance, the one custom of the Mohammedans to call the faithful to prayer with the human voice, as over against a bell. In some countries, especially in Turkey, Mohammedans have declared that they believed the good Mohammedan turns over in his grave whenever he hears a church bell ring. Unquestionably they are deeply prejudiced against the bell, and, as has already been stated, against styles of construction that include images or pictures of living things. In Mohammedan countries especially, the Oriental churches have often been over-decorated in a way that repels the Mohammedan and confirms him in his conviction that Christians are idolaters, — that they worshipped images and pictures, contrary to the instruction of their own sacred book.

It would be well for those who wish to get near to the Mohammedan and to remove prejudice and win his confidence, seriously to consider whether the buildings which stand for Christianity cannot wisely, and should not, for psychological purposes alone, be shorn of their ornamentation which is repulsive to those whom they wish to win This is a matter for careful consideration in the construction of churches and all places of worship in countries where the Mohammedan is the special object of approach. Is there any reasonable objection, as many workers among Mohammedans have already suggested, to using the Moslem method of calling to Christian services? The minaret is a graceful addition to the place of worship What could be more impressive than to have the call go out from the minaret in the name of the God of heaven and the Savior of men, to all within the sound of the voice, summoning to the worship of God through Jesus Christ? Here, too, the Christian prejudice against Mohammedanism would need to be laid aside, and this custom of the Moslems, which has much to commend it, and nothing to which valid objection can be raised, made to serve the cause of Christ.

Another point that has been discussed at considerable length is the use of the Bible in Christian schools, especially in the colleges within Moslem lands. It has been the custom, in most Christian colleges, to insist that the Moslem students must study the Bible as a part of the curriculum. There are few probably today who would favor the elimination of the Bible from the Christian college or Christian schools even of lower grade. Since Christianity has won such a large portion of the world, this fact alone is adequate ground for insistence upon the study of the content, claims and promises of that religion by all who expect to rank as educated men and women. But, in addition to this, one may raise the question as to whether the candidate for scholarship ought not to study, in the East as in the West, other religions than Christianity. We in our American institutions have adopted the subject of Comparative Religion and the study of the world's great religions, as worthy and necessary. The subject is becoming increasingly popular, and renewed importance is laid upon it by Mission Boards as among the requirements for candidates who are to go out and live among these Oriental religions and try to win their followers to an acceptance of Christ.

Without advocating any policy here, it is suggested that, in Mohammedan countries, the study of the Koran be introduced into the colleges at least, and the Mohammedan students be given the opportunity of studying their own religious book by the side of the Christian book, that they may draw their own comparisons. Certainly the Christian has nothing to fear from a comparison of the two books, or of the two religions. There are many who believe that, by including the Koran as one of the studies in the regular course for Christian colleges in Mohammedan countries, the Mohammedans would come with greater readiness as they recognized the fairness and openmindedness of the Christian administrators of the school and would be in a much more open frame of mind to take up the study of the comparative values of Christianity and Mohammedanism. Possibly it might be well to add Buddhism and maybe other religious subjects. This is certainly a question worthy of careful thought on the part of Eastern educators.

There are certain doctrines which Christians put first in their discussions among themselves but which stir up animosity and opposition on the part of the Mohammedan. It would be most unscientific from a pedagogical standpoint, to thrust at the outset in the face of a man, whom one desired to win, a doctrine that would arouse his opposition if not his contempt. It is necessary to follow the instruction of our Lord, — " First the blade, then the ear, and then the full corn in the ear," and approach the Mohammedan mind from a Mohammedan point of view, with his prejudices and opposition thoroughly recognized, leading him on step by step by paths in which he is willing to walk, until he is able to bear the full truth. Why is it necessary to approach the Mohammedan first with the doctrine of the trinity, the Fatherhood of God or the Divinity and Sonship of Jesus Christ? There are probably few tried and experienced missionary workers among Mohammedans who would do this, and yet now and then one appears who feels it to be his duty to proclaim first of all that which he believes lies at the very foundation of the doctrine he is commissioned to preach, thus assuming that he fulfills his full duty and throws the responsibility of acceptance or rejection upon the one to whom he speaks.

These are only suggestions of concessions that may be made by those who are endeavoring to reach the Mohammedans with the Gospel message and to make permanent impression upon them. It must be borne in mind that there is no one method of approach or of concession that can be applied to all Mohammedan countries alike. Mohammedans differ materially in different countries with reference to their rites and ceremonies of worship, and whoever would approach them must learn the people among whom he lives and their method of thought, and use great wisdom in adapting to them his message and his method of life.

Already reference has been made to religious controversy, so we need not dwell upon it at length. The great trouble with controversy or debate with Mohammedans is the failure of the debaters on either side to understand the point of view taken by his opponent. So long as this misunderstanding exists, little will probably be accomplished by controversy except to drive the contestants farther apart. The traditional methods of Moslem argumentation are scholastic and pedantic, and not at all in harmony with modern methods of thinking. These methods to the Mohammedan are thoroughly convincing, but they can have little influence over the Western mind; while the principles of reasoning and the arguments used by the Westerner hardly touch the mind of the Oriental. Owing to this supreme difficulty in understanding each other in argumentation or in controversy, it is of great importance that only those should enter upon it who are able to put themselves completely into the atmosphere and method of thinking and point of view of the Mohammedan opponent.

A statement by Dr. George F. Herrick, in his "Christian and Mohammedan" upon this subject of controversy, is in point:

"To answer a sincere question is not controversy. It should be sympathetically given, and may solve a difficulty for the ignorant inquirer. But I would accept no challenge; it is seldom other than a defiance, in temper as well as in fact. To put it aside gently, and then to appeal to the conscience of the man in the presence of God is an excellent way. I have known this done with astonishing effect, the arrogant champion becoming, before the end of the interview, a deeply interested listener.

Attack has its use in disturbing unthoughtful confidence in an impregnable Islam, such as is prevalent among its votaries. Missionary brethren may deem it a necessary preliminary to the teaching of the truth. I thought so at one time, but now prefer to ignore Islam and address the man."

Controversy of this character should not stand out prominently as a prime method of approach to the Moslem, but it should be reserved for weightier matters and especially to be applied after the Mohammedan opponent has been lifted out of his antiquated scholasticism. There are those with whom controversy can be effectively carried on, if conducted from the proper point of view.

. The Mohammedans are more and more awakening to the value of controversy and are preparing and putting out controversial literature of a great variety. For instance, a leaflet was recently issued at Cairo on the subject of " Manners and Morals of the Prophet"; another on " Early Moslems and their Golden Deeds"; another on the "Principles of Islam"; another on " Women under Islam: their Social Status and Legal Right"; another on " Polygamy." A leaflet has been issued also answering Dr. Sells' book on Islam. All this opens a wide field for the production of a class of controversial literature which shall be fair, constructive, and prepared in a spirit of love and with full regard to the Moslem point of view. The same form of controversy may be carried into oral discussion, but largely in the form of personal discussion with individual leaders, and based upon unbiased scientific research, which the Mohammedans have hardly yet begun to apply to their sacred books and to their traditions.

We would therefore contend that there is a place, not regarded as primary, not to be used with the rank and file of Moslems, but with trained leaders, capable of entering into such controversy with a spirit of fairness, for a certain amount of controversial debate and discussion and of controversial literature. The Mohammedan must learn to appeal to the reason and not simply to tradition or to feeling, and he must learn that religion holds sway as it appeals to the moral consciousness, the intellectual integrity and the spiritual longings of men. And we should also bear in mind that much of this investigation, which shapes itself into the form of controversy, has its place in the class-room rather than upon the platform.

The Christian who would win the Moslem must be ready to lay aside many precedents and traditions and approach his task with an untrammeled mind ready to be all things to the followers of Mohammed if perchance some may be won for Christ.

CHAPTER XIX

THE CHRISTIAN MESSAGE TO MOSLEMS

There is an imperative need that every missionary to the Moslems should have definitely in mind the Christian message which he bears. It is easy to prejudice the minds of one's hearers and thus not only render the message inoperative but make it the agency for closing the door of approach for all time. Not every Christian truth should be preached at all times and to all hearers, and there are many of the truths of our religion that a Moslem is unable to bear until he has learned other truths that prepare the way for fuller knowledge. Christ addressed the parable of the lily and the sower to peasants, the taking of fish to the fishermen, and of the solidity of the great stones of the temple to his followers when in Jerusalem.

Well-known workers among Mohammedans who know well their doctrines and prejudices have suggested that the following aspects of Christianity should be presented to Moslems with caution, and then only after special and unusual preparation:

1. *Foremost among these are the doctrines regarding the person of Jesus Christ, like the immaculate conception, his sonship, divinity, his death and resurrection.*

Concerning these, progress must be made slowly and with a degree of caution that recognizes the deep prejudices that must be unseated before Christ can be enthroned. Here the Koran can be quoted in regard to the divine nature of Jesus and his prophetic rank. After that a positive preaching of the manhood and nobility of the person will necessarily lead to an acknowledgment of his divine character. It is well here to follow the suggestions of Christ himself and so lift up

Jesus before them that they will be led to acknowledge him as Lord.

2. *Another doctrine is the fatherhood of God.*

The gross and literal method among Moslems of interpreting the doctrine of the fatherhood of God has made it impossible for them, at the outset, to regard the declaration in any other than a sensual manner. As the Koran always speaks of Jesus as the son of Mary, the declaration that he is the son of God makes Mary the consort of Deity, and against this interpretation they rebel. In the same way and for the same reason they deny that God is the father of men. Their conception of Allah is so exalted and his position is so vastly above all human relations, that they find it difficult to put him into paternal relations with men. They recoil from the first words of address in the Lord's prayer and ought not to be asked to repeat it until they begin to grasp the meaning of the Christian interpretation of God as the father of all mankind. This alone when understood and accepted will undermine much of the fundamental theology and philosophy of Islam.

3. *Prejudice is also aroused by the doctrine that redemption comes only through Jesus Christ.*

Redemption through Christ is a long way from a belief that redemption is possible only through the repetition of the creed of Islam and the performance of its five fundamental acts of worship. To ask a Mohammedan at the outset to abandon every essential doctrine of his ancestral religion and put into its place another doctrine, which from childhood he has been taught to regard as the very essence of falsehood, is to violate the law of human thinking and every rule of religious pedagogy. We may claim that the Holy Spirit can and will prepare the way for the reception of the most radical doctrines of Christianity, and yet it is difficult to believe and presumptuous to assume that the Holy Spirit can be relied upon always to intervene as a corrective of our failure to make use of the divinely given faculties with which we are endowed.

4. *Another cause of stumbling is the denial that Mohammed was a prophet of God.*

This does not even suggest that Mohammed's divine character should be proclaimed or conceded. At the same time one is forced to acknowledge that he did have a message for the pagan tribes of Arabia that was superior to the religion they formerly held and practiced. His proclamation of the one great overruling God was a step far in advance of the many deities worshipped by the Arabians. There are passages in the Koran worthy to be read in the pulpits of our Christian churches, and exalted conceptions of duty and sacrifice that the centuries have not dimmed. There is a wide field in which the Christian preacher may present the claims of Christianity upon the Moslem without condemnation of their revered leader who has been almost deified among some sects. It is better not to make attacks upon the prophet of the Mohammedans, but leave it to them, after they have caught the transcendent beauty and felt the infinite power of the living Christ in their own lives, to draw the inevitable conclusion that Mohammed could not have been and is not now the prophet of the living God.

5. *It is also unwise to claim that Christianity is the only true religion.*

Such a proclamation, if it did not at once repel all listeners, would precipitate a bitter controversy. One would not begin here in preaching Christ to the followers of any other religion, much less to Moslems. The appeal must be to the desire in the soul of every man to find rest and peace in God, and the Mohammedans know that this desire has not been gratified through observing the exactions of their faith. The proclamation that Christianity is a great and satisfying religion that has met the demands of multitudes and is meeting those demands today, is the positive message that must end in the recognition that it alone is from God and leads to God.

6. *The use of wine at the Sacraments is repellant to Moslems.*

It is fully realized that we are here treading upon ground that, among Christians, is controversial, and yet there is no sound reason for insisting that fermented wine shall be employed among Mohammedans to celebrate the sacraments when such use runs directly counter to their highly commendable ideas of temperance. There are some who contend that Christ himself did not use fermented wine: and even if he did, does it follow that he would have us do so if it were to make our Moslem brothers to offend, or even to stumble and fall? It does not need to be stated here that all Christian workers among Moslems should abstain from all use of wine; which use the Moslems believe is contrary to the teachings of Christianity as it is to their own religion.

There are several difficulties standing in the way of the Mohammedan's quick acceptance of Christianity besides his inherent prejudice. Many of these are perfectly honest and need to be cleared up before Moslems can take their stand for Christ. We can here name but a few of these.

1. *Foremost among these is the high state of morality demanded of men by the life and teachings of Christ.*

To many this seems to be an unrealizable ideal and so far beyond the possibility of human attainment that they feel it to be useless to make the attempt at all. That Jesus achieved it is encouraging, and that many others have approached unto the perfect life gives hope. The doctrine, however, to the Mohammedan who is conscious of gross failure in attaining unto the lower standards of his own religion, is a severe one.

2. *The failure of Christianity actually to win all the western world presents another difficulty.*

It is but natural that the Mohammedan should seek to know why it is that all America and all Europe are not yet truly followers of Christ. He is also asking how it is possible that the entire non-Christian world has not even yet heard of Christ and had an opportunity to accept or reject him.

3. *The supposition that Christianity has passed the zenith of its power and is now a waning religion presents often a real difficulty.*

Many Moslems believe this, both because of its failure in all of the centuries since Christ to win the world and also because of the many divisions that have entered into the Church, breaking it up into different and not infrequently mutually antagonistic sects.

4. *The composite authorship of the Scriptures also offends many.*

In comparison with their Koran written by their prophet's hand alone, our Scriptures seem to them fragmentary, un-correlated and unauthentic.

5. *Perhaps the greatest difficulty is the relation of Christian nations to Mohammedan countries.*

Since Moslem conquests ceased it has been the Christian nations that have encroached upon Mohammedan countries, gradually usurping their authority. This seems to them like the spirit of the crusades inaugurated in the name of Christ for usurping the national control of the world. They see that today most of the Mohammedans are under the rule of Christian nations and are beginning to feel that in time there will be left no Mohammedan country that is ruled by the law of the Koran. It is natural that they should regard this as the fixed policy of the Christians, as it was their own in the early days of Moslem supremacy. It is difficult for them to see that this has not taken place under the dictates of Christianity.

The following fundamental truths and principles of Christianity have been suggested by a large number of experienced workers among Moslems as containing that which appeals to the Mohammedan's religious sense and that have in a large number of instances received his hearty approval, and yet even these should not be preached indiscriminately and without regard to local environments and prejudices. The list is not exhaustive but is suggestive of many applications and divisions of these great themes that lie at the foundation of our faith.

1. *The unity of God* is the most important of these. The Moslems are so convinced that Christians are polytheists that it is well at the outset to let it be known that we believe in one eternal, all-powerful ruler of heaven and earth whose we are and whom we serve. There is little if anything in the Mohammedan conception of the Godhead that we cannot affirm with equal emphasis, and to this we have much to add. A bold presentation of the great truth of the one great overruling God of heaven and earth cannot fail to disarm the hearers of the objection that Christians have three Gods.

2. We may also insist with advantage upon the *divine omnipotence coupled with divine goodness*. Here we move away from and beyond the Moslem position which has little to say about the goodness of Allah. They affirm his power and his justice, but doubt his love. It is not difficult to establish from the Old Testament and from nature the fact of divine goodness which is a step in the path of the revelation of paternal compassion. The Moslems believe in a great God, but not a loving God. When they catch a vision of the inherent goodness of the Godhead they will have begun to break with the cold severity of Islam.

3. *The use of miracles by Christ and his apostles* has, in many countries, proven to be of much value in establishing the divine character of Christianity among both Moslems and other non-Christian peoples. Whatever we may claim as to the evidential value of Christian miracles, we know they had a large place in the life of Christ and his apostles and that they are no less effective today upon the mission field. The

Moslems believe that Christ wrought miracles but they know little of the benevolent character of these mighty works.

4. *The Christian doctrine of the future life* is, some missionaries report, generally accepted by Mohammedans as superior to their own paradise. In it they find an uplift and joy that is far above their own sensual and sensuous conceptions of the future. Some of the passages in the Gospel of John and in the Revelation come to them with a mighty appeal.

5. *The purity and nobility of the moral ideas set forth in the teachings of Jesus* may be urged to advantage.

This does not presuppose the divinity of Jesus. His teachings can be presented as the utterances of a man who, in the midst of the moral degradation of his times, set before the world ideals of living of the highest and most exalted character. Here is an inexhaustible field for instruction in which no place for controversy can be discovered and through which the Christ can be revealed in his beauty, grace and power. In the minds of the hearers this will be set over against the teaching and practices of their own prophet which many Moslems fail to endorse as an ideal for the world.

6. *The fact that Jesus practiced what he taught* never fails to make a profound impression upon a people who for generations have divorced principles from practice. The Moslem will state principles of living that are not second to those taught by Christ himself, but at the same time he acknowledges that no one has lived in accordance therewith — not even their prophet. This fact in the life of Christ, which they do not deny, kept to the front, coupled with the teachings themselves, awakens a consciousness of his nobility of character and sinlessness and tends to lead to adoration.

7. *Moslems are also attracted by love expressed in beneficent deeds and in unselfish character*.

While Mohammedans admire unselfishness, their legends being full of records of those who have unselfishly served their fellow men, they have come almost to deny that it today exists. Their theology aids to this conclusion. It is difficult for them to conceive of an unselfish act calling for personal sacrifice. It is at this point that the devoted life of the missionaries, given to acts of beneficence, appeals to them with tremendous power when they are convinced that their deeds are unselfish and prompted only by love. No one who has not lived among Moslem peoples can realize how devoid is their life and character of this Christian virtue. We have often misinterpreted Moslem acts of what appeared to be supreme unselfishness, like the giving of alms and general hospitality, as a demonstration of Christian virtue, forgetting that through these acts he believes he is accumulating credits in heaven by which his sins may be cancelled.

8. *Christian secret prayer and worship* is designed to fill a need in Mohammedan life. The many modern movements towards various forms of mysticism demonstrate the sincere desire of multitudes of Moslems for a spiritual life not provided for in the tenets of Islam. His set forms of worship, mechanical and at stated periods, do not seem to satisfy the conscious needs of his soul. Christianity assures him that he who would worship God in spirit and in truth can do so at any time and in any place; that the soul can be in constant communion with its God, requiring no set form and demanding no ritual. Christianity offers all that the many mystical movements have sought to supply and much more. The Mohammedan has from the beginning believed that he can draw near and speak to his God without the aid of priest or mediator, but at the same time he has been taught that times, seasons and forms are imperative. Consciousness of an ever-present God with ear ever open to the cry of his soul comes as a revelation from heaven full of beauty, comfort and power.

9. *Christian institutions for the relief of ignorance and suffering* are of great importance.

Here we come to a practical demonstration of what Christianity has done in accordance with the principles taught by Jesus. The benevolence of Christendom in founding and supporting educational institutions, asylums, places of refuge, hospitals and many other similar lines of work, is capable of endless demonstration. What has been done in this direction in Christian countries carries much weight, and yet here it is more difficult to separate the act from a selfish purpose, since Christians and their families enjoy the privileges afforded by such institutions. When however the gifts of Christendom are given for similar institutions in foreign countries for the help and relief of peoples whom the donors have never known and probably will never see, it is impossible to assign a selfish purpose to the act. It is not difficult to connect these deeds of Christians with the teachings and example of Christ and to show that such institutions of benevolence, pity, and charity spring from the very essence of the teachings of Jesus and that a Christianity professing to be true to Jesus that did not thus express itself would be false, and not Christianity at all.

10. *Freedom of worship from casuistic demands* is a counterpart of the place of secret prayer. It is difficult for the Mohammedan to bring himself to realize that acceptable worship must not be offered in a formal way and that religious acts must not be in accord with prescribed rules. He has been held all his life in the trammels of form and ceremony and the greatest aims of which he has been conscious are the sins of omitting to keep all the demands of his religious laws. Form and ceremony have been to him priest and mediator. Christianity sets him free and brings him face to face with his God.

11. *The possession of and reliance upon a book* is in accord with the predilections of all Moslems. They are ready to accept the Book as containing the content and claim of the Christian religion. They require no proof of its divine

character since their own Koran refers to the Bible as the word of God and to the Hebrew prophets and Jesus as prophets of God. They are already predisposed to look upon the Book favorably although they may deny some of its teachings. The preacher should be clear in his own mind that his book contains the revelation of God to men and that in it is revealed the plan of salvation for the race. He should utter no uncertain message as he offers to the Moslems the Bible in the place of the Koran and assures him that it is the word of God.

There will be no call for the missionary to go out of his way to introduce to the Mohammedans the principles and methods of higher criticism, for they are not ignorant of those principles and will undoubtedly begin to apply them in investigation, in their own way, as soon as they have sufficiently advanced in Christian studies. Already they find difficulty in the composite authorship of the Christian Scriptures and the widely separated periods in which the different books were written. Still they are ready to accept the Book and it is the task of the missionary to guide them into an earnest study of its teachings.

12. *The realization of a strong, free, pure Christian womanhood* may with advantage be held before Moslems as an ideal.

Here again we are face to face with historical records which have grown out of Christian teaching. The attitude of Christ towards women is clear and there follows the necessity of showing how that teaching has resulted in the elevation of womanhood in all Christian countries. One of the chief difficulties will arise from the presupposition, upon the part of the Moslems, that their women are incapable of attaining to the same high state that the women of Christian lands have reached. Among Moslems they have never known such women as Christendom possesses and it is easy and natural for them to conclude that their women are intellectually and morally inferior. It is not, however, impossible to prove, through examples taken from among races formerly pagan, that whenever and wherever Christianity is accepted by a people and they begin to live in accordance with its precepts, womanhood begins to emerge from its former state of suppression and depression into new forms of beauty, strength and grace. There is a boundless field here for proving the practical value of Christianity in elevating the mothers of future generations and thus recreating the race.

13. *That Christianity awakens social aspirations, leading to reforms* is a fact that should be insisted upon. There is nothing in Islam that leads to effort or sacrifice for the help of the community. Not a little has been done by them in aid of other Moslems at times when this seemed necessary to protect their religious establishments. A Moslem community is essentially selfish. In times of severe famine among them distributors of relief have frequently remarked upon the impossibility of securing the services of any Moslem to aid in saving life except by paying large prices. Moslem nature seems to lack that to which appeal can be made for a service of pure philanthropy. Human suffering as such seems to make little or no impression. A community appeal falls upon dead ears. It will be a long and difficult task to impress upon them the brotherhood of humanity and to engender in them a genuine desire to improve the social order and eradicate its evils. What has already been done in this direction in Christian lands can be cited with great force and cannot fail to make an impression.

14. *That Jesus came not to destroy but to fulfil the best and highest aspirations of every man and of every religion* should also be set forth. It will not be an easy task to move the Moslem from the position that it is the chief function of Allah miserably to destroy all those who are not Moslems, to the position that God cherishes and desires to preserve all that is good in all lands and among all peoples, and condemns everything that is evil wherever found. That Christianity

does not universally and indiscriminately condemn all Mohammedans to eternal destruction and assign all professing Christians to an eternal paradise is a startling revelation. That Christianity aims to reveal to every soul seeking after God, be he Moslem, Buddhist, Hindu or pagan, the very God he hopes to find comes with mighty force. It is a gospel of joy to know that Jesus came not to condemn the world, but to seek out the needy and the lost and to bring them into the abundant life. This message will meet an immediate response in many a Moslem heart that has been staggering under the condemnation of his own religion while longing for something that will show him the way to higher and better living. It is here that the Gospel has a special message for Moslems today wholly discouraged as to the national supremacy and coming to doubt the spiritual adequacy of Islam.

15. *The presentation of Jesus Christ as a mediator and intercessor between God and man* should be constantly made.

One of the supreme difficulties of Mohammedanism is that Allah is so exalted and powerful that in his presence man is but a slave too degraded to look even into the face of his master. There is an awful gulf that separates between the worshipper and his God. Realizing this fact, a multitude of sects or divisions have arisen, all of them more or less mystical, but providing some way by which man in his low estate may come nearer to God. Some of these make Mohammed an intercessor between man and God. Others provide a Mahdi or some other leader who claims to have special power of intercession or who claims for himself an unusual portion of divine favor. In a peculiar sense the Moslem world is seeking for some mediator between themselves and God and are marvelously ready for the message that tells them of the existence of that for which they seek. This presentation will answer the cry of the soul of many who are seeking in other ways to find access to their God who is afar off. There is hardly another phase of Christianity more suited to the present hour for which the Moslem world has been in unusual preparation for a generation and more.

Growing out of the experience of missionaries in their attempt to reach the Moslems most effectively with the message of the Gospel of Christ, sufficient data has not been gathered to make clear all those phases of the Gospel which most appeal to the Moslem mind. We must bear in mind that there are so many different grades of culture among Mohammedans, that they belong to so many different races and have come up in the midst of such varied environments that we should hardly expect one method of approach or one phase of the Gospel to appeal equally to all classes and during all periods of their life. At the same time, there are undoubtedly certain phases of the teachings of the New Testament that are calculated to make a stronger impression upon the Mohammedan hearers than other phases and that too because the hearers are Mohammedan. It is this point to which attention should be called, with the possibility that missionaries having this subject in mind will experiment with Mohammedan hearers until some conclusion can be reached which will be of constructive help to those who would reach the Moslem heart.

Dr. Harrison in Arabia has made some experiments in his hospital along the line of this suggestion with the endeavor to discover what are the chief living forces of the Gospel as applied to the mind of the Arab. In this plan some aspects of the Gospel were presented to each individual patient in the hospital in a personal and friendly way daily and the results were carefully noted and recorded. These different presentations were along the line of the distinct doctrines of the New Testament teachings, the idea of sin and need of salvation, the holiness of God and the demand for forgiveness, the historical presentation especially with reference to the historic Christ, the parables and the lessons which they teach. These experiments were so limited in range and brief in period that it is impossible to draw any general conclusions from them, and yet it was evident to those who were closest to the plan that some phases of the Gospel held attention more closely and made impression more deeply than others.

The same experiments could be tried perhaps to better advantage on groups of Moslems where the dogmatic, the historical, the pictorial, the emotional and the mystical phases of Christianity were presented at different periods, observing and noting down the conclusion of the speaker or of one who faced the audience with the speaker as to which presentation seemed most deeply to hold attention. This would be only one of the results of the presentation and would need to be followed up in order to discover which presentation tended the most to inquiry for further light or guidance. There seems to be a field here for a legitimate and necessary experimentation.

These are but suggestions for the consideration of those who have opportunity for presenting the claims and promises of the Gospel of Christ to Mohammedans. They are the result of wide observation and experience upon the part of different experienced workers among them. While there is much in Christianity, even in the fundamental doctrines, that is not here mentioned, there is yet enough to call to the attention of all to whom these great truths are preached that Christianity offers to the individual and to society that which transcends everything Islam possesses and that meets the cry of the heart after a closer walk with God. We need not hasten to the more controversial questions until minds and hearts have been prepared for the more difficult and more personal truths.

CHAPTER XX

PROGRAM OF EVANGELIZATION

In discussing the evangelization of the Mohammedan world, it is essential that we discuss methods of approach which give promise of rewarding returns. There has been much theoretical endeavor to reach the Mohammedans, much of which has seemed utterly to fail.

Special preparation and a special study of the Mohammedan problem in all of its historic setting and all of its peculiar local and present conditions is required in order to devise ways and means of successfully reaching the Mohammedan mind and especially the Mohammedan heart. The time has passed when missionary work, in any country, can be successfully carried on in a haphazard way without scientific investigation, careful and thorough preparation, and the adoption of methods of approach to meet the requirements of the case. No longer is it assumed that the missionary who is successful among the Hindus will necessarily be successful with Mohammedans, or one who is able to preach with great effectiveness to the Japanese will be able to convince a Mohammedan of the truth of Christianity and the consequent insufficient character of the religion in which he has hitherto believed.

There is probably more necessity of careful preparation for making a successful missionary to the Mohammedans than in the case of any other of the great religions, since Mohammedanism is, more than all the rest together, deeply, bitterly and fundamentally opposed to Christianity. Its opposition is so deep-seated that methods must be devised for breaking it down before the door of approach to the heart can be unlatched. We will consider a few of the methods of approach which have already proven to be successful to a greater or less degree, and which, after careful preparation and investigation, may be made vastly more successful in the future than they have been in the past.

(1) The first is the use of the Bible, and especially of the New Testament, accurately translated into the vernacular of the people to be won.   Without the Bible in the vernacular there would be little use in attempting to build up a Mohammedan in a strong Christian faith, and much less to build up a church or a Christian community from Mohammedan people.

The Christian who approaches Mohammedans with a book that is open and easily understood, has a peculiar advantage, since their own sacred book, except to those who are able intelligently to read the Arabic, is closed to them. This from the very beginning gives the Christian missionary among Mohammedans an advantageous start.   It is not difficult to arouse an interest in a Mohammedan population in the written word of the Christian book, and the more they can be led to read and discuss it, the more the truths of the Bible will penetrate.

It is a fact demonstrated from experience that the Mohammedans have been more fundamentally moved by reading parts of the New Testament than they have by the oral presentation of Christianity or by the use of the Christian literature hitherto provided.

We would therefore place first emphasis upon the translation and wide dissemination of the New Testament at least in the vernaculars spoken by the Mohammedans whom we are seeking to win.

(2) Other Christian literature should also be provided. The printed page must necessarily take a preeminent place in all endeavor to reach the Moslem world.   Beyond the Bible in the vernacular, there is a great field for the production and distribution of an explanatory literature setting

forth the teachings and principles of Jesus Christ and of Christianity, in a positive, constructive way, prepared from the Moslem point of view and in a way calculated to remove prejudice and to give the reader a reasonable conception of that for which Christianity stands. Such literature is more important in dealing with Mohammedans than with any other of the great Eastern religions, because the Mohammedan starts with a long-time prejudice, deep-seated, often bitter in the extreme, and the mission of the literature that is first put into his hands is to free his mind of some of these prejudices and to put him into a frame of mind capable of understanding and appreciating the positive teachings of Christianity.

There is considerable difference of judgment as to how much controversy should enter into this literature. Viewed from one standpoint, and with one interpretation of controversy, we would unhesitatingly say that there should be none; that it is not the province of the Christian teacher either by pen or by word to attack any religion. But from another standpoint, and especially from the Mohammedan point of view, almost any kind of a positive statement with reference to Christianity would probably be looked upon as controversial. The border line between noncontroversy and controversy is dim and uncertain in dealing with the Moslems, but as a general principle, most of the workers among Mohammedans would undoubtedly agree that the controversial element should not be made the prominent feature, but that the literature produced should breathe the loving and fraternal spirit of Christ Himself.

This literature should include both periodicals and books. In addition to the religious discussions contained in the periodical literature, an unusual field is open for the discussion of questions of the day from the Christian standpoint. Social, educational and historical questions may be treated in such a way as not to arouse antagonism, but gradually to open the mind of the Moslem reader so that the truths of the modern world may find entrance. Missionaries have not given due weight to the demand and place of a strong, aggressive, general Christian periodical literature, to be circulated among Moslems, always in their vernacular. The editorial management of such periodicals should be statesmanlike and the material calculated to meet the mental, social, physical and spiritual condition of the Moslems among whom it is to circulate.

But beyond this, and of equal importance, although not taking the place of the periodical, is the necessity for a carefully prepared permanent literature, calculated to reach the more educated classes. Much has been published already in the Arabic, Turkish, Persian, Urdu and other languages spoken and used by Moslems. Much of this has, however, been prepared by those who were not fundamentally familiar with the Mohammedan point of view and method of thought, and, too frequently, these productions have been slavish translations of English books which were originally written without reference to Moslems, and consequently often of no value at all.

It is of first importance that a literature to prove effective among Moslems of every character should be prepared by those who have made a special study of Mohammedanism. They should be familiar with the Mohammedan objections to Christianity as well as the beliefs and doctrines of Islam, not only among Mohammedans as a whole, but of the particular class sought to be reached. The best and most effective literature will probably yet be written by Moslems who have become Christians.

We will not endeavor to discuss here the question as to how much of the dogmatic doctrines of Christianity shall appear in this literature. It is the opinion of the writer that too much of this has been included hitherto, forgetting the practice of St. Paul who fed milk to babes and meat to strong men. Altogether too frequently the traditional doctrines of Christianity, not emphasized by Christ or the apostles, and sometimes hardly referred to by them, have been put to the front in the endeavor to win the Moslem.

The purpose of the literature should be to win, and there are elements in Christianity which appeal with tremendous force to the Mohammedan. If these are stressed until prejudice is overcome, then will he be in a frame of mind to consider the doctrines upon which the very foundation of our Christian faith rests.

(3) Christian education is another powerful instrument for evangelizing. It is only in recent years that the Mohammedan world has aroused itself to the importance of modern education. In fact Mohammedanism has been opposed to modern learning from the first, under the theory that whatever is important to know was revealed in the Koran, and that everything taught by Western learning that is contained in the Koran does not need to be taught by outside books or outside methods, and whatever is taught that is not in the Koran is irrelevant if not opposed to true religion. This statement fairly represents the thinking of the great majority of Mohammedans. There is no class of people in India that have remained so backward under the great forward movement in that country during the last century as the Mohammedans. Their schools are the poorest and the most feebly supported of any, and the state of illiteracy among them is appalling. Even today the Mohammedans of India have not aroused themselves to the importance and value of modern education.

The situation in Turkey has been practically the same. Mohammedanism, in all the history of Turkey, has never advanced modern education. The ordinary training of the Moslem youth was obtained in connection with the mosque and began with learning to read and recite the Koran. This was followed by a study of the commentaries and other books on the law, and never extended much beyond that.

Under the great combination of influences that have been sweeping over Turkey, and in fact most of the Mohammedan countries, there is beginning to dawn an awakened intelligence in the minds of many, though not yet the majority, by any means, who are seeking better opportunities for their children to gain the benefits of Western education. At the same time, the Mohammedans themselves have little ability to develop and conduct a system of education. They seem to be helpless in this respect and look to outside assistance in order to secure modern facilities for educating their children.

The educational system of Turkey, as developed by the Government, has been borrowed from Christian schools established within the country, and has not been established and conducted with the general approval of the Mohammedan hierarchy, but usually in opposition to it. The advance made in the last few years, in Turkey, Persia, and in Egypt, and which is just beginning to appear in India, manifests itself in the presence of more Mohammedan pupils in existing Christian schools. From the kindergarten to the highest college grade more students are being received. The changes in this respect that have taken place during the last ten years are sufficiently convincing to warrant a united endeavor on the part of the Christian missionary forces to establish kindergartens and schools of primary and intermediate grades in vastly increased numbers. They should be especially adapted to Mohammedan children. There is every reason to believe and expect that these schools, properly conducted, would soon if not immediately become popular with Mohammedan parents and would be abundantly patronized.

The Mohammedans have recently started, in some places in Turkey, kindergartens for their children, but have been compelled to turn to the Christian schools for teachers. This fact is suggestive of the method by which Christian missions can control the situation by preparing teachers to go into Mohammedan schools of all grades and character and help them develop an educational system for themselves.

This introduces us to the second stage in education, namely, the preparation of teachers, which is probably one of the most important phases of missionary educational work. It stands next after the preparation of men for the Christian ministry. The strength with which the desire for modern education is taking hold of the Eastern races, and the readiness with which the people turn to the Christian missionaries for the training of their young, opens a door of approach to the home and to the heart of the non-Christian population. No approach could be more effectual among the Mohammedans, since they have from time immemorial held the teacher in highest esteem.

The Christian teacher, coming daily into contact with the pupils, will be able more fully and completely to turn their minds favorably toward the teachings of Christ and away from the teachings of Mohammed than any other class of Christian worker, not excepting the Christian doctor. Undoubtedly different forms of educational work will be more prominent in all plans for work for Moslems in the future than in the past. They will increase in force and power as the minds of the Mohammedans open, their sympathies broaden, and their ambitions for the advancement of their children enlarge. As the horizon of Mohammedans widens, the more will they be ready to welcome anyone who has ability to aid them in the accomplishment of their new-found purpose to develop in harmony with the rest of the world, and the more will their old superstitions and traditions of hostility to Christianity be removed. They will come into more complete relations of fellowship and brotherhood with those whom hitherto they have regarded as their traditional foes.

The Christian school and the Christian teacher are bound to exercise mighty influence in breaking down not only the intellectual antipathy of the Mohammedan world, but in opening the door to their confidence and affection.

The statement is often made that in general education there is a force adequate to Christianize the world. Perhaps this is proclaimed more frequently with reference to Mohammedanism than to any other of the great religions on the ground that Islam is the traditional opponent of modern learning. We must not lose sight of the fact that education is not Christianity, and that to deprive one of the faith he formerly had in his religion is not necessarily to lead him to Christianity. Almost any religion to which a man loyally adheres is far better than a religionless life. Every religion interposes restraints of one kind or another, while an absence of religion is liable to lead to an absence of restraint.

A Mohammedan may be educated out of his faith in Islam and be left in a far worse moral condition than before. It is stated upon unquestioned authority that the twoscore men who, under the name of the Young Turk Party, controlled the fate of Turkey for several years and especially after the outbreak of the war, were men without belief in Islam or in any other religion. Talaat Bey, the Minister of the Interior, and later the Grand Vizier under whose direction the Armenian atrocities were perpetrated, is characterized as wholly destitute of religious impulse and without belief in God or religion.

Modern education alone tends to shake the Moslem's confidence in his sacred books and traditions, and is in danger of causing him to cast off all religious restraints.

The *Islamic Review* recently stated:[1]

" The truth is that Western education as imported at present (in India) demolishes the old building of one's beliefs, but does not arrange for the construction of another and more beautiful. The mind is unhinged; it knows not where to go to find repose. The consequence is not very pleasant to look upon. The Hindu rails against the rulers, the Muslim

[1] Quoted from *The Moslem World*, Jan. 1916, p. 2.

Three Indian Students, a Hindu, a Christian, a Mohammedan

turns traitor to the traditions of unflinching loyalty to Islam. Islam is a dead letter in educated circles. Where the Koran was read daily in the morning formerly, there, now, the *Pioneer* (newspaper) has taken its place." When men have lost their moorings and are adrift it is our duty to try and give them a new anchorage, especially as the West itself has caused them to lose faith in the old traditions.

Lord Bryce's words are terribly true: " We have disturbed their ancient ways of life for our own interests, because we went among them, some few doubtless with a desire to do good, but the great majority from a desire to make money and to exploit the world's resources for the purposes of commerce. . . . Are we to do this and yet not be responsible in God's sight, if we fail to exert all our efforts to give these people by our conduct a just view of the Christianity we desire to impart to them?"

All educational work for Moslems must therefore be aggressively and constructively Christian. This does not mean " offensively Christian." But it must mean that when a follower of Mohammed begins, through the processes of education, to question the basis and teachings of Islam, he must be shown a more excellent way. As Islam fails to satisfy the questionings of his awakened intellect, he should be directed to the Christ who meets the requirements of the mind as well as of the heart.

(4) Another successful avenue of approach is found in Medical Missions. Medical work is most quickly appreciated and most effectively breaks down the inherent opposition of Moslems to Christianity. Islam has almost nothing to offer its followers in times of physical distress, and it is just at that time that the Christian medical missionary can approach the suffering Mohammedan with that which his own religion fails to provide but which he is quick to appreciate. It is also true that in the person and the work of the medical missionary, the Mohammedan is able to grasp something of the conception of the Christian compassion and of the teaching of our Lord that it is more blessed to serve than to be served, to give than to receive. The testimony of medical missionaries over the world practically agree in this.

The American Board of Commissioners for Foreign Missions began medical work in Turkey more than half a century ago. At first few Mohammedans were reached, but gradually prejudice was removed, and in later years every missionary hospital has had an increasing attendance of Mohammedans, both in the clinic and as regular patients in the wards. In increasing numbers Turkish officials, strong in their Mohammedan belief, have opened the doors of their homes to the Christian medical missionary, sometimes calling for service in the harem, but more generally for the men of the household.

As an illustration of the way in which prejudice has been removed, the experience of Dr. Arthur Lankester, of the Church Missionary Society, in Peshawa, on the Afghan frontier is a good illustration. In 1912 Dr. Lankester visited the town of Charsadda, with some 20,000 inhabitants, twenty miles away from Peshawa. He had the greatest difficulty in getting permission from the Mohammedans of the place to use a vacant warehouse for hospital purposes. After only three years of experience of the benefit and favor of the mission hospital, the inhabitants of the town made a public demonstration as an expression of gratitude for the work of the medical mission, and Dr. Lankester and his associate were received with great honor and enthusiasm. In this the Mohammedans and the Hindus alike joined. In the brief period of three years, the attitude of the people had been changed from one of suspicion and even open hostility to one of cordial goodwill and friendship, and this was due to the work of the medical missionary.

During fifty years of experience in the Turkish empire, similar testimony could be given with reference to nearly every one of the mission hospitals, which were reared not wholly for the Mohammedans but which are open to people of all races alike.

The Church Missionary Society began in 1864 to send

medical missionaries to Kashmir, and since then a chain of medical missions stretching across the Northwestern frontier of India has been established. In every one of these centers the medical missionaries are recognized by the Mohammedans as among the best friends of the people, and in not a few of the places their most earnest supporters are Moslems.

The same Society opened medical work in Persia, as has also the Northern Presbyterian Mission Board, and in that stronghold of Mohammedanism, covering Ispahan, Yezd, Kerman, Teheran and Tabriz few missionary undertakings have been fraught with more striking consequences than these medical missions. These medical centers, during periods of great political upheaval, have exerted a mighty influence in maintaining order.

Palestine and Turkish Arabia were entered by the Church Missionary Society of England and the Board of Foreign Missions of the Reformed Church in America, where the medical missionary has thoroughly established himself even among the fanatical Arabs. The Bishop of London, after a recent visit to Egypt and the Holy Land, said that, so far as he could see, the most influential people in the Near East were the Christian doctors.

This state of affairs is equally true of the medical work carried on in Egypt, in Cairo, Omdurman, Alexandria and other centers, as well as the medical missions of the Church Missionary Society in Bagdad and Mosul. These all have the enthusiastic support of the people, and announce that their chief difficulties have not arisen from Moslem opposition but from the failure of the home church to supply the needed recruits and necessary financial support. The same is true of the medical work in East equatorial Africa, in Uganda, Northern Nigeria, and other parts of North Africa, although in the last mentioned case they have not become so thoroughly established as in some of the instances already mentioned.

The citation of these few facts is sufficient, in the absence of any evidence to the contrary, to make clear the importance of medical missions in opening the door to the Moslems of any and all countries. No people suffer more than they in times of sickness; none are more superstitious with reference to the treatment of disease. To such the medical missionary comes as an angel of light and a bearer of infinite blessing.

(5) Personal relations may be made the means of evangelism. Much emphasis is laid everywhere in the West upon social service, and many have seemed to assume that it is something new, discovered within the last generation. It is well known in foreign mission circles where great stress has from the first been placed upon the personal contact of the missionary with a non-Christian population brought about by his residence in their midst, and the daily contact of himself and his family and his home with the life surrounding him. The importance of this method of approach to the Mohammedan can hardly be over-stated. It gives the Mohammedan an opportunity to see the daily acts of a Christian, and the way in which a Christian home is ordered, with a wife and mother holding her proper place in the household. Such contact with a Christian home speaks more loudly than words can utter, of the place of the woman in Christian society and especially in the home.

While this method of approach is not new, and not necessarily peculiar to Mohammedanism, it is one that needs to be mentioned here as a method upon which emphasis will necessarily be placed in any united effort to reach the Moslem world with the direct teaching of Christ as it displays itself in the life of the individual and in the home. This point is not here enlarged upon because it is too obviously true to require it. Mohammedans must and will be convinced by what they see rather than by what they hear, and the life of a Christian passed in their midst will preach more mightily than a thousand oral sermons. Christianity must be lived into the confidence of Moslems before they can accept the Christ.

Methods of personal approach are suggested by the following from Rev. John Van Ess of Arabia and quoted in the *Moslem World:*

" Islam is vulnerable from four points of view — (1) As a theology; (2) as a science; (3) as a philosophy; (4) as a code of morals. Christian missionaries should, I think, attack the citadel from four sides. All missionaries should, of course, present Christ, but each of the established agencies can do so in a way peculiarly its own. The clergyman can demonstrate that it is impotent as a way of life; the physician can authoritatively point out that polygamy and the legislation with regard to women are opposed to sound, scientific principles; the teacher can show that its geography, cosmogony and history are faulty; then last of all the itinerant, merchant believer, whom, I think, we should subsidize as a mission agency, with his small stock of wares, emulating the example of the early Waldenses, can show by an upright life and Christian standards, the power of the Christ life. In brief would it not be better that the various kinds of missionaries and helpers should specialize in methods with which they are best acquainted and on which they can speak with authority? I have heard one of our mission doctors effectually silence an opponent with whom I had been discussing hours without effect, by pointing out the Prophet's ignorance of medicine.

City Evangelistic Work. (1) Advertising is good business and good religion. How to let people know we exist and what we stand for is a problem in a big city. A few years ago I started a campaign against the use of spirituous liquors, drawing up a petition in the name of all the spiritual heads, asking the governor to take steps toward the abolition of the liquor traffic. The various spiritual heads, the mufti, the priests, the rabbi refused to sign, so I presented the petition in the name of the Mission, with the result that a marked decrease in the number of liquor shops was noticeable. But the chief gain lay in the fact that the Arabic papers took up the matter, roundly denouncing those who had refused to sign, and calling attention to us and our work." [2]

(6) The missionary to the Moslem will always be a preacher, but many of his ideas of a sermon and of preaching will undergo radical modification, and probably must undergo radical modification before the Mohammedan can be generally reached by the spoken address. It may even be necessary, in order to secure a sympathetic hearing from the very

[2] *Moslem World,* July, 1913, pp. 324–5.

beginning, to take a text, not necessarily from the Bible, but from the Koran, or some traditional saying of Mohammed or from the Sheriat, or some other Mohammedan source. There certainly can be no fundamental necessity for beginning a sermon to a Mohammedan, or to anybody else, for that matter, with a quotation from the New Testament or the Old. Missionaries to other peoples have often found it wise and rewarding to take a text from something outside of Christian writings. The missionaries in China and Japan frequently take their texts from some of the writings of Confucius. Is there any reason why some of the statements of Mohammed, wholly true, and capable of wide and large Christian development should not be made the basis of a Christian sermon to Moslems? It would not be difficult, in probably every case, for the thought expressed by Mohammed to be reinforced by some corresponding expression of Jesus Christ or the apostles in such a way as to show the existing harmony between the declaration of Mohammedanism and the declaration of Christianity. No suggestion is made here that the sermon may not, and will not often be based upon a text from the Christian Scriptures, but the contention here is that it need not be, and that often it ought not to be, if the preacher wishes to start with a sympathetic bond between himself and his hearers.

Then, too, there is no absolute necessity that there be any text whatever, but the sermon may be announced as a lecture and be treated as such from beginning to end. There are many Mohammedans who would listen to a lecture, who would not entertain the thought of going to a Christian place of worship and listening to a sermon. There is no reason why Christian truth cannot be impressed just as effectively under the title of a lecture as under the title of a sermon. It is results that are sought rather than the perpetuation of a traditional idea or a custom that has prevailed for centuries in Christian lands.

Unquestionably the worker among Moslems will find that his most effective sermons are preached to an audience of one or two, or to a small group of men, accompanied by no formality. We must remember that one of the most impressive addresses ever given by Christ was spoken in conversation to the woman of Samaria by the well, and in many other instances our Lord addressed small groups of men, revealing to them the most fundamental of Christian truths. Can the missionary to the Moslems have a better example than that of their Lord, who was ready to give the choicest truth to a small group, even to a single person? It is probably in this way that the most alert leaders of Islam will be reached, and it is well worthy the careful consideration of all missionaries living and working among Mohammedan peoples.

A veteran in missionary work has suggested that, in approaching Moslems with the Christian message, only one fundamental idea, the very essence of the Gospel, be presented, namely, the love and compassion of Jesus Christ. He would exclude all other questions of theology and bring to the attention and the consciences of all Mohammedans, in private conversation, in daily contacts, in public address, by word and action and life, this one eternal, burning message which has in it power sufficient to conquer the world.

To others than Moslems he would accompany this with the message of God the Loving Father of all, Who watches over and cares for His children. To Moslems who violently reject the idea that God is the Father of mankind, this doctrine would need to be presented later, when the hearers were prepared in mind and heart to receive it.

This suggestion is worthy of careful and prolonged consideration. It is possible that to the Moslems we have befogged the real issue by the preaching of confusing and often irritating doctrines, some of which are of doubtful value, if not actually harmful. If Moslems can be led to catch something of the beauty of the Love of Christ and begin to attempt to reveal that love in their own lives, other essential doctrines will present to them little or no obstacles. The love of Christ will constrain them.

Rev. John Van Ess of Arabia speaks from his experience of the value of itinerating preaching:

Itineration. This constitutes the rural problem, and since nine-tenths of the field is rural it constitutes nine-tenths of the problem, besides being an emulation of the example and method of our Lord who spent so much of His time by the wayside, in villages, and at the seaside. Some observations stand out prominently after several years spent in itineration: (1) A good detailed map of the field, containing names of tribes and sheiks, and their attitude, should be prepared. (2) Thirty days spent in one place is better than one day spent in each of thirty places. (3) One should always aim at the individual. A card index should be kept of the most promising inquirers, purchasers of Scripture, etc., together with details of each case. These should be followed up, revisited, and, in fact, never let go. These individuals should always be mentioned by name in prayer between missionary and helpers. Nathanael wanted to be noticed, and thus Christ drew him. I have known a fanatical opponent to become a friend because after six years I have not forgotten his name. (4) In one of our stations we keep a guest-house with accommodation for fifty or sixty men. Food and sleeping mats are provided, and a helper is always in attendance. Thus we can return the hospitality we receive. The guest-house has proved itself a mighty agency.

(7) During the last ten or fifteen years some of the missionaries in Turkey have had remarkable success in getting hold of Moslems through the organization of clubs, so-called. This plan is unique, but has been sufficiently tested to prove its effectiveness among the Mohammedans of Turkey, who in some respects are as prejudiced against Christianity as any class of Mohammedans in the world.

The Mohammedan shuns the chapel or the church. He is often watched and persecuted if he puts himself in a position to hear a Christian sermon or come into contact with the Christian preacher. There is, however, latent in the Mohammedan mind, especially in Turkey, and in other countries as well, a desire for sociability and contact with his fellows, and at the same time a curiosity to hear and know about the outside world.

Seizing upon this fact, missionaries in several places in Turkey, have engaged a building, and organized a club, somewhat upon the basis of the Young Men's Christian Association. They have had their committees on entertainment, etc., and have supplied their building with a certain amount of reading matter and with amusement rooms. In connection with these clubs the missionary acts as a member, perhaps at first the head of the organization, but not necessarily the one who dominates it.

These clubs have invariably taken up the idea of having lectures and public entertainments. Usually the missionary has been called upon to lecture, as he was the best educated and unquestionably the best able to bring the members of the club into contact with the outside world. They have been called upon repeatedly to speak on a great variety of topics, as, for instance, upon different countries of the world, education and its place in modern civilization, the life of Christ, the life of Paul, the teachings of Christ on different social questions, and a large number of topics beside. In this way a wide field is opened up in which the missionary appears as a lecturer, at the invitation of the committee in charge of the entertainments and with perfect freedom, he has been able to speak about Christianity and of Christ. There have been few cases where offense seems to have been given. In most cases a large measure of hearty approval has been manifested.

The stereopticon has been brought into requisition in many of these entertainments, as one can readily see it might be, and while some of the Mohammedans have been strongly prejudiced against pictures, yet they have been so completely overruled by the great majority that it has caused no break, but has proven to be an opening wedge to the confidence and interest of the Moslem community.

In one instance, the missionary was asked to give a series of addresses on the life of Christ, which he did, the Moslem audience increasing until they numbered something like 200 on the last night. These addresses were given on Sunday evening, in the club rooms, of course, and were lectures but in every respect real sermons to Moslems.

This method of approach to the Mohammedans has not been fully tried out. There are great possibilities in it, especially with the moving pictures which will soon be available, if they are not already available, for use in Mohammedan clubs. The phonograph also gives an opportunity for wide use in such clubs and has its place unquestionably in opening and enlarging the mind of the Moslem, a most important step before it acquires capacity to hold and appreciate Christian truth.

Some might say that this method should be left to the Young Men's Christian Association. There is no reason why it cannot be used and applied by the missionaries vastly more widely than would be possible under the Y. M. C. A. Such a club could be set up in every mission station among Moslems, and also at many of the out-stations. To many of the out-stations, unquestionably native teachers in mission schools would be repeatedly called upon for lectures, as the missionary himself would probably be, thus widening the opportunity and giving the lecturer the advantage of having been invited by the Mohammedans who would feel an obligation to listen. There are great possibilities for opening a new door of approach to Mohammedans through the club organization, which is capable of a great variety of modifications.

(8) The use of Christian music also affords great possibilities. Many opinions have been solicited from a great variety of sources, in the consideration of this subject, and these opinions as expressed have grown out of a wide experience in contact with Mohammedans.

It is an interesting fact that some missionaries who have

lived in Mohammedan countries all their lives have insisted that there is no music among Mohammedans, that in their worship and in their home and social life, music plays no part. On the other hand, many who have had the same experience, often in the same place, but more frequently in different countries, have stated that music plays a large part in the Mohammedan life and especially in his worship.

One missionary, who has spent fifty years in Constantinople among Mohammedans, reports that he knows of only two kinds of music: first, the military, which is an importation from Europe; and, second, a kind of drum used from earlier times, played with a fife and flute, and employed largely by the dervishes in their ceremonies. Dr. J. K. Greene adds, that music implies a joyous disposition which the Turks do not possess.

Dr. H. O. Dwight, who spent some thirty years in Turkey, speaks of the Turks as having a considerable number of ballad tunes which they greatly love. Their scale differs materially from that in use in the West, and consequently is not appreciated outside of Asia as music. He reports that it is difficult to take this music seriously, although the Mohammedans stated that their hearts are stirred by it to the very depths. Dr. Dwight suggests that Christian ideas might well be adapted to the music which Mohammedans love, and that, thus adapted, they would become effective and forceful.

Another missionary from Turkey suggests that Turkish music is probably borrowed from the Persian and is difficult to reduce to any regular scale known to the West. It seems to be without system or rule. It is reported that the Turks have used music in war, perhaps they were the first to do so, and which is characterized by weird, passionate strains calculated to stir the warlike feeling of the combatants.

The whirling dervishes always accompany their graceful revolving movements by instrumental music, already referred to, the drum and flute. The howling dervishes use a kind of monotonous chanting with the word Allah constantly repeated; this is accompanied by the swaying of the body until consciousness is lost in religious ecstasy.

It is difficult for the Turks as a whole to appreciate our Western music, even hymn tunes. They do not take to it kindly. Hitherto in all of the mission schools in Turkey, Eastern music is excluded and only Western church tunes have been requisitioned. Greek and Armenian schools, not under missionary control, still cling to their Oriental ecclesiastical music, thus demonstrating the natural tendency of the Oriental to prefer the more weird and unrhythmical music of the East to the music which is more appreciated in the West.

Dr. Dwight suggests that the task of reaching Mohammedans with spiritual music is awaiting some inspired poet and musician of the East, very likely a Mohammedan who has caught the vision of the Christ, to provide this for the Christian church.

Mr. Gairdner, of Cairo, discussing the question, says that metrical rhythm plays but a small part in Moslem music, and he gives this as the reason why our metrical hymns and psalms seem to have less effect than is ordinarily expected. At the same time he suggests that their unmetrical rhythm is unsuitable to congregational singing. He adds, however, that there are metrical melodies in the East which have their place in worship, but which are, in the minds of the people, closely and intimately associated with secular and sometimes unchaste and worldly ideas. His idea is that Western melodies, depending as they must on harmony, are not generally accepted by the Eastern mind at the present time. Missionaries seem to him to put unnecessary value on harmony as the most important thing for the church worship, he regarding it as unnecessary and as sometimes presenting a barrier to the approach to the Moslems.

Mr. Trowbridge, of Cairo, who has lived many years in Turkey, speaks of the Javanese music as a distinct type, accompanied by unique instruments. He calls attention to the fact that none of the moslem nations have made any worthy contribution to the world's music, citing the interesting phenomenon that the Christian Hungarian, who is racially very close to the Turks in Russia have developed most beautiful Christian music, whereas the Turkish music has not developed at all from the primitive habits of central Asia.

Nearly all of those who have written on the subject speak of the powerful effect of the chanting of the Koran and the deep hold which this has upon the Moslem imagination and spirit of worship. The Mohammedans have severely criticized some of the ostentatious music practised in Catholic churches, on the ground that it was unfitting to a congregation that was coming into the presence of the great God, and suggesting that on such an occasion the music should be humble and shot through with the spirit of homage and devotion.

Rev. Mr. Goodsell, who has been several years in Turkey, puts emphasis on the fact that rhythm and not harmony seems to fascinate the Moslem; that his sense of harmony is rudimentary, but that even the wildest dervishes in their chants profoundly impress all who hear them, because of the accuracy of the rhythm of their exercises and chants and songs, while at the same time there seems to be an absolute disregard of harmony. He speaks of the fact that the Turks make no use of hymns in their worship and have not attempted to introduce anything of the kind. Those whom he had met have looked with contempt on Christian hymns and tunes. On the other hand, there are many evidences that the Moslem villagers and more simple peasants have been greatly impressed with simple Christian singing. There are many indications of this coming from various sources in the Moslem world.

Dr. Watson, who has been a careful student of Mohammedanism, reports the chanting and recitation of the Koran in cadence as music of a high order to the Mohammedan, and as representing a complicated science requiring years of training to perfect. He speaks of paid singers, who have practised for years to reach their high position, and who hold permanent place in leading the Mohammedan festivals. Their product would not be called music from the Western standpoint, for it is frequently more a form of recitation with musical intonations, often occupying an entire evening, and yet it holds the audience and draws in outsiders to listen. He says that he himself has been wonderfully impressed by this Moslem music, and a Moslem convert in Cairo testifies to the wonderful beauty and pleasure he has found in such recitations, even after he became a Christian.

Professor Macdonald of Hartford Seminary, after a wide study of the subject, expresses the opinion that music and singing play a large part in the life of Moslems, and especially in their religious life. He entertains a strong conviction that, through music, their religious imaginations are deeply moved, and that through these imaginations their wills can be influenced.

The music and the singing which will influence Moslems must be of their own kind, that to which they are accustomed and which appeals to them. It is vain to try to capture Mohammedans with Western music, hymns and tunes. He thinks also it is equally vain to attempt to carry to them translations of our hymns written in our tongue; he hopes that the time will come when there will appear among the Christian converts from Islam those who are poets and musicians and who will be able to produce for their fellow-men hymns of Eastern meters, set to Oriental music, and that these hymns will pass into use in all missions to Mohammedans. It is his deep conviction that there is a great field for development of Christian music among Moslems, but of the kind that he has indicated.

This discussion is perhaps sufficient to reveal the fact that the subject of music has not yet been adequately considered by those who would reach Mohammedans and that here is a large field for future development, promising reward to those who are able to solve the question and produce a Christian music that will command the admiration of Mohammedans.

The following is a song of devotion translated from the Turkish, remarkable for its fervent aspirations after God. It was sung by a Turkish woman in a Christian hospital in Turkey. This is a demonstration of the mysticism in Mohammedanism and of the spirit of genuine piety and devotion that is kept alive especially in the hearts of the common people; it also suggests the possibilities of poetry and music as yet undeveloped, almost undiscovered among Moslems:

> Tread my face underfoot, make my head a pathway,
> Burn me with Thy fear.

(Chorus)
> If only I may find Thee my God,
> Let me once see Thee my Lord.

> Throw me into the fire with Ibrahim,
> Hold me back like Moses.

> If only I may find Thee my God,
> Let me once see Thee my Lord.

> Hang me upon the tree like Jesus Isa,
> Like Mansour make me poor.

> If only I may find Thee my God,
> Let me once see Thee my Lord.

> Cause me to be beaten by the hands of others,
> By thy command cause tongues to slander me,
> Thou hast made me to wander in distant ways.

> If only I may find Thee my God,
> Let me once see Thee my Lord.

Make me to fall into the pit like Yousouf,
Like Yakoub make me to weep and be overwhelmed.

If only I may find Thee my God,
Let me once see Thee my Lord.[3]

---

[3] *The Moslem World*, October, 1914, p. 413.

CHAPTER XXI

REORGANIZATION FOR CONQUEST

It remains to make some suggestions as to what the church and the missionary organizations of the church can do to meet the Moslem call for Christianization. We are agreed that the Moslems need Christ; that their own religion has failed to lead its devotees into a pure, positive, developing, spiritual life. We do not need to argue that fact.

We are also agreed that the church, and the societies that represent it in the work of missions, have not risen to the height of their privilege in carrying the Gospel to the Mohammedans, but that they have taken hold of this colossal task in a desultory, half-hearted way, demonstrating a lack of comprehension of the difficulties faced and the urgency of the call.

In view of the sweeping changes taking place in the Moslem world and the new opportunities for reaching the Moslems in many countries, and in view of the failures of the past to grasp the situation, and the demands of the present that the Christian world arouse itself as it has never done before, the following distinct steps are urged as presenting a partial solution at least for this old and difficult problem:

1. A plan to be devised and put into execution by which a complete survey of the Mohammedan world shall be made and published. This should cover every part of the world in which Mohammedans dwell, and every Moslem race and people, with their physical, social, intellectual, linguistic and religious status. All of the facts necessary should be assembled for a full knowledge of the people to be reached by missionary effort, with adequate facts and data to enable a missionary organization intelligently to plan for work among them. The

survey should point out the strategic centers of Islam from and through which the greater numbers could be reached. It should also show what Christian influences, if any, are already brought to bear upon the country or upon any particular races or peoples. In a word, this survey should be as complete, scientific and comprehensive as united Christendom can make it.

2. The survey would provide the foundation and basis for a comprehensive Mohammedan prayer cycle or intercession calendar intelligently covering the entire Moslem world. This should be used by the entire Church of Christ so as to concentrate, especially upon Fridays, the united prayers of Christendom upon the whole Moslem world. This could not be brought about in a day, or a year, but there should be no cessation of endeavor until the Universal Church recognizes its universal responsibility to exalt the Mohammedan world and its need before the God of all men and races and religions, until it shall see and recognize the divine and redeeming character of the Lord Christ.

3. The preparation and publication of a comprehensive statement of the failure of Islam as a religion. This is necessary for the church at home in order to counteract an impression that exists in many places that Mohammedanism is almost as good as Christianity; that it is a stepping-stone to the Christian faith, a door through which the pagan may advance from the degradation of his heathenism to a better civilization and a nobler religion. The Church needs to be awakened to the facts of Islam and its failures, in all history, to lift and save a people. This need is not fully realized at the present time, but it is demonstrated in a large degree by the lethargy of the church when it stands face to face with the opportunities offered among Moslems.

4. A united appeal on the part of the church to so-called Christian nations, which rule over Moslem peoples, to put no hindrances in the way of bringing to bear upon Mohammedans

the influence and power of the Gospel of Christ. The attitude of the British Government in the Sudan and of the French in Africa shows the need of enlightening government leaders and demonstrating that Christian missions do not, even among Moslems, make the people less loyal citizens to the Government under which they reside, but quite the contrary. There is too much apprehension upon the part of many local officials that the presence of Christian missionaries among fanatical populations may cause local disturbances if not general uprisings against the Government itself. Such conditions and opinions are capable of correction if properly approached, but it can hardly be accomplished if the only petitioning body is the one desirous of conducting the mission. No reasonable Government would persist in this attitude of exclusion or repression, if approached by a representative body reinforced by arguments based upon the facts of Christian missions for a century and accompanied by a carefully wrought out program of procedure.

5. Equally important is agreement among Missionary Societies as to the standard of preparation necessary for the best success of the missionary to Moslems. It is only during the last few years that this subject has had any consideration whatever either by the church or by missionary organizations. Even now it has attracted the attention of but a few educational and missionary experts. One of the reasons for the small returns for the already large expenditure of life and treasure upon Moslem work must be due to the fact that no adequate preparation was made upon the part of the missionaries or of the Societies sending them.

Since the task is a peculiar one, presenting obstacles and difficulties nowhere else manifest, the preparation also must be unique, suited to the difficulties and varied character of the work to be done. It is imperative that intellectual, physical, linguistic, temperamental, Biblical, as well as spiritual qualifications of the missionaries to the Moslems be standardized, and that standard recognized by all who would enter upon that work.

6. In order that such standardization may be actual and not theoretical, schools in countries in which Moslems dwell and for which the missionaries are to work, will need to be opened, for the completion of the training every new missionary requires for his most perfect furnishing. These field schools would present the practical side of the theoretical training each new missionary would have received in his home land. Here he would be brought face to face with the problems he will be called upon to solve and in contact with the people he is sent out to reach. With expert and experienced leaders, he will be trained to avoid errors, so easy to make, and to comprehend the delicacy of his mission so difficult to grasp.

7. There must be a willingness on the part of the Church of Christ to pay the cost of a united campaign to win the Moslem to Christ. One of the reasons why so little missionary work has been done formerly for Mohammedan peoples is that the returns are so slight, while pagan races seem to offer a more rewarding field. The missionary endeavor for and among Moslems must, for many years yet, meet with the most violent opposition and maybe, persecution. The work must be undertaken with a consciousness that a long time may be required before the returns will be striking or sufficient to provide much encouragement to those who are giving money and life. They must also recognize that much money must be given where it will seem for a time as if it is thrown away, as foundations are being laid and plans matured.

The missionaries who enter into this service must enter with a consciousness that they may put their whole life in without any large or startling returns to announce to the world. The real work among and for Moslems must begin where the work in China began more than a century ago, where a whole life-time of effort and of treasure and of missionary sacrifice was given apparently without results. The Church must enter upon this work with a firm conviction that it is a campaign not of a decade or even of a generation, but of a century, and that a vast amount of treasure, both of life and of money, may be required before there is any great yielding of the barriers that separate the Moslem and the Christian world.

8. There will be need of an international and inter-denominational body representing all the Christian forces united for the Christian conquest of Islam. This body, or board of strategy, or whatever it may be called, should have its headquarters in the home land, but, at the same time, be in touch with the entire Moslem world. It should have before it as its field of study all parts of the world in which Moslems dwell and its chief task will be to direct the Christian forces that are available for the work. This organization seems essential for the proper placing of the Christian forces so that they may accomplish the largest possible results with the least waste.

This Board would need to lead in the preparation of permanent Christian literature for the use of Moslems in different countries. Not that the members of the Board would produce the literature which, of course, must be prepared in the field, but it would provide for its publication in other countries and in other languages. It would keep the constituency at home informed of the opportunities and needs abroad.

It is possible that ultimately all of Christendom would unite in one supreme effort to bring to bear upon the Moslem world the undivided force of the Church. Already Mohammedans in different countries, noting the Edinburgh Missionary Conference, as well as the two conferences upon work for Moslems, held, the one in Cairo in 1906, and one in Lucknow in 1911, are beginning to deplore the divided state of Islam and fear the effect of the united Christian Church. Hitherto they have boasted of their strength in comparison with the divided state of the Church. The effect of such a united Board, representing the combined energy and devotion and external resources of the Church, all for the purpose of presenting to Islam the beauty and the saving power of the Christ, would strike consternation into hearts of scattered Moslems and make them see and feel the power of the Church.

9. A survey would be of no permanent value unless it led to a mobilization of the forces of the Christian church and the organization of those forces for the speedy and adequate occupation of the strategic centres of Islam. It will be a mistake to assume that favorable conditions following the war will continue to be equally favorable for an indefinite period of years. Before five years have elapsed there should be a strong body of well equipped and thoroughly trained men and women ready to enter, occupy and permanently hold at least a score of these centers. To this initial number there should be added new recruits annually, amounting to not less than 10 per cent of the number already on the ground, and this rate of increase should be continued for twenty-five years. This body for occupation, demonstration and proclamation would, by the end of the 25 years, have the avenues and methods of approach to the Moslems well in hand in all of the larger centers of Moslem influence and power. The children first taught would be coming into maturity and the mission to Moslems would then be well entering upon the second stage of development, namely, that of advance through an educated and consecrated native Christian leadership. This would necessarily mean the planting of institutions that characterize all Christian lands, like hospitals, asylums, schools of all grades, and the printing press. In some countries, like Africa, industrial enterprises that promote the purity, unity and prosperity of Christian society would be called for, and everywhere the church, so organized as to meet the prejudices and answer the cry of the Moslem heart

for a mediator and redeemer, would be the goal to which all other efforts would lead.

It is only through the adoption and use of a program of this general character that we may hope to make an immediate and lasting impression upon Islam. Our efforts hitherto have been feeble and scattered, with results far out of proportion to the sacrifice made. The times call for a new strategy calculated to break down opposition, command a hearing, and compel the Moslems to recognize and confess that Jesus Christ is Lord to the glory of God the Father.

APPENDIX

Proclamation of the Shereef of Mecca

" In the name of God, the Merciful, the Compassionate."

This is our general proclamation to all our Moslem brothers.

" O God, judge between us and our people in truth; Thou art the Judge."

The world knoweth that the first of all Moslem princes and rulers to acknowledge the Turkish Government were the Emirs of Mecca the Blessed. This they did to bind together and make strong the brotherhood of Islam, for they saw the Sultans of the House of Osman (may the dust of their tombs be blessed, and may they dwell in Paradise), how they were up right, and how they carried out all the commandments and ordinances of the Faith and of the Prophet (prayers be upon him) perfectly. Therefore they were obedient to them at all times.

For a token of this remember how in A.H. 1322 I with my Arabs helped them against the Arabs, to save Ebhah from those who were besieging it, and to preserve the name of the Government in honour; and remember how again in the next year I helped them with my armies, which I entrusted to one of my sons; for in truth we were one with the Government until the Committee on Union and Progress rose up, and strengthened itself, and laid its hands on power. Consider how since then ruin has overtaken the State, and its possessions have been torn from it, and its place in the world has been lost, until now it has been drawn into this last and most fatal war.

All this they have done, being led away by shameful appetites, which are not for me to set forth, but which are public and a cause for sorrow to the Moslems of the whole world, who have seen this greatest and most noble Moslem Power broken in pieces and led down to ruin and utter destruction. Our lament is also for so many of its subjects, Moslems and others alike, whose lives have been sacrificed without any fault of their own. Some have been treacherously put to death, others cruelly driven from their homes, as though the calamities of war were not enough. Of these calamities the heaviest share has fallen upon the Holy Land. The poor, and even families of substance, have been made to sell their doors and windows, yea, even the wooden frames of their houses, for bread, after they had lost their furniture and all their goods. Not even so was the lust of the Union and Progress fulfilled. They laid bare all the measure

313

of their wicked design, and broke the only bond that endured between them and the true followers of Islam. They departed from their obedience to the precepts of the Book.

With the connivance of the Grand Vizier of the Ottoman Empire, the Sheikh el-Islam, the Ulema, the Ministers and the Notables, one of their papers called the *Ijtihad* published in Constantinople unworthy things about the Prophet (The Prayer and Peace of God be upon him) and spoke evil of him (God forbid!). Then the Union and Progress rejected God's word, " A man shall have twice a woman's share," and made them equal. They went further, and removed one of the five corner-stones of the Faith, even the Fast in Ramadan, by causing the soldiers in garrison in Mecca, Medina, and Damascus to break their fast for new and foolish reasons, taking no account of the ordinance of God saying, " Those of you who are sick or on a journey. . . . " Yea, they went further. They made weak the person of the Sultan, and robbed him of his honour, forbidding him to choose for himself the chief of his personal Cabinet. Other like things did they to sap the foundation of the Khalifate.

For this it had been clearly our part and our necessary duty to separate ourselves from them and renounce them and their obedience. Yet we would not believe their wickedness, and tried to think that they were the imaginings of evil-doers to make a division between us and the Government. We bore with them until it was apparent to all men that the rulers of Turkey were Enver Pasha, Jemal Pasha, and Talaat Bey, who were doing whatsoever they pleased. They made their guilt manifest when they wrote to the Judge of the Sacred Court in Mecca traducing the verses in the Sura of the Cow, and laying upon him to reject the evidence of believers outside the Court and to consider only the deeds and contracts engrossed within the Court. They also showed their guilt when they hanged in one day twenty-one of the most honourable and enlightened of the Moslems, among them Emir Omar el Jazairi, Emir Arif el Shahabi, Shefik Bey Moayyad, Shukri Bey el Asli, Abdel Wahab, Tewfik el Bassat, Abdel Hamid el Zahrawi, Abdel Ghani el Areisi, and their learned comrades. To destroy so many, even of cattle, at one time would be hard for men void of all natural affection or mercy. And if we suppose they had some excuse for this evil deed, by what right did they carry away to strange countries the innocent and most miserable families of those ill-fated men? Children, old men, and delicate women bereft of their natural protectors were subjected in exile to all foul usage and even to tortures, as though the woes they had already suffered were not chastisement enough. Did not God say: " No punishment shall be inflicted on anyone for the sins of another"? . . . Let us suppose they found for themselves some reason for ill-treating the harmless families of their victims; why then did they rob them of their properties and possessions, which alone remained to keep them from death by famine? And if we suppose that they had also some excuse for this evil deed, how shall we find pardon for them for their shattering of the tomb of our most righteous and upright Lord and Brother, El Sayed el Shereef Abdel Kader el Jezairi el Hassani, whose bones they have polluted and whose dust they have scattered abroad?

We leave the judgment of these misdeeds, which we have touched upon so briefly, to the world in general and to Moslems in particular. What stronger proof can we desire of the faithlessness of their inmost hearts to the Religion, and of their feelings towards the Arabs, than their bombardment of that ancient House, which God has chosen for His House, saying, " Keep my House pure for all who come to it," . . . a House so venerated by all Moslems? From their fort of Jyad, when the revolt began, they shelled it. The first shot struck a yard and a half above the Black Stone. The second fell three yards short of it, so that the flame leapt up and took hold upon the Kiswa. Which, when they saw, the thousands and thousands of Moslems first raised a lamentable cry, running to and fro, and then shouted in fierce anger and rushed to save it. They had to burst open the door and mount upon the roof before they could quench the flames. Yet a third shell fell upon the Tomb of Abraham, and other shells fell in and about the precincts, which they made a target for their guns, killing every day three or four who were at prayer within the Mosque, till they prevented the people coming near to worship. This will show how they despised His House and denied it the honour given it by believers.

We leave all this to the Moslem world for judgment.

Yes, we can leave the judgment to the Moslem world; but we may not leave our religion and our existence as a people to be a plaything of the Unionists. God (Blessed be He) has made open for us the attainment of freedom and independence, and has shown us a way of victory to cut off the hand of the oppressors, and to cast out their garrison from our midst. We have attained independence, an independence of the rest of the Ottoman Empire, which is still groaning under the tyranny of our enemy. Our independence is complete, absolute, not to be laid hands on by any foreign influence or aggression, and our aim is the preservation of Islam and the uplifting of its standard in the world. We fortify ourselves on the noble religion which is our only guide and advocate in the principles of administration and justice. We are ready to accept all things in harmony with the Faith and all that leads to the Mountain of Islam, and in particular to uplift the mind and the spirit of all classes of the people in so far as we have strength and ability.

This is what we have done according to the dictates of our religion, and on our part we trust that our brethren in all parts of the world will each do his duty also, as is incumbent upon him, that the bonds of brotherhood in Islam may be confirmed.

We beseech the Lord of Lords, for the sake of the Prophet of Him who giveth all things, to grant us prosperity and to direct us in the right way for the welfare of the faith and of the faithful.

We depend upon God the All-Powerful, whose defence is sufficient for us.

Shereef and Emir of Mecca

25 Shaaban, 1334.   HUSSEIN.

Date Loaned
